RADICAL HISTORY Review

Truth Commissions: State Terror, History, and Memory

Editors' Introduction

Extrajudicial investigations into political violence date back at least to the Carnegie Endowment for International Peace's inquiry into crimes against civilians committed during the 1912 and 1913 Balkan Wars, but the modern truth commission form has a much more recent genesis, primarily associated with what is often called Latin America's transition to democracy. First established in 1982 with Bolivia's small Comisión Nacional de Desaparecidos (National Commission on the Disappeared) and in Argentina in 1983 with the more well-known Comisión Nacional sobre la Desaparición de Personas (National Commission on Disappeared People), nationally- or internationally-administered truth commissions did indeed mark a particular moment of transitional justice — but not in the way legal theorists and social scientists like to use the term: to reference the evolution of particular nation-states from repressive and unrepresentative to liberal and constitutional forms of government. Rather, truth commissions, adopted in one variant or another in more than twenty Latin American, African, Asian, and Eastern European countries over the past two decades, indexed the shift from the global crisis of the 1970s — where escalating cycles of conflict and polarization often led to either repressive dictatorships or deadlocked civil wars — to the post–Cold War would-be *pax* neoliberal. Marking this transition, the utility of truth commissions, in retrospect, seems to have been exclusive to it, having exhausted their potential as instruments, however limited, of consolidating the norms and institutions of liberal jurisprudence. Consider two cases at opposing ends of today's global political spectrum: U.S.-occupied Iraq and Venezuela. In the former, the victorious (briefly at least) invaders felt no need to implement a truth commission as an exhortatory body to foster a culture of respect for human rights. Instead, they moved to invoke the more confident time of the Nuremberg and Tokyo trials, putting Saddam Hussein and a number of high-ranking Baathists on the dock to submit to the sword of justice. In the latter, in the wake of

Radical History Review
Issue 97 (Winter 2007) DOI 10.1215/01636545-2006-010

the 1998 elections that brought Hugo Chávez to power and signaled the collapse of a corrupt two-party monopoly, there have been few calls to set up a truth commission to investigate political violence that took place under the old regime (particularly the murder, by some accounts, of over a thousand people during the 1989 riots against an austerity program imposed by the International Monetary Fund) or to invoke the language of reconciliation to solidify social cohesion. Rather, while there have been a few isolated attempts to investigate the pre-1998 repression, supporters of Chávez, having shattered the previous political order, frame justice nearly exclusively in terms of social and economic rights.

The structure and work of truth commissions took many forms throughout the 1980s and 1990s—some mandated by national legislators, others brokered and administered by an international arbiter such as the United Nations—but in general, they have gathered testimony from victims and witnesses in order to document political violence committed by state and/or nonstate agents. While rarely invested with the legal authority to indict or to prosecute perpetrators, commissions nonetheless usually conducted their investigations within a framework supplied by national or international human rights law, making individual decisions on each case presented to them, similar to a panel of voting judges. When the investigative period ended, the commissions often issued final reports that quantified violations, typically with the aid of a statistical data base, and assigned global institutional responsibility. The UN-administered Commission on the Truth for El Salvador, for example, established as part of the peace negotiations between the state and the insurgent Farabundo Martí National Liberation Front, found that government forces were responsible for 85 percent of human rights abuses, charged the rebels with 5 percent, and left the remainder "undetermined."

Yet the explicit mission of truth commissions to lay an ethical foundation on which to establish liberal constitutional polities differentiated them from more routine bodies of legal inquiry. Increasingly, as it evolved throughout the 1990s, the truth commission form was presented as a way to forge future social unity, constructed from both an official recognition of past human rights abuses and the supposed collective healing that comes from telling one's story to an official body. The early architects of Latin American truth commissions—Carlos Nino and Jaime Malamud-Goti in Argentina, for example, and José Zalaquett in Chile—were self-conscious political liberals, seeing themselves as opposed not just to right-wing terror but to what they believed, in Nino's words, was an "epistemic elitism regarding facts and morality" on the part of the Left, which justified violence in pursuit of a greater good.[1] Heavily influenced by Émile Durkheim's arguments about the role of the rule of law in the formalization of social solidarity, these legal theorists laid the philosophical foundation of subsequent truth commissions. They understood the function of such commissions to be, first, the healing of the psychic damage caused by repression and, second, the deterrence of similar repression in the future. These two goals were said to be mutually dependent in that officially sanctioned inquiries into the past, followed by public acceptance of the conclusions of those inquiries, would not only heal wounds but also help generate a culture of liberal tolerance and thus prevent future transgressions. "The truth in itself is both reparation and prevention," Zalaquett, a professor of ethics and human rights at the University of Chile, believed.[2] Truth commissions, he wrote, "help to create a consensus concerning events about which the community is deeply divided. . . . The purpose of truth is to lay the groundwork for a shared understanding of the recent crisis and how to overcome it."[3]

The ethical charge of the truth commission form meshed with post–Cold War political liberalism in two principal ways. First, truth commissions worked, at least in theory, similar to other myths and rituals of nationalism, to sacramentalize violence into a useful creation myth. To do so, they often embraced historical analysis, but they did so precariously, at the risk of undermining their stated goal of establishing social solidarity. History and law may share many methodological procedures—reliance on eyewitness accounts, corroborating evidence, reasoning by analogy, and the laying out of plausible sequences of events "in accordance with the rules of rhetoric, an art of persuasion"—yet historians usually reach conclusions not about an individual event, as lawyers often do, but about larger social, economic, or cultural patterns and phenomena.[4] As the burden of proof widens from the individual to the social, historical conclusions are inevitably less verifiable than legal rulings and therefore more open to conflicting interpretations. Likewise, historical conclusions are divisive, for they usually rest on a multifaceted analysis of how economic, cultural, and political power is distributed within a given society. As such, they suggest a more profound degree of social responsibility than do legal judgments of individual actions and tend, as E. H. Carr remarked some time ago, to side with the "losers."[5] In order to avoid such divisive conclusions, truth commissions, for the most part, presented history not as a conflict of interests and ideas within a context of unequal power, but as a parable of illiberal intolerance, distilling a nation's recently ideological feverish past into a useful moral, one that portrays terror as an inversion of a democratic society, a nightmarish alternative of what lies ahead if it does not abide by constitutional rules.[6]

Second, truth commissions have tended to disaggregate the collective nature of social justice struggles. In many instances, they forced victims to submit their experiences to the procedural and doctrinal compartmentalization of liberal jurisprudence: Julie Taylor argues that the Argentine truth commission abstracted human rights violations from dynamics of social power and conflict, in a way reproducing the logic of a repression that was intended to break down networks of political solidarity. She writes that all "who passed through this process, then, accused and accusers—actors in highly political dramas where they had represented clashing world views and collective strategies for implementing them—were refigured as innocent or transgressing individuals with individual rights and obligations." The truth commission's "opposition of the order of law and the chaos of violence further led to the omission of collective motivation not only of victimizers . . . but of victims as well, who were defended as individuals whose human rights had been violated rather than as political activists."[7] In other cases, they denied the validity of collective forms of social organization and struggle, which, as mentioned above, the early theorists of truth commissions felt would not only reproduce the conflict but would also open the door to justification. One notable exception to this occurred in South Africa, where the Truth and Reconciliation Commission (TRC) did admit that the struggle against apartheid was morally just.[8] But the righteousness of the antiapartheid movement was assigned nearly exclusively to its antiracist content, drowning out its socialist and communist impulse. Thus was the officially sanctioned process of national catharsis synchronized with the African National Congress's capitulation to free-market economics.

But that the time of truth commissions seems to have passed suggests that Cold War triumphalism was in fact more fragile than it appeared during the years following the collapse of the Berlin Wall, and that to whatever degree truth commissions were used to subsume the remnants of the Cold War left into an imagined new postideological liberal polity, they were also meant to leash the Cold War Right—the military states and death squads that by eliminating nationalists and socialists served as the shock troops of neoliberalism. The latter proved more difficult than the former. It is often overlooked that not only did the Argentine theorists who designed the first major truth commission not believe that efforts to hold individuals accountable for human rights violations had to be sacrificed to the needs of national reconciliation, but that any attempt to do so would undermine both. Nino criticized what he believed to be the absolutism of groups like the Madres de la Plaza who, he wrote, "invok[ing] Kant" asked "for the punishment of every last individual responsible for the atrocities, even if society were at the brink of dissolution."[9] But despite this criticism, Nino, along with others in Raúl Alfonsín's administration, felt that for their National Commission on Disappeared People to have effect, it would have to be supplemented by the prosecutions of high-level junta officers who set policy, as well as of those soldiers who tortured and killed with excess zeal.

Finding a proper balance between prosecutions and reconciliation, however, proved to be impossible. By 1986, following the convictions of General Jorge Videla and Admiral Emilio Massera, sectors of the Argentine military launched a series of failed but threatening coup attempts, forcing Alfonsín first to pass the so-called full stop law, which imposed an absolute cutoff date for the trials, and then to call a halt to military prosecutions. Before leaving office, he signed the so-called law of due obedience, which allowed military officers to argue in their defense that they "had acted under orders and thus were not punishable."[10] In 1990, his successor, Carlos Menem, pardoned in the name of national reconciliation all those either awaiting trial or already convicted, including Videla and Massera. By the time of the installation of the next significant commission—in Chile in 1990, the first to call itself a "Truth and Reconciliation" commission—the strength of the Right vetoed any attempt to complement a broader inquiry into human rights violations with targeted prosecutions. Moreover, many in Chile's post-Pinochet political class, including those involved with the Truth and Reconciliation Commission, refused to recognize that the inability to prosecute human rights violators was a realpolitik concession to the ongoing strength of the military, rather ideologizing it as a preferred option in the quest for national catharsis.

The very weakness of the post–Cold War liberal order was often manifested in much of the advocacy and theorizing of the truth commission form, which prioritized catharsis and forgiveness over punishment, and tended to gloss over the de jure or de facto amnesties that often came with it. This is perhaps clearest in the case of the much-lauded South African TRC, which set up a number of mechanisms that pressured victims to abandon a desire for vengeance for the sake of national reconciliation. The progressive hollowing out of the truth commission form was further revealed either by attempts to impose it on shattered nations such as Sierra Leone and Rwanda—where viscous reconciliation talk seemed but a parody of its use, however problematic, in Argentina, Chile, and South Africa—or to introduce it in countries where impunity has long been institutionalized. In 2004, for example, Indonesia passed legislation that would create a truth and reconciliation commission to investigate pre-2000 "gross violations of human rights," including the 1965 executions of hundreds of thousands of communists and suspected communists, "in order to establish national peace and unity" and to achieve "national reconciliation" in the "spirit of mutual understanding."[11] Following the logic of similar truth commissions, the law explicitly prohibits situating the crimes in their larger historical context, limiting truth to "the truth of an incident." If it comes into being, Indonesia's commission would provide for the same kind of truth-for-amnesty swap pioneered by South Africa's TRC, including, in violation of international law, reprieves for perpetrators of genocide that would restrict the right of victims to seek redress in the judicial system. Where, in South Africa, amnesty decisions were decided on by the independent branch of the TRC, however, the Indonesian legislation invests the power to grant clemency to the executive branch. Worse still, it would condition a victim's right to reparations to a willingness to sign a formal statement of forgiveness.

. . . . .

The three feature articles in this special issue highlight the internal contradictions and tensions in truth commissions' historiographical projects, raising a number of questions about the role of historical narratives in legitimizing state rule. For the most part, in the context of post–Cold War reckonings with the past, truth commissions have served as instruments for reestablishing political and institutional stability according to liberal democratic norms. In countries ranging from South Africa to Chile and Guatemala, the foundation of this liberal constitutional order has also been viewed as essential to the implementation of market reforms according to hegemonic neoliberal economic development theory. Reconciliation, forgiveness, and political consensus have been understood as the basis for moving forward into an era of market-driven economic progress. The historical "truths" mobilized by commissions function, then, within serious limits. Indeed, in the case of commissions whose charge is both truth and reconciliation (Chile and Peru, for example, and forgiveness in the case of South Africa), it might be argued that the goal of reconciliation imposes profound obstacles to the production of historical truth.

Truth commissions' primary mode of evading a confrontation with the structural socioeconomic and ideological conflicts that created the conditions for political violence has been to focus on verifiable and documented individual cases of human rights violations. The microscopic and forensic approach, combined with the collection of testimonial evidence and documenting violence, often precludes an analysis of the structural historical processes and political conflicts that gave rise to human rights violations. And the imperative to build forgiveness and reconciliation translates individual modes of working through trauma to the national social and political sphere in the name of building social and political consensus. In the end, the focus on specific cases, individual victims, and individual perpetrators abets the slippery move from individual experiences of trauma and healing to social structure and political process. The historian's problem of analyzing the relationship between structure and experience, between individuals, individual events, and broader socioeconomic and political processes tends to remain unacknowledged and unresolved.

The anthropologist Alejandro Castillejo-Cuéllar poses critical questions about the use of the South African TRC as a model for other countries, including his native Colombia. Castillejo-Cuéllar makes a number of important points about the South African TRC by focusing on the case of the Gugulethu Seven, one of the TRC's window cases. He shows how the transformation of the case into a symbol and icon of the TRC's focus on reconciliation and forgiveness, often articulated in a Christian idiom, elided the voices and experiences of victims and their surviving relatives. He examines the shifting focus and nature of evidence and the tension between testimonials that foreground victims' subjective experience and forensic and scientific, supposedly objective, forms of knowledge and proof. By foregrounding forensic evidence in the service of a historical narrative organized teleologically to lead to reconciliation, Castillejo-Cuéllar argues, the South African commission marginalized the experiences of victims. While the TRC's reliance on testimony reduced its focus of analysis to the individual and to the subjective process of working through trauma, it also provided a window onto the ways in which the apartheid regime committed systematic and broad violence that affected all areas of everyday life, which, Castillejo-Cuéllar cotends, suggests that testimonial may be the only way to gain access to and document the daily violence lived by Africans under apartheid. Yet at the same time, he suggests that by placing emphasis on certain kinds of historical evidence, by limiting inquiry into circumscribed acts of violence, and, finally, by placing these cases in the context of a historical narrative designed to produce reconciliation, the structural and systemic violence of apartheid—its underlying class structure, for example—remains obscured in the South African TRC report.

The Gugulethu case also raises the question of the relationship between narrated stories and history. It focuses on the tensions implicit in the equation "truth and reconciliation," between the imperatives of state formation and regime legitimation and the narratives of subjective and individual process of working through trauma. As the article shows, it is difficult, if not futile, to project the individual or subjective psychoanalytic process of coping with a traumatic experience onto a state level. Indeed, Castillejo-Cuéllar's article implicitly challenges any direct employment of psychoanalytic categories in the broader context of social trauma caused by state terror. By examining an internationally distributed film documentary on the TRC and the Gugulethu Seven massacre, Castillejo-Cuéllar extends his analysis from the nation-state to the global human rights community, focusing on how certain historical narratives about state violence achieve a certain hegemony through their transnational circulation. The South Africa commission is frequently invoked as a model for application elsewhere in Africa and in Latin America, and Castillejo-Cuéllar demonstrates how the distribution of the documentary at international conferences—the documentary was produced with an international audience in mind—served to disseminate the TRC report's focus on cases ending in supposed reconciliation and forgiveness.

The issue of the reception of the histories consecrated in truth commission reports is taken up by Elizabeth Oglesby in her article on Guatemala's ambitiously named Comisión para el Esclarecimiento Histórico (Historical Clarification Commission, or CEH). How the histories these reports produce become hegemonic is a key question: How do they both impose a historical narrative of the past, setting the limits of what can be said and known, and create spaces for discussing an otherwise repressed traumatic past? How do they become known nationally, as well as internationally? Oglesby raises the issue of how the histories produced by truth commissions are used and implemented, noting that the Guatemala commission's report opened an important space in Guatemala for acknowledging and discussing the state-directed terror and genocide of the late 1970s and 1980s. Despite all expectations to the contrary, the CEH broke with past truth commissions to present political terror not as a Durkheimian breakdown of social cohesion but as both an instrument and reflection of class exploitation and racial domination. It fixed overwhelming responsibility for political repression on the Guatemalan state and military and avoided falling into a narrative of a Mayan peasant population caught between and victimized by two opposing armies (the thesis advanced notoriously by the anthropologist David Stoll). Yet Oglesby shows how the circulation of the CEH's report, rather than its production, limited the possibility of confronting the structural and political origins of genocide in Guatemala.

Oglesby shows that efforts to make the findings of the CEH, along with those of the Catholic Church's own historical memory project, part of national teaching and curriculum standards were frustrated by the entrenched power of the Guatemalan Right. As efforts to disseminate the history of state and military repression documented by the CEH through textbooks and teaching standards floundered, programs directed by international organizations like the United Nations Educational, Scientific, and Cultural Organization (UNESCO) and the U.S. Agency for International Development (USAID) produced their own version of the CEH report's findings in proposals for training and education. These proposals diluted the strong historical conclusions reached by the CEH to a watery opposition of a so-called culture of peace and a supposed culture of violence, attributing the genocide to the latter rather than to the Guatemalan state and ignoring histories of political struggles. These proposals even went as far as purging the role of the United States in the 1954 overthrow of the democratically elected Jacobo Arbenz, the effects of which the CEH documented in great detail. As part of the cultural project of neoliberalism, Oglesby writes, the culture-of-peace framework not only helps to instill a highly individualized doctrine of rights but also, by ignoring traces of collective or class mobilization, draws explicit and implicit boundaries for what is acceptable in the current context. Oglesby's article highlights the question of mediation and reception: Who are the brokers who translate and distribute truth commissions' findings to national and international audiences? What are the means through which the histories produced by the reports are communicated (theater, film, school textbooks, soap operas, advertisements)? In the case of Guatemala, the important work done by the CEH is limited by the powerful role played by international agencies in appropriating its report and imposing their own, neutered version of Guatemala's history in the name of peace.

Finally, Brian Loveman and Elizabeth Lira's article on Chile underlines the ways in which, at least in the Chilean case, truth commissions are a new incarnation of a policy that was central to modern nation-state formation during the nineteenth and twentieth centuries. Rather than a major break with the past, the Chilean truth commission was one in a series of government commissions and policies designed to bring together the "Chilean family," foment healing, and reestablish governability. What then, Loveman and Lira ask, is new in truth and reconciliation commissions? Are not all states founded in both violence and necessary forms of reconciliation between contending political and social groups? Loveman and Lira's argument about Chile coincides with Benedict Anderson's contention that all nations and nationalisms require political routines and rituals for forging reconciliation and political stability in the wake of the violence that lies at the origin of modern state formation. Furthermore, Loveman and Lira argue that in the case of Chile, rituals of reconciliation have been historically predicated on amnesia and amnesty as much as on historical truth. Oblivion, an erasing of histories of political violence, has been the historically necessary condition of governability.

Yet Loveman and Lira also show that in Chile, efforts to establish historical truth about political violence have a long history embedded in the juridical mechanism of the constitutional accusation. Chile's truth commissions were not the first legal bodies designed to establish the truth about state violence as a precondition for the establishment of a stable political order. Throughout the nineteenth and twentieth centuries, government commissions and constitutional accusations sought to make uncovering histories of political violence central to building a liberal political system. But these efforts, Loveman and Lira contend, ran up against the constant imperative to bury the past with amnesties and pardons in the name of reconciliation or the unity of the national family. They suggest that at least since its early nineteenth-century independence, there has been no reconciliation between truth and reconciliation in Chile as the historical condition of reconciliation has been oblivion.

Loveman and Lira's article raises an important question for historians: if institutional mechanisms and political routines of reconciliation and forgetting have laid the foundation for modern nation-state formation everywhere, what distinguishes the proliferation of truth commissions during the 1980s and 1990s? As tools for reckoning with the political violence of the Cold War, are they distinct from earlier methods of confronting state violence and political upheaval? In addition, what difference does a post-Nuremberg international juridical human rights framework make in the establishment of truth commissions? Finally, the specificities of the Chilean case raise the issue of historical comparison. Does the tension in modern Chilean history between institutional routines of reconciliation and procedures for establishing the history of political violence shed light on the experiences of other nations? How are specific Chilean national political traditions articulated to transnational juridical human rights discourses and institutions, as well as the post–Cold War organization of truth commissions globally? What is Chilean in the Chilean truth and reconciliation commission, or can Chile be understood as just another arena of Cold War struggle and international efforts to build liberal democracies and neoliberal economies following the fall of the Soviet Union?

—Greg Grandin and Thomas Miller Klubock

Notes

1. Carlos Santiago Nino, *Radical Evil on Trial* (New Haven, CT: Yale University Press, 1996), 170.
2. Quoted in Lawrence Weschler, *A Miracle, A Universe: Settling Accounts with Torturers* (New York, 1990), 243–45.
3. José Zalaquett, "Truth Commissions: A Comparative Assessment" (paper presented at an interdisciplinary discussion, Harvard Law School, May 1996), www.law.harvard.edu/programs/HRP/Publications/truth3.html.
4. Carlo Ginzburg, *The Judge and the Historian: Marginal Notes on a Late-Twentieth-Century Miscarriage of Justice*, trans. Antony Shugaar (London: Verso, 1999), 12.
5. E. H. Carr, *What Is History?* (New York: Knopf, 1962), 102.
6. Guatemala's Comisión para el Esclarecimiento Histórico (Historical Clarification Commission) was an exception to the tendency of truth commissions to avoid a rigorous engagement with history. See the discussion in Greg Grandin, "The Instruction of Great Catastrophe: Truth Commissions, National History, and State Formation in Argentina, Chile, and Guatemala," *American Historical Review* 110 (2005): 46–67.
7. Julie Taylor, "Body Memories: Aide-Memoires and Collective Amnesia in the Wake of the Argentine Terror," in *Body Politics: Disease, Desire, and the Family*, ed. Michael Ryan and Avery Gordon (Boulder, CO: Westview, 1994), 197.
8. Hesitantly so: The TRC's official Web site announces that the commission was "set up by the Government of National Unity to help deal with what happened under apartheid. The conflict during this period resulted in violence and human rights abuses from all sides." See www.doj.gov.za/trc (accessed May 8, 2006).
9. Nino, *Radical Evil*, 136.
10. Ibid., 101. See also Kathryn Lee Crawford, "Due Obedience and the Rights of the Victims: Argentina's Transition to Democracy," *Human Rights Quarterly* 12 (1990): 17–52.
11. See the Web site of the Asian Legal Resource Centre at www.hrli.alrc.net/mainfile.php/indonleg/131 (accessed August 8, 2006).

Knowledge, Experience, and South Africa's Scenarios of Forgiveness

Alejandro Castillejo-Cuéllar

The law selects among these voices, silencing some and transforming others to conform to legal categories and conventions. Most voices are silenced; those that do survive do so in a barely recognizable form.
—John Conley and W. O'Barr, *Rules versus Relationships: An Ethnography of Legal Discourse*

In the early hours of Monday, March 3, 1986, seven young activists from Old Crossroads and Gugulethu Townships in Cape Town were led by *askaris* into an ambush where members of South Africa's security branch and covert operations forces killed them during a joint operation. Official reports maintained that they died as a result of "multiple bullet wounds sustained in the course of S.A. [South African] Police activities for the purpose of combating terrorism." The Gugulethu Seven incident, as it came to be known, has since been surrounded by controversy and debate about the specific circumstances that led to the assassination of these youths. For more than a decade, this incident remained engulfed in an atmosphere of permanent denial.[1]

During that time, one of the most controversial issues was the circulation of two different versions. One maintained that the shoot-out started as a direct response to supposed terrorists who, finding themselves surrounded by the police, reacted by

Radical History Review
Issue 97 (Winter 2007) DOI 10.1215/01636545-2006-011

shooting at members of the Murder and Robbery Unit. This version contradicts the second one, in which eyewitness testimonies reported seeing "a white man shooting one of the men in the head while he was lying motionless on the ground."[2] Another eyewitness, from a nearby hostel, maintained that a group of policemen threw a man onto the ground and shot him three times at point-blank range, execution style. The police version differed from these testimonies that attested to the brutality and callousness of the security personnel. Ten years later, Zenzile Khoisan, the Truth and Reconciliation Commission (TRC) officer in charge of the investigation, wrote in his report to the head of the Western Cape Investigation Unit that "it is our view that these young men were led into an ambush by the security forces after they had been infiltrated by *askaris* from Vlakplaas, who participated in the training of these men and provided them with weapons."[3] The complexities involved in the Gugulethu Seven case placed it center stage in a series of public debates, ranging from the role of doctors and the media during the apartheid era to the use of death squads by the former government during the later years. The history of the case spans two decades of South Africa's political process.

In this article I explore how, after more than ten years of virtual silence, the Gugulethu Seven resurfaced through the process of the TRC. In the same way that the TRC constituted, among other things, a major attempt to rewrite an authoritative history of South Africa between 1960 and 1994, it also indexed certain incidents as part of the history of the struggle against apartheid. The TRC was simultaneously a technology that rendered visible certain forms of violence while obliterating others. Of the twenty-two thousand official victims, for instance, the killings of the Gugulethu Seven were a case of human rights violation given special attention by the commission. In this way, the Gugulethu Seven became an institutionalized yet contested site of remembrance in Cape Town. This institutionalization, and the particular discourses in which the Gugulethu Seven became embedded during the mid-1990s, came as a consequence of their inscription into the TRC's general goal of promoting reconciliation and revealing the truth of the past.

At the time of the general hearing in April, the investigation was still at a preliminary stage. By late September that year, the investigative team had already made major advances into the clarification of the incident. In an internal memo, the head of the Western Cape Investigative Unit proposed a "Special Event Hearing" to be held in November 1996 in Cape Town, as part of the Human Rights Violation Hearings. Special event hearings were selected as "window cases and aimed to provide detailed insights into particular incidents that were representative of broader patterns of abuse."[4] The commission only held ten of these hearings, among which one finds major events: the 1976 Soweto student uprising, the 1986 Alexandra six-day war, the 1960 Pondoland rebellion, and others. The Gugulethu hearing finally took place on November 27, 1996, and included testimonies from the families (only five of them gave testimony), as well as from the journalists and eyewitnesses. All alleged perpetrators were subpoenaed and questioned by the commission. From this moment on, the Gugulethu Seven emerged from relative invisibility to become a major TRC event and was written into the new authoritative historical narrative produced by the commission as an emblem of the amorality and evil nature of apartheid.[5] The Gugulethu Seven reappeared to the broader South African audience as an icon, a landmark, a site of resistance, and as an example of the state abuse of human rights.

In this essay, I pose the following question: How was the Gugulethu incident framed by the commission's institutional discourses so that, by the year 2000, it had become an emblem of reconciliation and forgiveness?[6] The discourses about the case framed the manner in which the Gugulethu Seven were represented and codified (as an example of human rights violations, for instance) and also shaped the way the incident was remembered by the society at large. I approach this question by analyzing a series of sites that fostered an iconic quality of the Gugulethu Seven. Aside from the TRC final report's particular ways of representing the killing, the transnational, iconic quality of the Gugulethu incident could also be easily perceived as it was crystallized and reinforced in a well-known documentary directed by Frances Reid and Deborah Hoffmann, *Long Night's Journey into Day* (2000), produced under the auspices of the TRC. In this article, I explore the political assumptions underlying this film, a particular kind of mediation that depicts and represents a series of "scenarios of forgiveness," and the ways they interconnect with the commission's general goals.[7] What kind of political *artifact* is this documentary, as well as the other memory sites that will be analyzed, and what kind of narrative do the images and texts weave? What kind of "Gugulethu Seven" is produced and articulated in this narrative? And finally, what kind of historical artifact was this scenario of forgiveness?

I pursue these questions for two reasons. One has to do with the transnational circulation of ideas and concepts regarding political transitions, and the prospect of reconciliation and forgiveness in societies characterized by political violence and war. Over the past year or so, while writing this essay, I had the opportunity to participate in several conferences on issues of collective memory, transitional justice, reconciliation, and postconflict situations as an academic who has worked on Colombia and South Africa in different academic scenarios, from Argentina and Colombia to the United States, the United Kingdom, and Germany, among others. The concern I have expressed elsewhere—that in the circuits of transitional justice theory, South Africa held a particularly important status as a reference point—became all too obvious in the context of these conferences and workshops.[8] Aside from the idea of the country's supposedly peaceful transition, a notion debated at the grassroots level in South Africa, the TRC and its discourse on social and individual reconciliation always came up as models.

I found it rather interesting how, at many of these conferences, Reid and

Hoffmann's documentary was screened, always sparking a handful of hopeful, sometimes even naive, assessments of the future in other war-torn countries such as Colombia. One of the reasons organizers screened the film was that its ending apparently opened a door. While looking at the complexities of forgiveness, it established a moral ending, showing that, despite differences, there was a light at the end of the tunnel: the prospect of forgiveness. The Gugulethu Seven, one of the cases presented by the documentary, represented that light. I found particularly revealing the fact that the film circulated more widely abroad than in South Africa. I wondered what the conditions for such circulation were, and what gave these images so much momentum. Proof of this power of circulation can be demonstrated by the fact that in November 2005, the Gugulethu Seven and the Amy Biehl cases, the latter also part of the documentary, formed part of a special television report entitled "Can South Africa Be an Example to Follow?" and broadcast by a local Colombian television network. In an evident attempt to give credence and some kind of factual grounding to the government's current and highly criticized peace process with paramilitary squads, the report presented South Africa as a country where differences between blacks and whites had been overcome due to the implementation of the law (in South Africa, the National Unity and Reconciliation Act of 1995, and in Colombia, the prospect of the Ley de Justicia y Paz [Justice and Peace Act] of 2005).

The second question concerns the historical claims of communities of apartheid survivors in South Africa and the importance of recognizing these people as agents in history. This was brought to the fore during long interviews with friends closely related to the Gugulethu families as they spoke and reflected on the meeting between the Gugulethu mothers and one of the *askaris*, and particularly Reid and Hoffmann's depiction of this face-to-face encounter. The general opinion, contrary to what I had heard at international conferences, was that *Long Night's Journey into Day*, rather than offering a hopeful comment on South Africa's transition, was "reconciliation propaganda," a phrase so straightforward, so loaded—and a *narrative gesture* so complex—that it certainly required further unpacking to make it intelligible. My friends felt that too much attention on the light at the end of the tunnel trivialized and abstracted the suffering and the occluded historical conditions of such encounters. This essay constitutes an attempt at understanding the semantic density of this gesture as a way to comprehend the historical character of these scenarios of forgiveness.

As a consequence of the particular dynamics of violence during the apartheid years, the families of the Gugulethu Seven embodied the experience of historical and endemic silence, witnessed the defilement and public mistreatment of their sons' bodies, and encountered the blatant manipulation of facts and the censorship of the truth about their children's deaths. During the TRC process, these issues resurfaced, but this time they became articulated in the language of sacrifice (as a way of speaking about and rendering intelligible the tension between a painful past and an uncertain present) and restoration. The demands of the families regarding the acknowledgment of these two registers of experience met the commission's general goals and main institutional discourses. The term *restoration*, then, came to encompass the families' expectations about the restitution of "voice" (and the recognition of the experience of suffering under apartheid), the restoration of human dignity, and the restoration of truth. It was precisely around these three vertices that the commission was structured from the moment of its inception. In some ways, the families' experience of historical dislocation found a home in the commission's language of restoration.[9] The language of sacrifice, on the other hand, to which I will return in the final comments of this article, was strongly embraced by one of the families during the private unveiling of a tombstone in March 2005 as a way to address and balance the price paid for liberation.

In this essay I point out that the TRC's discourse of national unity and reconciliation framed the Gugulethu Seven and, in doing so, created a particular idea of the Gugulethu Seven as a beacon of reconciliation. This Gugulethu was later taken by other mediators (such as filmmakers) and stripped of any historical context. In some ways, it was re-presented as an icon of reconciliation but emptied of historical content, creating the conditions for its circulation in a number of national contexts. This text then fleshes out the conditions for such circulation and the ways in which discourses of transition and reconciliation, postconflict and peace, have not only come to form part of the only transnational and hegemonic language to speak about political change but have also defined the technologies applied in other national contexts.

The Prospect of Restoration: On Truth, Voice, and Human Dignity

Three of the Gugulethu Seven mothers approached the TRC staff in 1996. Their intention was clear: to request assistance from the commission to clarify the circumstances that led to the killing of their sons and to hold the perpetrators accountable for their acts. In the preface of the National Unity and Reconciliation Act of 1995 (hereafter, the Act), the act that gave birth to the TRC, the centrality of the search for factual clarification was clearly established from the outset. One of the goals of the commission, and I quote extensively, was

> to provide for the investigation and the establishment of as complete a picture as possible of the nature, causes and extent of gross violations of human rights committed during the period of March 1, 1960 to the cut-off date contemplated in the constitution [May 1994], within or outside the Republic, emanating from the conflicts of the past, and the fate and whereabouts of the victims of such violations . . . it is deemed *necessary to establish the truth* in relation to past events as well as the motives for and the circumstances in which gross violations of human rights have occurred.[10]

The commission established a series of mechanisms to provide such a supposedly complete picture of the apartheid past: first, a research and corroboration process — triggered by victims' and deponents' testimonies, and carried out by the Research Unit — assisted in localizing and mapping certain incidents within the general coordinates of human rights violations defined by the TRC's mandate. This mandate not only identified specific acts as violations (which defined the meanings of violence) but, in doing so, it constrained and defined the nature of the TRC's endeavor, disconnecting it from lines of causality that may have explained, for instance, the historical interrelations between apartheid and its recourse to other forms of less visible violence and previous forms of segregation.

Second, much detail came from perpetrators who applied for amnesty, for which sworn affidavits, hearings, and on-camera interviews were used to collect information. The interconnection between these two mechanisms produced the commission's findings, or knowledge, distilled out of a social process of inquiry. However, in the context of rendering this factual picture to the broader society, in the case of specific incidents during the apartheid years, the amnesty process played a far more central role in its production. This process created a specialized knowledge about the past, rendering cartographies of certain notions of violence and dislocation and presenting them in particular ways.

These mechanisms, which coexisted during the commission's life span, weighed differently during different stages of its process. The victim-centered testimonial process central to the first stages of the TRC gave way to the more legalistic and forensic concept of truth developed by the Amnesty Committee. Even if, during the process of knowledge production about the past, the testimonies helped to visualize certain uses of apartheid violence, and in this way triggered a process of truth recovery, in the end the testimonial process had no epistemological weight in the final report. Yet if at one point testimonies were more concerned with narrative, dignity, and voice, as many authors have stressed, they also formed part of, even if tangentially, the general process of knowledge production in which specific information was extracted from them, organized, and interpreted. Both of these mechanisms, which rely on two concepts of what constitutes sources, laid the foundation for the prospect of the restoration of truth and the production of knowledge about the past.

The Act speaks, in this regard, about the idea of factual or forensic truth within the temporal confines of the mandate period (March 1, 1960 to May 10, 1994) and concentrates its effort on establishing a comprehensive account of certain kinds of acts, typified as gross violations of human rights. These violations are defined by the Act as well, and are confined basically to "(a) killing, abduction, torture, or severe ill-treatment of any person," on the one hand, and "(b) any attempt, conspiracy, incitement, instigation, command, or procurement to commit an act referred in paragraph (a)," as well as a series of subcategories emanating from these general terms developed by the commission's information and classification system.[11] For instance, killings may be subclassified according to the specific procedure: by beating, electric shocks, and so on. For these actions to be classified as gross violations of human rights, they had to be performed in the context of the "conflicts of the past" (that is, the mandate period) and be associated with a "political objective."

As I have stressed, the commission basically had two mechanisms available to carry out this mission. On the one hand, it collected evidence on the basis of a standardized process of statement taking from deponents. Subsequently, the investigative unit would corroborate the information gathered in this way. This process consisted basically of filling out a protocol that would describe and capture specific kinds of information on gross violations of human rights: dates, the nature of the violation, the names of the victims, a brief summary of the incident, and the place at which it occurred. These testimonies were produced during the statement-taking process when people came forward to call the commission's attention to the killing, abduction, or torture of a relative, and they were mainly the responsibility of the Human Rights Violation Committee. Although these testimonies concerned themselves with what was known as "narrative truth," I also see them as part of the commission's broader goal that sought to unveil forensic or factual truth regarding the conflicts of the past.

Richard Wilson has succinctly pointed out that the protocol itself underwent a process of transformation (and technical refinement according to certain pragmatic necessities) during different moments of the commission's life.[12] Initially, in early 1996, when the Gugulethu Seven mothers appeared before the commission, statement takers, trained especially for the job, were responsible for gathering general narratives or testimonies from the victims themselves, surviving relatives, or other deponents in connection with past events. These proved long, personal, and detailed renderings of the context that surrounded particular incidents. Like all testimonies—and at the time there were little practical constraints regarding form and content—these often constituted complex textures that wove time and space in a not necessarily linear fashion, hovering around minutiae not specifically connected, in the legal sense, to the violation of human rights. At that moment, the commission was certainly interested in encouraging this cathartic exercise, replicated in the ritualistic space of public hearings.[13] Testimonies would divert, so to speak, from the actual incident into other dimensions of experience. Public hearings may give an example of what these sorts of testimonies looked like. One of the Gugulethu mothers, for instance, in her public testimony (and this implies a constraint in itself, when compared to the intimate face-to-face relationship with statement takers) took little time to describe her son's killing, and rather focused extensively on the consequences of his death: family dislocation, economic fragility, scarcity, orphanhood, loneliness, and so on. Certainly, one of the problems around statement taking was the fact that the definition of an "act" was so narrow that it could not take into consideration the web of effects constituting the lifeworld of the extended family.

If the idea of statement takers was to gather very precise information regarding human rights violations, the time needed to gather the information, as well as that required to process this information, made it a difficult and time-consuming job.[14] Statements could take any time between two to three hours to complete, and they could run thirty to forty pages. Given this pace, and the narrative nature of the information gathered, by September 1996, the commission did not have the number of deponents they had foreseen at the beginning of their work. Much of the shortfall was blamed on the statement takers themselves. As an investigator commented, "statements were coming in with no date of violations, no names of the victims or witnesses, and *meanderings in the story*. We should have trained lawyers taking statements. They were of very poor quality."[15]

If the first year of the commission's work was a victim-centered process, allocating a great deal of resources and time to listening, by the second year the process had already shifted dramatically. Hardly any findings, one of the commission's goals, could be drawn from the material extracted from the first kind of testimonial process. Strong criticisms came from different quarters, mostly from investigators, data analysts, and lawyers, concerning the "useless," in the legal sense, nature of this kind of information. According to this view, the commission could not fulfill its mandate because it could not make any serious, legitimate, and impartial findings based on a process that, first, involved a lot of emotions and produced a text that seemed to allow too many inconsistencies and contradictions, and second, could not yield any relevant or significant "facts" to identify perpetrators and hold them accountable for their acts.

The change in the protocol not only reflected a particular technical transformation and the refinement of information-gathering tools based on bureaucratic rationalism but was also an expression of deeper cleavages within the commission itself as to the notion of truth and the sources of knowledge. The notion of truth, and hence the idea of an authoritative knowledge about the past, was embedded in complex political tensions. The debate centered on which concept of truth—forensic or narrative—held more legitimacy in the process of providing a supposedly complete picture of the past, and it was an expression of the differing social contents assigned to the notion of truth. The very fact that the commission grew out of a last-minute compromise, relating to the question of amnesty for perpetrators, and was decided on at a late stage during the negotiation process, made it an institution susceptible to criticism regarding issues of justice in which the amnesty provisions were viewed as favoring the perpetrators. In the final analysis, as far as perpetrator findings were concerned, a forensic-factual notion of truth seemed more consistent with the goal of producing an accurate assessment of the conflicts of the past. In this regard, the changing of the protocol, and the role of experience as a source of knowledge, constituted a response to social and political prerogatives.

Be that as it may, on one side of the debate about notions of truth reflected in the changing form of the protocol were those who defended a truth based on experience and narrative as an exercise in a process of the restitution of human dignity, centered on the victims' voices. The other side of the debate was more concerned with "factual" truth, devoid of any subjective content and necessary to uphold not only the commission's legitimacy but also the goal of making any findings regarding gross human rights violations. Many commentators on the TRC process relate to this dual register of truth recovery that informed not only the actual process of the commission but also its final distillation into the report.[16] As Graeme Simpson has pointed out, "At the heart of this hybrid approach [between amnesia and prosecution embodied by the TRC] was a reliance on a notion of 'truth recovery' as a restorative alternative to punitive justice—through full disclosure by perpetrators (and their supposed shaming) in exchange for amnesty as well as through voluntary testimony about apartheid's gross human rights violations given by victims (and their supposed healing)."[17] The protocol as an artifact of truth recovery reflected this duality.

As I remarked earlier, during the first year of the TRC, protocols were geared toward gathering full voluntary testimonies from victims and witnesses. The information would then be registered, photocopied, and archived. Subsequently, the testimony rendered by the victims' relatives, witnesses, or the victims themselves would be separated into different categories and subcategories or subtypes of violations, namely "killing" (by different means), "torture" (also by different means), "abduction," and severe ill-treatment.[18] This information would then be entered into a general database, using the Information Management System that allowed regional offices to exchange and compare sensitive or relevant information via computer networks.

The statement before the commission's staff constituted a first step in the unveiling of truth and the clarifications of the circumstances that may have led to gross violations of human rights. It was also a first step into the production of specialized knowledge about the past. After this initial step, the commission, through its investigative unit, would start a process of corroboration and investigation based on the powers conferred by the Act: powers to subpoena potential witnesses and to seize documents in any archive or holding, whether private or public. The information captured at local TRC offices could be *translated* into local and regional findings, statistics of gross human rights violations, particular patterns of abuse, and so on.[19] Comparisons among regional offices would inevitably lead to national generalizations regarding the phenomenon in question during the mandate period of the commission. The final report, the final "complete picture," was produced out of these forms of fact collection and translation.

However, as the process of shifting the protocol took a definite turn, and as its inherent conception of truth shifted from open-ended testimony to factual truth, the process relied more heavily on categorical classification and a "controlled vocabulary" in which testimonies would be boxed into narrower definitions of acts of violence. The shifting of the protocol generated a sea change in the procedure, including the training of the statement takers, making the process of recollection more expeditious. In this context, in late 1997, the commission had engaged in a complex process of perpetrator findings, and it required more precise information during the process of statement taking so that the final picture, identifying victims and perpetrators of gross human rights violations, could be produced. To do that, the statement-taking process changed dramatically, according to new necessities. If at the beginning of the TRC, experience as a source of knowledge on the past constituted a central element, by 1997, experience had been scratched off the script. The notion of truth recovery, as part of a broader healing process, depended also on this specific path to collecting information.

The shifting form of the protocol to serve the needs of lawyers and analysts had its consequences. It became a questionnaire with very specific entries that could easily be handled by data analysts. The testimony would be reduced to its simplest form: a brief summarized version of the incident. In the words of one Johannesburg data processor, "When we started it was narrative. We let people tell their story. By the end of 1997, it was a short questionnaire to direct the interview instead of letting people talk about themselves. The questionnaire distorted the whole story altogether, it destroyed the meaning."[20] The protocol became an instrument of reduction, a particular technology that grasped historical causation, interrelatedness, and complexity by fragmenting a narrative texture into smaller clusters of significant or relevant information. By doing that, acts were decontextualized, dehistoricized, and treated as discrete, universal categories. Acts of gross violations of human rights, the smallest unit of analysis, came into existence only as they were inscribed into the system of classification. Data collection was further narrowed by the analysis of summaries on the basis of a rigid, controlled vocabulary.

The emotional character disappeared altogether, and the problem of the person's articulation of experience in language became irrelevant. The initial cathartic character of the testimonial experience became an exercise of data extraction, decontextualized and stripped of personal, meaningful detail. The whole process changed from a three-hour interview to a half-hour one. As the process became more and more impersonal, the less cathartic it became. The more impersonal and directed it was, the more useful and legitimate a source of knowledge it became. "Factual truth" grew out of an aseptic process that would cleanse a constellation of historical, personal, and existential factors from its subjective burden. In a country like South Africa, this particular practice reinscribed silence at the very moment the experience was articulated. As Wilson succinctly states, "What was lost in the data processing and the urge to generate acts that could be counted were the existential truths contained within complex narratives. The processors destroyed the integrity of the narrative by chopping it into segments and 'capturing' discrete acts and types of persons."[21]

In the final analysis, this process implied a series of translations: from the first testimony, itself framed by the informational necessity of the statement-taking process, into the findings, from experience into knowledge. The final report, as I will show later, reflects this banishment as the information regarding the Gugulethu Seven was certainly reduced to basic factual information. During the process of knowledge production, the mothers' experiences were displaced by the commission's need to establish legal evidence. However, these testimonies also constituted a fundamental source in grounding it, even if only partially and at the beginning of the process (although they—in the long run—were not recognized as such by data analysts). In this regard, as far as this knowledge is concerned, they had a rather liminal status, simultaneously central and peripheral, present and absent. In any case, had it not been located by the mothers' experiences and voices within the commission's coordinates, forensic truth would never have emerged at all. It seems to me that despite the fact that the commission had very different definitions of truth at this point, two of the definitions, narrative and forensic, seemed to intersect.[22] However, in the long run, the TRC process would take both of these truths along different paths.

The fact that the Gugulethu mothers contacted the commission's staff at an early stage meant that they had the opportunity to experience the process of statement taking in its initial form rather than in its more restricted and technocratic one. This allowed, simultaneously, the prospect of knowing what had happened to their sons and the possibility of telling their own stories. In conversation, the mothers described how they retrospectively evaluated the work of the commission in this manner, as a space to speak and as a space to uncover the past, as painful as it may have been.[23] The problem was that over the course of the TRC process, their experiences and voices, and what the Gugulethu Seven came to represent, became plotted into the commission's historical narrative, where these testimonies were either exiled from the findings or strategically used as a moral bedrock or emblem.

But the weight of uncovering what the commission called forensic truth did not come from families' testimonies. In fact, a great deal of the information regarding the Gugulethu case came either from the investigations carried out by the commission's Research Unit or from amnesty applications. In the latter case, provided that the acts for which amnesty was requested were politically motivated, perpetrators were granted amnesty on the basis of a full disclosure of the nature and extent of the violation they committed. The Gugulethu mothers' testimonies brought the incident to the attention of the commission, generating a thorough investigation including the seizing of documents from police stations, magistrate courts, and other venues, and eventually leading to the draft proposal of a special hearing where all the policemen involved were subpoenaed. The amnesty application from the *askaris'* handlers further revealed some details.[24] Taking all these elements together, the process of the commission, at the very least, helped answer, as Archbishop Desmond Tutu put it while introducing the special hearing, some of the questions that had remained in the air for more than a decade (as well as posing new ones), at least from the point of view of the families. Although the Gugulethu families' legal representatives contested the decision, the two amnesty applicants were finally granted amnesty in 2001.

This process, however, was not easy. The mothers testified in public, in November 1996, and, as the special event hearing unfolded, they had to cope not only with the act of retelling their experiences in front of television cameras and the perpetrators but also had to endure viewing the images of their sons being dragged around the streets of Gugulethu, as well as the photographs taken after the killing. This was obviously so painful that while watching the police video with its gruesome images of the crime scene, one of the mothers threw a shoe and hit the head of one of the policemen present, disrupting the proceedings. The hearing was adjourned and the families had to be escorted out of the room to be debriefed by TRC staff before the hearing resumed. In addition, they had to cope with the policemen's half-truths, evasive testimonies, and their lack, on the surface at least, of any kind of remorse. Except for one *askari* who asked for forgiveness during an encounter with several of the mothers weeks later, the policemen either reiterated the old version or simply denied any knowledge of the involvement of covert operations squads. Forensic truth, the product of a complex process of gathering, classifying, and analysis of information — a partial and incomplete process in itself — proved a painful, wounding experience. The media's gaze certainly captured this wounding experience, disseminating it to all those interested in the work of the TRC.

I shall not dwell on the proceedings of the special event hearing or the details of the amnesty process. What must be pointed out is that at the juncture of these two processes, a space was created that allowed a clarification of the context surrounding the Gugulethu Seven killings. This was in accordance with the mothers' requests to know what had happened. The product of this juncture constitutes the essence of the commission's findings, the distilled knowledge it produced. The point that I want to emphasize, however, is that in this process, the mothers' testimonies had an ambiguous status in which their experiences proved central to the general endeavor of uncovering truth, but remained irrelevant in the final authoritative history represented in the final report. The findings on the Gugulethu Seven were voided of experience, and, as I will show, denied an epistemological status within the process of producing knowledge about the past. In this regard, there was a cost to be paid for this knowledge. Besides issues widely debated at the time (such as granting amnesty in exchange for truth), there was a price paid for the way the

Gugulethu Seven were inserted into the TRC report and "written into history as evidence" of gross violations of human rights.[25]

In the official interpretation, these voices were more connected to "restoring human dignity," with "letting people tell their stories," than with forensic truth. Personal and narrative truth was one of the dimensions that the TRC strongly, and structurally, encouraged, an avenue to a particular kind of truth, to an existential universe inevitably defined by harm. The commission functioned as a space for listening to South Africa's multiplicity of experiences of apartheid. Personal truths, particularly from those victimized by apartheid, were rendered in public and transmitted through the media. They were selected from thousands of possibilities. "The stories told to the Commission *were not presented as arguments* or claims in a court of law. Rather they provided unique insights into the pain of South Africa's past, often touching the hearts of all that heard them."[26] In this regard, the submissions during the public hearings concerned the validation of the persons' experiences of violence, and about public acknowledgment. As Archbishop Tutu pointed out during the Gugulethu Seven hearings, it was simultaneously an exercise that sought validation as well as factual truth:

> In this hearing we do not make a *finding*. We will be listening to evidence and *testimony* and we will then, later on, be making a finding. It is not a court of law, but we want to indicate that, first of all, we hope that out of solidarity and respect for those who have come to testify about their pain and suffering, we would be able to conduct ourselves in an appropriate manner. . . . As part of the process of healing in our land we hear the stories of what took place and the chief aim is reconciliation. We are searching for the truth, and what we want is actually healing and reconciliation in our land.[27]

The possibility for victims to speak up, to let their voices be heard, formed a major component of the commission. The TRC constituted a mechanism that allowed the recognition of those experiences of harm and suffering silenced by the apartheid regime.[28] However, the temporal and spatial coordinates of the commission's mandate, as well as the conceptual limitations of the hearings—focusing on gross violations of human rights and certain forms of political agency, for instance—determined the nature of the testimony and the acknowledgment it sought. As Premesh Lalu and Brent Harris pointed out few years ago, as much as the TRC opened up spaces to speak, it also created certain forms of silence. The fact that the hearings were concerned with specific forms of violations of the body, and not concerned with wider, communal effects of apartheid, might serve as an example.[29]

From the TRC's point of view, testimonies were more about "opening and cleaning the wounds," about "acknowledgement" of the other's experiences, about telling a personal truth, about "reconciliation," and about "affirmation of humanity and dignity" in the very process of speaking, rather than, strictly speaking, about "facticity" and "knowledge."[30] Moreover, as a "window case," the Gugulethu Seven had all ingredients for an iconic and representative story of apartheid horror: death squads collaborating with security forces, institutionalized cover-ups, the defilement of corpses, the suffering of families, the evasiveness of factual truth, the mothers testifying to the commission, and the social resonance of the case.[31] It was in this discursive context that the Gugulethu incident was heralded onto the screens: as a tale of terror and survival, of suffering and forgiveness. Not only had the appearance of the Gugulethu families placed them at the forefront of broader public interest but also the encounter they had with one of the *askaris*, a story presented in the documentary *A Long Night's Journey into Day*, reaffirmed the place of the Gugulethu Seven as an emblem of reconciliation.

In summary, in the report, testimonies of the past are displaced from the wider findings the report established. Testimonies only appear to highlight and validate a broader viewpoint regarding some of the conceptual guiding lights of the TRC's work. As an emblem, as an icon, the Gugulethu Seven testimonies are presented as having a pedagogical role to fulfill: to show South Africa the possibility of forgiveness and the prospect of reconciliation, at a personal level, between victims and perpetrators. Reconciliation and forgiveness are viewed as two of the pillars of the new South Africa, the *rainbow nation*.

First Scenario: Encountering the Other; A Phenomenology of Reconciliation

In 2000, the filmmakers Frances Reid and Deborah Hoffmann released their documentary *Long Night's Journey into Day* (subtitled *South Africa's Search for Truth and Reconciliation*) onto the international scene. Over the years, the documentary has won a number of international prizes, from the Grand Jury Prize at the Sundance Film Festival to the *Berliner Zeitung* Reader's Jury Award at the Berlin Film Festival and the Golden Spire at the San Francisco International Film Festival. It was also an Academy Award nominee for best documentary feature. The film was a coproduction between Iris Films and Cinemax, a major cable television network based in the United States. The documentary traces the development of four stories as they unfolded during the TRC process over a period of two years, from the initial moments of victims' testimonials to the amnesty process.

The film establishes a parallel between four different scenarios as South Africa traveled from the seemingly ever-lasting darkness of apartheid into the early light of a new South Africa by the hand of the TRC. The documentary concentrates on what one might call stories of reconciliation and scenarios of forgiveness.[32] One of them treats the Gugulethu Seven. The story is organized around a particular linear chronology: first, a summary of the incident including some historical background information; second, a moment of truth revealed during the TRC hearings; and finally, the prospect of forgiveness and personal reconciliation. The four cases are summarized along these lines and show, in general, the complexity of facing the past, in its most literal sense, and the challenges that a society undergoing political and social transformations may run into.

Of the historical part, the documentary gives just enough information to render the story legible to foreign viewers. For example, at the beginning, it makes reference to the existence and role of the TRC, an almost unnecessary piece of information for a South African viewer at the time. The content concerns itself primarily with the TRC process, a process that, one infers, opened up spaces in which victims and perpetrators faced each other. In the Gugulethu Seven case, the directors decided to unravel the historical context while simultaneously presenting the developments of the TRC victims and amnesty hearings. As they follow the path of the hearings, the historical context emerges.

This process is punctuated in all four sections by footage of victims, from amnesty hearings, selections from testimonies, and in some cases, images of the general atmosphere: the intrinsic tensions of an emotionally charged process. Reid and Hoffmann also conducted several interviews, with victims as well as with perpetrators of gross violations of human rights, in order to understand different points of view, particularly those of the victims and their personal and existential predicaments, but also those of the perpetrators, exploring the reasons why they finally came forward and told the truth. In general terms, of the four stories, two are ones of reconciliation and forgiveness, or at least this is how they are depicted: Amy Biehl's parents finally meet the killers of their daughter, former members of the armed wing of the Pan-Africanist Congress (PAC), in Gugulethu.[33] In the other encounter, the Gugulethu mothers speak to one of the *askaris* involved in the killing of their sons. The remaining stories are, from this point of view, about failure.

Long Night's is a tale of victims encountering perpetrators. It is certainly a world of discrete opposing racial categories, of victims and perpetrators, and of precise contending political affiliations, where history is revealed in all its brutality and drama. Despite this seemingly moral organization of the world, mainly three subtle protagonists emerge from the documentary. The first, it seems to me, is *experience* as articulated in an individual *voice*. Second, is the recovery or the revealing of *truth*, in a factual sense; and finally, the prospect of *forgiveness*. I wish to discuss very briefly these three issues only to highlight that in the moral message emanating from this documentary, one circulating in contexts of transitional justice theorizing, the Gugulethu Seven case stands as a "beacon of hope," to use the final report's own phrasing.

Long Night's has no narrator in the formal sense telling the story.[34] This is not to suggest the absence of an intellectual authority, in the sense of an authorship organizing the footage, fragments, and stories told, in short, accommodating these elements along certain thematic lines. But the only voices that serve the purpose of recounting, at the immediate level of the viewer, were witnesses speaking in their own terms. Every piece of footage was plotted within the general structure of the narrative to build and articulate a linear, chronological continuity. From conflict to reconciliation and forgiveness, the viewer is taken through these people's personal histories by the hands of the witnesses themselves, by their experiences, feelings, and opinions. The use of testimonies, of firsthand witnesses, gives the film a strong emotional weight, as well as a sense of being driven into the details and minutiae of people living under abnormal circumstances during the apartheid years. Voices speak about past sufferings while images of burned and desecrated bodies, bombs and destruction, visually substantiate the content of the witnesses' words. There are also the voices of the perpetrators, either extracted from the TRC's hearings or from the interviews themselves, trying to explain their deeds. In any case, these voices were plotted in such a manner that their very presence not only gave the film a sense of realism and temporal sequence but also legitimacy.

Another relevant protagonist was truth. As people came to the commission, details from particular incidents began to emerge. In all cases, truth was obviously a painful encounter, not only in the sense of clarifying the incidents of the past but also in the sense of meeting the other, sometimes with his indifference, sometimes with his remorse. The Gugulethu Seven mothers' encounter with truth meant meeting the killers, facing their contradictions, their words, the public scrutiny, after years of silence (although they had seen them before in the context of Tony Weaver's 1987 trial when he was accused by the government of publishing a series of opinions from families and local residents regarding the actions taken by the security forces during the Gugulethu shooting). One of the mothers encapsulates this ambiguous encounter when she says,

> Whatever he [the informer] has been saying, is just eating me up inside. He was the cause of this whole thing. He is like a wolf wearing a sheep's clothing. The informer was meeting with them [our children] and milking them for information. The children poured everything out because he wanted to get the job done. Every time they say something, the informer goes and reports it to the authority. It makes me so bitter and angry, why entrap children like that?

With truth came the possibility of locating responsibility, of holding someone accountable, of facing for the first time the person who, whether willing or hesitant to acknowledge this responsibility, produced harm. The film producers indexed this first distant encounter when they registered the way victims looked at the deponents while they spoke. Gazes full of anger and bitterness were fixed on the other's face.

In the chronological sequence of the documentary, the victims' encounters with truth and otherness play as a prerequisite for the possibility of forgiveness and healing. In two of the cases, this possibility never emerges for different reasons. In the remaining ones, it does. In the case of Amy Biehl, her parents met the family of their daughter's killer. Not only did they not oppose Mongezi Christopher Manqina's amnesty application but they also, when he was released from prison, encouraged his own community to receive him. The two families approached and embraced each other, as a "way to honor Amy," according to her father.[35]

However remarkable this scenario of forgiveness may be in the context of South Africa's conflict, it seems a rather strange example to be included in the film. Besides the fact that the encounter between a black family and a white family certainly stands as a metonym of the nation's racial conflict, and that the killing of the American student was a mistake (she was taken as a white settler, when in fact she lived in South Africa to support the country's political transition), the encounter—as a juncture of two different yet deeply entwined histories—is abstracted from the historical and sociological backgrounds of those taking part. The encounter between the Biehls and the Manqinas is not about former South African enemies, one representing the monopoly of a racial elite, the other representing the oppression of a majority. It is, in my view, only a face-to-face encounter between whites forgiving blacks, as discrete categories of racial classification, not an encounter between two different yet deeply entwined histories. This is a scenario of forgiveness and reconciliation in a minimalist sense, where the encounter is completely voided of its sociological context.

The main conceptual basis for this representation, its "arti-factuality," is that reconciliation is a personal, deep engagement with the Other, an almost ontological transformation in which the seemingly impossible happens. In this transcendental context, personal histories do not necessarily inform the nature of the encounter. As the Reverend George Molebatsi during an interview suggested to me, "it comes from the heart."[36] In some sense, although it deals with reconciliation, this section of the film is not about South Africa. The only moment during which whites and blacks are shown embracing is here. Problematically, it only involves *one* South African family, while the other is an American family that had never visited the country before their daughter's death. The centrality of this case in the film's narrative makes it even stranger. It is the first optimistic scenario presented, and the story also serves as the documentary's epilogue, the last sequence of the film depicting Manqina's release from prison, a moment of renewal: from forgiveness to a new beginning. Yet the diverse historical experiences of blackness and whiteness, or any other racial category, as they developed specifically during the apartheid years in South Africa did not form part of this particular scenario. To put it bluntly, during their meeting, neither family saw stereotypes: the Biehls did not see "kaffirs," and Manqina's family did not see "white settlers." *Long Night's* certainly does not give us any details about the historical and sociological texture of this face-to-face encounter. History remains absent. The documentary itself is a historical artifact, and one of the representational devices it uses to consider the nature of reconciliation and forgiveness is the exiling of the historicity of the encounter, as well as the historicity of the representation.

But any possible doubts regarding the problem of facing the Other and the prospect of reconciling the nation in the Biehl case, at least for an attentive reader, might be lifted by the Gugulethu Seven scenario, especially when contrasted with other failed stories of reconciliation.[37] The TRC and the Reverend Molebatsi facilitated the encounter between the Gugulethu mothers and one of the *askaris*, Taphelo Mbelo, who was involved in the setup. Pumla Gobodo-Madikizela, who served on the TRC's Human Rights Violations Committee, initially informed the mothers of Mbelo's request. The mothers initially discussed the issue, and although unsure as to what to expect from such an encounter, they finally faced the man. Through Mbelo, the whole incident was clarified. Wilhelm Riaan Bellingan, the other amnesty applicant for the Gugulethu case, appeared evasive and hesitant during the process, always giving the impression of withholding information and avoiding full disclosure, one of the requirements for granting amnesty. Both Bellingan and Mbelo were Vlakplaas (the notorious apartheid covert-operations death squad located near Pretoria) operatives in 1986.

The encounter between the mothers and the amnesty applicant was filmed, although there had been some debate as to whether to allow media presence. Finally, Reid and Hoffmann were granted entry. Mbelo, a black man in his mid-forties, states in the documentary,

> My name is Taphelo Mbelo. I am ashamed to look you in the face. I know it is painful for you to be faced with the person who has done you wrong and to talk to you. Others may never forgive me. I know I have done wrong, that I have done evil things on this earth. I want to say to you, as parents of those children who were there that day, I ask your forgiveness from the bottom of my heart. Forgive me, *my parents*. (emphasis added)

And then a long silence engulfed the room, a calm tension, the Reverend Molebatsi remembers. Reid and Hoffmann's documentary is mostly concerned with the verbal exchange that followed. While Mbelo avoided eye contact, looking to the floor, one of the mothers clearly, in a very straightforward way, stated that she did not have forgiveness for him. It is obviously impossible to know what really happened that day, whether all mothers spoke or not, in which order, and what they said. In speaking with the Reverend Molebatsi, I learned that the exchange had been much more complex. From the point of view of the filmmakers, there were only two sections worth showing. The mothers had a negative reaction: they spoke of the unbearable pain of seeing how their sons had been treated, how their bodies had been defiled, and how death had broken relations. Even their current financial circumstances stood as a reminder of the past, another form of reliving it. The camera captured these moments of tension. Time seems to elongate, to unpack endlessly, slowly. Mbelo's reference to the mothers as *his* parents, to reconnect to his "own blood," to reconnect the severed relations, to be reincluded in the moral community he diverted from, did not have the expected effect. Then, when everything seemed to have fallen apart, when the meeting was about to be adjourned, Christopher Piet's mother, the mother who watched her son being "treated like a dog" on TV, a committed religious leader in her community, abruptly spoke and voiced a remarkable, complex statement embracing him.[38]

> Just a minute *my son*, doesn't Taphelo mean prayer? I see what your name means. I don't know whether you follow this or not. Speaking as Christopher's mother, I forgive you *my child*. And the reason I say I forgive you is that my child will never wake up again, and it is pointless to hold this wound against you. God will be the judge. *We must forgive those who sin against us, even as we wish to be forgiven*. So, I forgive you, Taphelo. I want you to go home, knowing [that] the mothers are forgiving the evil you have done and [that] we feel *compassion* for you. There is no place for throwing stones at you, even though you did those things. So Jesus told us when he was on the cross "forgive those who sin against you." Because we want to get rid of this burden we are carrying inside, so we, too, can feel at peace inside. So, for my part, I forgive you, *my child*, yes, I forgive you; go well, *my child*. (emphasis added)

The documentary ends with this statement. Mbelo stands up and leaves the room after hugging the mothers who allowed him to. I do not want to comment on these words, and I have decided to transcribe them with the speaker's permission. The genealogy of some of the phrases and words emphasized speaks to the possible textures of not only these words but also to the texture of something called forgiveness. Behind this act there is certainly a world condensed and a number of different referents socially available to speak about the past. The statement constitutes a complex articulation. It speaks of moral principles, of Christianity, of living by the word, of kinship, and of the role of elders.

In summary, the documentary delivers a moral lesson. Encountering an other who has done wrong, even in the most profound ways, is a plausible scenario. In the midst of much fear and resentment, forgiving is possible, embracing is possible. One of the Gugulethu mothers rose up from her own feelings of despair as she remembered her son Christopher being dragged "like a dog," and despite the reactions against Mbelo, she finally embraced him. This scenario, to be a lesson, had to be abstracted from its specificity. The sociohistorical context of this encounter was erased. What could have been the historical conditions of her words? There was only remorse from Mbelo, and forgiveness from her. This moral ending, this scenario, was sealed and legitimized by the families' own words, by their experience of suffering as they were played out in the documentary, a site where the Gugulethu Seven became an icon to be shown elsewhere.

Second Scenario: Stripping History of Experience

The TRC's final report contains several references to the Gugulethu Seven scattered throughout the seven volumes. Six of the ten references are photographs of

Cynthia Ngewu and Eunice Miya, the mothers of Christopher Piet and Jabulani Miya, respectively.[39] Another photograph depicts Sergeant John Martin Sterrenberg standing by Christopher Piet's bullet-ridden corpse.[40] Nine of the ten Gugulethu Seven references appear at the beginning of texts they do not necessarily seem to relate to. However scattered, they portray three different moments of the Gugulethu saga within that of the TRC. On the one hand, there is Sterrenberg's image: a time and space of horror, a portrait of death's ineluctable and irreversible presence. Second, there are a few other photographs depicting a public display of suffering, a portrait, for example, of Mrs. Miya crying as she recounted, during a human rights violations hearing, the day Jabulani was killed. It is an image of an old black African woman weeping inconsolably, a scenario repeated many times during the life of the commission. In the institutional discourses of the commission, this represented a moment of catharsis, of the mothers "bearing witness to their own suffering," as Archbishop Tutu declared the first day of the Gugulethu Seven hearing, and bearing witness to their sons' lives as well: a step toward healing.[41] Finally, images of Mrs. Ngewu walking to the Gugulethu graveyard, together with representatives of different religious denominations and TRC staff during a memorial service in 1996, stood as a tribute to the deceased, a step toward restoring human dignity.

The Gugulethu Seven case was one of the most frequently represented incidents among a couple of dozen introduced by the report. Although images are scattered throughout, they could be organized along a temporal continuity: first, the moment of death; second, the painful moment of the recovery of truth and voice; and finally, the forward-looking moment of restoration: from the darkness of the past depicted by Sterrenberg's cynical posture into the future of reconciliation. The photographs represent what, in my view, could be called the commission's essential Gugulethu Seven moral "story," though narrated in the language of images: the prospect of restoration in the midst of much (state-sponsored) suffering. It is only embedded in this visual narrative that the witnesses' sense of the world and emotions seem to fulfill a role, albeit a subordinate one, within the commission's findings, and within the report itself in particular. These represent instances of emotions indexed as capturing the "essential" moments of this moral story. The pictures are, as far as the Gugulethu Seven are concerned, technologies of memory in themselves, almost like mnemonic devices placed there for the rainbow nation to remember, to trigger a series of memories and associations about a traumatic past. The report, on the other hand, constitutes a technology of circulation; it disseminates a history of abuse carried out by the evil and inhumane system of apartheid. From the commission's final report, one learns what apartheid did at a certain level, and to a limited extent, who did it and how. However, the reader is never introduced into its genealogy as a legalized system of segregation that extended its sphere of control to the minutiae of the everyday, or as a historical artifact. The report nonetheless disseminates and speaks to a history of horror and rebirth in which the Gugulethu Seven are introduced as a symbol.

But the *reduction to the essential* is an abstraction that has been subtracted from its broader context. From the outset, the commission's mandate restricted its domain of inquiry to certain kinds of acts, and to a particular kind of causality: certain forms of violence on specific people produce certain kinds of acts, gross violations of human rights, and they in turn generate certain consequences, such as post-traumatic stress disorder. In this case, the notions of violence underlying the idea of gross violations (largely around personal and individual bodily mistreatment) and the category of *human being* that emerged from the infliction of this pain—the subject ironically and tragically formed out of this process of dislocation, the victim—ruled out other mechanisms through which violence (and apartheid itself as a concept that seeks to regulate otherness, or what I have called elsewhere a social form of the administration of otherness) could have been conceptualized and understood.[42] The human beings classified as the objects of a terrorizing system, the official victims of apartheid, constitute only a fraction of those who suffered in regard to apartheid's actual and destructive sphere of influence over the population since 1948, when the National Party came to power and devised the concept of separate development, one of the theoretical pillars of apartheid. The report overlooked these other systemic registers in which violence intersects with the human being and his or her experience of the world, and with the law that sought to determine experience itself.

Moreover, if the subject of the law—a subject partly constructed through its enunciation and representation within particular discourses—becomes the object of terror on whose body the memory of such violence is literally carved (as it happened during the emergency period), and, if the experience of the conformation of this subject is simultaneously the experience of subjection to and the contestation of power in its different registers, what sense of identity, community, and experience, of survival, of being in the world may be formed at the juncture between apartheid's disciplining discourses and its practices? Discourses that construct the subject by naming it (terrorist, for example), in doing so, render it partly invisible at the very moment of its enunciation. And bodies, on the other hand, are permeated by this "ecology of invisibility" in which "bare life" dwells on the threshold of terror (invisible yet brutally there, lying dead) as part of the social distribution of inequality and suffering.[43] From the moment of its inception into the social space, and particularly during the emergency years, Gugulethu inhabited such a threshold. What is the profound sense of being, of existence, formed and dislocated simultaneously under the aegis of apartheid?

By reducing to the essential, the report certainly overlooked questions regarding the historicity of apartheid as a multifarious and multilayered experience. It did not study the violence inherent to the permanent, daily enforcement of apartheid laws. Nor did it address the objective conditions for the production of experience and subjectivity as a way to grapple with the systemic nature of the phenomena, an issue much discussed by many commentators and analysts. The scope of the mandate hardly allowed a careful examination of phenomena located beyond the limited definitions of the National Unity and Reconciliation Act, such as other forms of violence that were constituent with apartheid itself. The inquiry left out the "social distribution of pain and suffering," to use Veena Das's phrase, through dislocation, displacement, dispossession, and the experience of a systemic, overarching, and all-embracing segregation system.[44]

The experiences of an unjust system were not, theoretically speaking, part of the knowledge and history produced by the commission.[45] If they emerged in the text, as they certainly did, they mainly meant to illustrate a point, to add eloquence and a sense of realism by assigning a voice to an argument so that the "facts" presented by the text acquired legitimacy. The practice of including extended excerpts from the testimonies had a strong impact on the reader, and on the existential and authoritative quality of the findings. However, testimonies in and of themselves were not, strictly speaking, the center of the inquiry. What can, for instance, testimony—as a particular artifact, a particular form of articulating experience—teach the student of violence and trauma about meaning, community, agency, subjectivity, power, and the systemic character of apartheid itself? The potential that testimony may have had at the beginning of the inquiry was dissolved along the way as facticity and perpetrator findings became central protagonists.

These problems could not be explored simply because the theoretical framework did not render the pertinent phenomena visible. The text does, for example, include transcripts from hearings describing torture techniques and other abuses, as well as other themes related to the commission's findings, but the former appear to illustrate the latter. The experiences of suffocation, anguish and humiliation, and of sexual abuse transcribed in the report speak more about the factual reality of torture than about *experience* per se. People's narratives remained subservient to the broader agenda of describing abuse, as defined by the commission's framework. As Mahmood Mamdani has so eloquently stated:

> Injustice is no longer the injustice of apartheid: forced removals, pass laws, broken families. Instead, the definition of injustice has come to be limited to abuses within the legal framework of apartheid: detention, torture, murder. *Victims of apartheid are now narrowly defined as those militants victimized as they struggle against apartheid, not those whose lives were mutilated in the day-to-day web of regulations that was apartheid.* We arrive at a world in which reparations are for militants, those who suffered jail or exile, but not those who suffered only forced labor and broken homes.[46]

This depuration of experience, this taming of the emotional, systemic effects of apartheid, at the very moment of its capturing during the statement-taking process and its subsequent analysis, finally crystallizes in the authoritative historic-teleological narrative of the report. The reduction to the essential, the iconic character of the Gugulethu Seven shooting as a history of horror and rebirth, as an example of abuse, defined and circumscribed by the language of human rights, extracted from broader experiences of apartheid, from the subtle, intimate, sometimes unintelligible sensory experience of dispossession—with which one, as a reader/viewer, only has a cursory, almost perfunctory relationship—is never granted the same epistemological status as the data gathered from the investigation process. Four additional written references to the Gugulethu Seven appearing in the final report, besides the photos mentioned earlier, show the displacing (and the disciplining) of experience and the victims' testimony from the historical narrative, the final product of the investigative process.

The final knowledge distilled out of the investigation process, which started with the mothers' submission to the commission, is presented in volume 6, a volume dedicated to revealing some of the findings of the Amnesty Committee and reporting on the work of the Reparations and Rehabilitation and the Human Rights Violations Committees. It was a much-expected document, for it included the commission's recommendations to the president. The reference to the Gugulethu Seven in this volume constitutes a summarized version extracted from the amnesty process, a condensation of the first two parts of Gugulethu's essential story depicted by the images themselves. Text and images are integrated: they speak about the recovery of truth and the unveiling of terror. The commission's findings answer the questions the mothers posed at the beginning of the process: What happened, when, how, and who carried out the operation? It is the final distillation of facticity.

> On 3 March, seven operatives were killed in Gugulethu, Cape Town, by a combined C1/Vlakplaas, Western Cape Security Branch and Riot Squad team. The group of youth activists had been infiltrated by C1/Vlakplaas operatives (working in conjunction with the Western Cape Security Branch) who provided them with weapons and training. Only one of the seven had apparently previously received military training from MK. The applicants presented conflicting evidence as to whether the intention had been to arrest or kill the activists. Two C1/Vlakplaas applicants were granted amnesty for this operation.[47]

Although the families' experiences and testimonies of loss had obviously proven central to the TRC process, in the final account, these experiences were left out. As is evident from the previous quotation, they had no epistemological status in the long run—other than when the Gugulethu Seven were included into the TRC knowledge-producing process through the statement. "Hearings," said the information manager in Johannesburg in an interview in 1997, "where not conceptualized as having any input into the production of knowledge—they had no epistemological status at all . . . [they] have to do with legitimation and recognizing people's experiences."[48] Nowhere do they appear in the findings of the commission, particularly in connection to the Gugulethu Seven. They were, rather, considered part of a narrative truth, a personal, subjective point of view whose articulation had more to do with the recovery of voice and dignity than with history, in the sense of a factual, forensic inquiry.

Experience, and the channel through which it was articulated, then, had an ambiguous status. On the one hand, it held a central position within the production of as complete a picture as possible of South Africa's past. Testimonies helped to localize the past the commission's mandate was looking for. However, during the process of production, their complexity was reduced to the terms, context, and institutional necessities of the TRC (even the few testimonies that were rendered in public hearings). What remained constituted narrative, subjectivity, deemed unnecessary as far as this knowledge-production process was concerned. In this process of the interpretation and institutionalization of evidence, testimony became domesticated by a state-sponsored commission of inquiry. Voices were restored—or, it seems to me, South African society also learned to listen to and render intelligible the unintelligible—at the price of domestication.

There is only one place in the final report where one of the Gugulethu Seven mothers is quoted extensively. She uttered her words during the sessions of the Forum on Reconciliation, Reconstruction, and Economic Justice held in Cape Town in March 1997 under the auspices of the TRC. By February 1997, there had already been two major TRC hearings on the Gugulethu Seven; the public prominence of the case was at one of its high points. The quote occurs in chapter 9, dedicated to the prospect of reconciliation.[49] One finds it under a subsection entitled "Towards the Restoration of Human Dignity: Perpetrators." The aim of the text, after a brief introduction highlighting the country's social divisions, is to show the complexity of the reconciliation process in South Africa. The editors of the final report selected "moments from the life of the commission" that "express significant steps in this reconciliation process."[50] The text openly refers to them as "beacons of hope," the light at the end of the tunnel, and "signposts on the long road towards . . . national reconciliation" (the "long road" is a dominant metaphor of South Africa's political process and an evident paraphrase of Mandela's autobiography) (5:350–51).

Again, excerpts from public testimonies only illustrate the ways the commission "helped people" to "restore their human dignity" (5:350–51). They also address the "willingness to forgive" and the "building and rebuilding of human relationships" as part of the reconciliation process (5:350–51). Categorizing along the same lines, describing the conflict of the past as having produced basically victims and perpetrators, the report is divided in two. The first one, "Towards the Restoration of Human Dignity: Victims," enumerates the different registers in which the "restoration of dignity" could be read. This section, perhaps the more programmatically important, claims that truth telling or "storytelling" leads to healing, the main assumption on which the whole TRC process was based.[51]

The document basically extracts from public testimonies sections that could display or substantiate the healing nature (or argument) of storytelling. It is important to note that if during the production of forensic truth testimonies had no epistemological status, as Richard Wilson has suggested, in the context of this part of the report, they are displayed as having an important bearing. Here testimonies are afforded what seems like an epistemological weight, a recourse that allows the pondering and confirmation of the main argument, namely, that truth heals. Again, as a rhetorical device, the story is detached from its context of enunciation, itself a space traversed by different forms of mediation, as the editor abrogates the right to frame the victim's voice, to define the reading and the interpretation of her or his words, and to con-sign or archive, à la Jacques Derrida, the Other's voice around an interpretative matrix.[52] Testimonies are presented as having, in this transitory epistemological space, an authoritative character. The supposed healing power of storytelling is reflected in the excerpts themselves. A number of references occur, sometimes not too clearly linked to the problem of healing, to a new life brought about by the revelation of the hidden, to the end of silence, to the cathartic dimension of speaking, and what seems to be, at first sight, an ontological transformation of the human being. Again, this is the realm of knowledge based on experience. However, the exercise of speaking is abstracted from the social conditions of its enunciation before, during, and after the actual rendering. One never knows whether these conditions actually determine, or at least inform, the nature and character of the rendering, the feelings involved during the aftermath, the medium-term feeling about it, and the retrospective evaluation of the experience of speaking. What at first sight could be cathartic and liberating, in the long run, given certain individual conditions, could be damaging. This is something that falls beyond the scope of the TRC mandate, and a self-assessment perhaps also beyond it. Yet the connections between storytelling and healing at the individual level were presented, ironically, as a finding. Only a very brief reference to the experience of the person right after delivering the testimony is sketched.

It is not my intention to trivialize the nature and complexity of delivering a public testimony or to judge or analyze its contents. My experience as a scholar in other countries, such as Peru and Colombia, has shown me how difficult it is, at the personal level, to speak about a painful past, and at the collective one, to listen to it, to understand the semantic density, the nuances involved, and especially to acknowledge the pain. Relatively recently, other scholars, too, have reflected on this kind of hermeneutics. Scholars of the Holocaust such as Lawrence Langer, Shoshana Felman, and Dori Laub, among many others, have emerged as central figures in these debates. I have also argued recently the extent to which truth commissions, and the institutional gathering of testimonies and victims' voices, have become a technology of legitimation, applicable to differing contexts. My purpose here is, rather, to highlight the context in which references to testimonies, voices, and experiences are placed within the report as a way of problematizing the political character of this location.

The transcript of the testimony from one of the Gugulethu Seven mothers mentioned earlier appears in the second part of the text, titled "Towards the Restoration of Human Dignity: Perpetrators." The mother's voice is taken as an example of someone suggesting that South Africans, in order not to return evil with other evil, accept perpetrators back into their communities as a different form of justice, not punitive but restorative, so that they can become human again. "Reconciliation," according the report, also means to "give the opportunity to become human again." From this point of view, it was the perpetrator who, in the capacity to exercise power and inflict pain on others, was dehumanized. Given the iconic character of the Gugulethu Seven's essentialized moral saga, conveying a history of silencing, the fact that one of the mothers "confirm[ed] this crucial insight [that perpetrators can become human again]" became iconic itself, a quotation reproduced by journalists and academic publications.[53]

The citation is taken out of its context of enunciation, and it appears as a confirmation of one the TRC's central arguments: that the restoration of humanity and forgiveness are not only interconnected but that both can be attained, even under extreme circumstances. The concluding note affirms that the nation can be reconciled. The paragraph ends with a remarkable phrase from Cynthia Ngewu that echoes the openness toward forgiveness she displayed during the encounter with Taphelo Mbelo: "We [victims] want to demonstrate humanness towards them [perpetrators] so that they in turn may restore their own humanity."[54] Ngewu certainly embodies the possibility of reembracing and reaccepting the other, an other that has done an irreparable damage to her. But what was the genealogy of this statement, of this particular articulation of experience and voice, and what was the constellation of factors that might have led to it? The report abstracted from this history.

The testimonies and voices from apartheid victims, particularly the ones coming from the Gugulethu Seven families, were used in specific ways within the report. They do not have to do, in the strict sense of the word, with the production of knowledge about the past. They were used, rather, as an authoritative device to highlight and substantiate some of the commission's main arguments regarding restoration and reconciliation. Who else could speak better about reconciliation than those who suffered the most? In this regard, the Gugulethu shooting—that is to say, the families' testimonies—was inscribed into the TRC's institutional discourses by becoming a "beacon of hope" and a symbol of what seemed impossible to attain, the light at the end of the tunnel, the prospect of reconciliation. As Michel-Rolph

Trouillot has pointed out in connection to history, "The naming of the fact . . . already imposes a reading and many historical controversies boil down to who has the power to name what."[55] This inscription, and this naming, mainly became possible because fifteen years of history were reduced to a single moral saga. Aside from that, the commission's report remains completely purged, so to speak, from the actual experiences, the cleavages, contradictions, and limitations of the story and the way it finally crystallized. If this held true for the Gugulethu Seven, a case of great prominence, it likely also held true for the majority of victims' testimonies who did not appear in any public hearings. Regardless of the fact that the mothers gave their testimonies at the beginning of the TRC process, the final Gugulethu Seven history embedded in the report not only occludes how personal histories interconnect global historical processes but also how these experiences, and what human beings in a particular language call or address as their experiences, are actually situated historically.

Final Comments

The Gugulethu Seven case has shown that a social tension exists between the idea of restoring voice, truth, and dignity and the languages available to speak about these issues. The prospect of the restoration of truth in the forensic sense, for instance, is partly achieved by stripping truth and history of experience. The recognition of other people's suffering might paradoxically only be possible through a particular kind of language, and a series of institutions, in which experience is reframed, mediated, and even domesticated. The Gugulethu Seven saga, particularly in those instances in which the mothers' voices and opinions have been emphasized as they faced one of the askaris involved in the killings of their kin, has come to represent, almost with paradigmatic force, a scenario of forgiveness, a guiding light, not only in the local South African context but also internationally through the circulation of Reid and Hoffmann's documentary. This circulation, and its potential intelligibility across transnational viewers, is only possible given the reduction of a complex, multilayered historical process into a single, essential, and teleological Gugulethu saga. In this process, voice and recognition are separated by a discursive abyss in which speaking about a painful past is, ironically, framed by the technical language of human rights violations. Silence acquires a different texture as the process of testifying unfolds existentially. To put it bluntly, it is this process of standardization, of the reification of the testimony to the detriment of its semantic density, that allows for its use under certain political conditions of enunciation as a legitimating technology. It is partly this reduction to the essential that transforms experience into knowledge about trauma, violence, and postconflict—a knowledge deemed transferable and applicable, according to administrators of conflict and managers of political transitions, to other national and historical realities.

Notes

I am indebted to the Solomon Asch Center for the Study of Ethnopolitical Conflict, University of Pennsylvania; the New School for Social Research; the Fulbright Commission; the Colombian Institute for the Development of Science and Technology; and the Wenner-Gren Foundation for their financial assistance during the different stages of this research. I must also express my gratitude to my colleagues at the Direct Action Centre for Peace and Memory, in South Africa, where I was a research fellow between 2002 and 2004. My work also benefited from a visiting research fellowship at the Institute for Justice and Reconciliation, also in South Africa (2001–3).

1. In South Africa, the use of the political term *askari* became widespread during the 1980s to describe guerrillas *turned* into police informers. The *askaris* from the Gugulethu operation came from Vlakplaas, a notorious apartheid covert-operations death squad located near Pretoria. The seven youths killed were Mandla Simon Mxinwa (age twenty-three), Zanisile Zenith Mjobo (age twenty-one), Zola Alfred Swelani (age twenty-two), Godfrey Jabulani Miya (age twenty-one), Christopher Piet (age twenty-three), Themba Mlifi (age thirty), and Zabonke John Konile (age twenty-eight). Official information comes from G. Hoffmann, "Kennis van Geregtelike doodsondergoek (14/86/7)" ("Notice of Inquest [14/86/7]"), Truth and Reconciliation Commission Archive, Pretoria.
2. Zenzile Khoisan, *Time of the Jacaranda* (Cape Town: Garib Communications, 1996), 12.
3. Report on the Investigation into the Gugulethu Seven, internal written memo presented by Zenzile Khoisan to the Truth and Reconciliation Commission's Western Cape Investigation Unit, September 19, 1996.
4. *Truth and Reconciliation Commission South Africa Final Report*, 7 vols. (Cape Town: Juta, 1998–2003), 1:148; hereafter *TRC Final Report*.
5. The historical narrative finally crystallized in the commission's final report. Critics of the report have pointed out its lack of a coherent, integrated historical narrative that connects and accounts for apartheid as a systemic phenomenon, looking into its complexities and fractures. The report is, as they have suggested, an aggregation of typologies of human rights violations organized around local, regional, and national findings regarding abuses, with very little insight into apartheid as a whole. In this regard, as Deborah Posel has suggested, the only possible narrative was a moral-theological one in which the explanation of apartheid as a systemic phenomenon is its evil nature and the moral wrongness of those who supported it. See Deborah Posel, "The TRC Report: What Kind of History, What Kind of Truth?" in *Commissioning the Past*, ed. Posel and Graeme Simpson (Johannesburg: Witwatersrand University Press, 2002), 148; and Richard Wilson, *The Politics of Truth and Reconciliation in South Africa* (Cambridge, MA: Cambridge University Press, 2001), 58.
6. It is important to note from the outset of this article that the measure of reconciliation and forgiveness that one of the mothers embodied during her encounter with one of the *askaris* involved in the killings seems to be exceptional when compared to the defilement and humiliation that the bodies of the dead were subjected to by the police. The more gruesome and callous the violation of the community and the body by the security forces, the more remarkable the potential for scenarios of forgiveness.
7. Jacques Derrida, *On Cosmopolitanism and Forgiveness*, trans. Mark Dooley and Michael Hughes (London: Routledge, 2001), 70.
8. Alejandro Castillejo-Cuéllar, "The Textures of Silence: On the Limits of Anthropology's Craft," *Dialectical Anthropology* 29 (2005): 159–80.
9. The interconnections between "intimate" and "personal" articulations of the past with broader forms of remembering are an avenue of research I am aware of. Looking into how

these two are in fact mutually constituent problematizes the dichotomies between collective forms of remembering as opposed to supposedly individual forms of remembering. As much as I found this a potentially fertile ground for inquiries, at the intersection of the mothers' experiences of historical dislocation and the commission's language of restoration, I was—for practical as well as ethical reasons—unable and unwilling to explore this complex interface. In any case, this essay gives a sense of such interconnectivity.

10. Republic of South Africa, Office of the President, "Promotion of National Unity and Reconciliation Act, Act 34 of 1995," July 26, 1995, 1; emphasis added.
11. Ibid.
12. Wilson, *The Politics of Truth*, 33.
13. Belinda Bozzoli, "Public Ritual and Private Transition: The Truth and Reconciliation Commission in Alexandra Township, 1996," *African Studies* 57 (1998): 167–95.
14. Laars Buur, "Monumental Historical Memory: Managing Truth in the Everyday Work of the South African Truth and Reconciliation Commission," in Posel and Simpson, *Commissioning the Past*, 66–93.
15. Quoted in Wilson, *The Politics of Truth*, 43; emphasis added.
16. Philip Bonner and Noor Nieftagodien, "The Truth and Reconciliation Commission and the Pursuit of 'Social Truth,'" in Posel and Simpson, *Commissioning the Past*, 173.
17. Graeme Simpson, "'Tell No Lies, Claim No Easy Victories': A Brief Evaluation of South Africa's Truth and Reconciliation Commission," in Posel and Simpson, *Commissioning the Past*, 221.
18. *TRC Final Report*, 5:15–23.
19. Wilson, *The Politics of Truth*, 33; Buur, "Monumental," 66.
20. Quoted in Wilson, *The Politics of Truth*, 45; see also Buur, "Monumental," 66.
21. Wilson, *The Politics of Truth*, 48.
22. *TRC Final Report*, 1:110.
23. By the time I did fieldwork in 2003, I only had the opportunity to interact, interview, and assist three of the Gugulethu mothers. I am aware of the impossibility of producing any kind of broad statement regarding the Gugulethu Seven on the basis of these connections to a few families, but they were the ones who took their plight to the commission and remained at the center of the process. The other four lived so far away, in other towns and townships difficult to access for me, that this distance made it very difficult to carry on any kind of sustained research with them. I did speak to these mothers on different occasions, but our relationship never went beyond those encounters. In some ways, my research was determined by the spatial arrangements set up by apartheid's distribution of space. I thus decided to work with the mothers that lived in the vicinity of NY1 and NY111, the corner where the seven young men died, in Gugulethu. Of the three remaining mothers, Cynthia Ngewu was the most outspoken and usually played the role of the families' representative. With the other two mothers, interviews were more difficult for various reasons, primarily ethical ones. The lack of direct references to these interviews or the mothers' voices and more explicit opinions in this essay is a silence I purposefully decided to integrate into my work.
24. Truth and Reconciliation Commission, amnesty application, W. R. Bellingan and T. J. Mbelo, cases AM5283/97 and AM3785/96, respectively, December 19, 1996.
25. Premesh Lalu and Brent Harris, "Journeys from the Horizons of History: Text, Trial, and the Tales in the Construction of Narratives of Pain," *Current Writing* 8 (1996): 25.
26. *TRC Final Report*, 1:112; emphasis added.

27. Gugulethu Seven hearings transcriptions, TRC electronic archive, 1; emphasis added. All transcripts of the TRC's hearings may be found at www.trc.org.za.
28. Alejandro Castillejo-Cuéllar, "Entre los intersticios de las palabras: Memoria, posguerra y educación para la paz en la Sudáfrica contemporánea," ("Between the Interstices of Words: Memory, Postwar, and Peace Education in Contemporary South Africa") *Estudios de Asia y África* 41 (2006): 11–46.
29. As I said at the beginning of this article, my intention is not to propose a description or an exegesis of the mothers' testimonies. I am certainly aware of the complexity of these personal, multilayered historical narratives and the sources they display in order to articulate experience. But given the uses their testimonies have been put to, I find such an exegesis a futile exercise. This is probably the point where such an endeavor would prove appropriate, but this interpretation falls beyond the scope of this text. However, extensive comments dealing with women's testimonies in general, and with the Gugulethu Seven mothers in particular, have been produced over the years. See Fiona C. Ross, *Bearing Witness: Women and the Truth and Reconciliation Commission in South Africa* (London: Pluto, 2003); Annalet Van Schalkyk, "A Gendered Truth: Women's Testimonies at the TRC and Reconciliation," *Missionalia* 27 (1999): 165–88; Martha Minow, *Between Vengeance and Forgiveness: Facing History after Genocide and Mass Violence* (Boston: Beacon, 1998), 82; Antjie Krog, *Country of My Skull: Guilt, Sorrow, and the Limits of Forgiveness in the New South Africa* (Cape Town: University of Cape Town Press, 2000), 109; Charles Villa-Vicencio and Wilhelm Verwoerd, eds., *Looking Back, Reaching Forward: Reflections on the Truth and Reconciliation Commission of South Africa* (Cape Town: University of Cape Town Press, 2001), 68.
30. *TRC Final Report*, 1:113.
31. Alex Boraine and Janet Levy, eds., *The Healing of the Nation* (Cape Town: Justice in Transition, 1995).
32. The four cases it deals with are, first, the killing of Amy Biehl in 1993, a U.S. Fulbright student working in South Africa at the time; second, the killing of the Cradock Four, Matthew Goniwe, Fort Calata, Sparrow Mkonto, and Sicelo Mhlauli, in 1985; third, the amnesty process of Robert McBride, a former Umkhonto we Sizwe (Spear of the Nation, or MK) operative responsible for the bombing of the Why Not bar in Durban in the mid-1980s; and fourth, the Gugulethu Seven saga.
33. Amy Biehl was a U.S. student conducting research in South Africa during the early 1990s. She was killed in the streets of Gugulethu in 1993 by a group of Pan-Africanist members who perceived her as a white settler. The killers were granted amnesty by the TRC.
34. In this context, I use the term *story* somewhat reluctantly (together with the contrasting word *history*), not to qualify what in fact were personal or collective histories of harm, oppression, or violence, but to highlight the fact that, out of a number of different sources, a single visual and textual narrative has been constructed in the video, with a beginning, a climax and tension, and a resolution. Histories of harm were translated into stories of reconciliation, according to the terminology used by the directors, and in this way, they became arti-facts.
35. Over the years, the Biehl family has run the Amy Biehl Foundation in Gugulethu, where Manqina and others participate in the development of sustainable programs.
36. Interview with Rev. George Molebatsi, conducted by the author, October 23, 2003, Cape Town.

37. I am not using the terms *successful* or *failed* as a qualification of these encounters. An uncritical use of them would certainly fail to see that failure and success represent overtly simplistic characterizations of what encountering the other may be about. I use the terms only to point out that this is how they are categorized and qualified in the film.
38. Interview with Cynthia Ngewu, conducted by the author, June 12, 2003, Cape Town.
39. *TRC Final Report*, 1:293, 3:451, 5:196–97, 5:304, 6:200, 6:444.
40. Ibid., 6:263. See also Alejandro Castillejo-Cuéllar, "The Archives of Pain: Essays on Terror, Violence, and Memory in Contemporary South Africa" (manuscript in preparation).
41. Desmond Tutu, HRV hearing transcript, Gugulethu Seven transcripts, 1996: 2. Available at www.trc.org.za.
42. The "subject," writes the philosopher Paul Smith, "on the other hand, is not self-contained, as it were, but immediately cast into a conflict with forces that dominate it in some way or another—social formations, language, political apparatuses, and so on. The 'subject,' then, is determined—the object of determinant forces." Paul Smith, *Discerning the Subject* (Minneapolis: University of Minnesota Press, 1988), xxxiv. See also Alejandro Castillejo-Cuéllar, *Poética de lo otro: Hacia una antropología de la violencia, la soledad y el exilio interno en Colombia* (*Poetics of Otherness: Toward an Anthropology of Violence, Solitude, and Internal Displacement in Colombia*) (Bogotá: Instituto Colombiano de Antropología, 2000), 173.
43. Giorgio Agamben, *Homo Sacer: Sovereign Power and Bare Life* (Stanford, CA: Stanford University Press, 1998), 71. Allen Feldman, "From Desert Storm to Rodney King via Ex-Yugoslavia: On Cultural Anesthesia," in Nidia Serematakis, ed., *The Senses Still* (Chicago: University of Chicago Press, 1994), 87.
44. Veena Das, *Critical Events* (Oxford: Oxford University Press, 1995), 37.
45. The notions of truth and knowledge conveyed by the public victims' hearings differed qualitatively from the notions instrumentalized by the commission's investigative unit. The latter were, as the commission's report actually stated, forensic and factual, and the "knowledge" the report produced was *inferred* from "methodological rigor" and a "scientifically valid process." *TRC Final Report*, 1:103. In the system of classification established by the commission's information system (infocomm), after a process of examination, only certain acts (defined by a number of coordinates) about the past could firmly be called knowledge. In the other case, victims' hearings, the idea of knowledge had more to do with encountering the other's experience in the past, with speaking what seemed to be unspeakable, as a window to that past, so that most South Africans *knew* what was happening then, a past that was occluded by power and silence. *Knowledge* here is not a technical term, but rather serves as a synonym for *uncovering*, *unveiling*, *restoring voice*, and *bearing witness*. In the context of the report, these notions of truth and knowledge remain unconnected, and they refer to qualitatively different processes: the first is a knowledge based on evidence and empirical research, in a positivist sense, on which the findings, the report, and an authoritative and official version of South Africa's recent past are grounded; the second is based on experience.
46. Mahmood Mamdani, "Reconciliation without Justice" *South African Review* 10 (1997): 22; emphasis added.
47. *TRC Final Report*, 6: 2003.
48. Quoted in Wilson, 2001, 41.
49. *TRC Final Report*, 5:366.

50. Ibid., 5:350.
51. I use the term *storytelling* in quotation marks because the word, it seems to me, gives the articulation of experience a misleading sense of fiction that fails to see the semantic and existential density of the voice. Whenever possible I shall use the term *testimony* instead.
52. Jacques Derrida, *Mal d'archive: Une impression Freudienne* (Paris: Éditions Galilée, 1995).
53. *TRC Final Report*, 5:67; for journalists and academics quoting the Gugulethu mothers, see also Minow, *Between Vengeance and Forgiveness*, 82; Krog, *Country of My Skull*, 109.
54. *TRC Final Report*, 5:367.
55. Michel-Rolph Trouillot, *Silencing the Past: Power and the Production of History* (Boston: Beacon, 1995).

Truth, Justice, Reconciliation, and Impunity as Historical Themes: Chile, 1814–2006

Brian Loveman and Elizabeth Lira

In the 1980s and 1990s, processes labeled "national reconciliation" became important elements in ending civil wars and framing the so-called transitions from military/authoritarian governments to elected civilian governments in much of Central America and parts of South America. National peace and reconciliation commissions were central to the end to warfare and the reconfiguration of regional political systems.[1] In all Latin American cases of reconciliation since the early 1980s, high priority was given to what was called "governability," a term that included the reestablishment of the rule of law, as well as the normal operations of government agencies. From Guatemala to Argentina, processes of political reconciliation have been challenged by demands for truth and justice, punishment of human rights violators, and reparations for injuries suffered during the recent conflicts.

The notion that reconciliation required forgetting the recent past, with the consequence of impunity for the guilty, was resisted by those who believed that true reconciliation required just the opposite. A small cadre of intellectuals and theologians even suggested that true reconciliation required eliminating the conditions that had given rise to the civil wars and political repression—defined as the evils of capitalism in an almost classical Marxist critique of capitalism and imperialism offered by radical Catholic theologians.[2] These apparently antagonistic moral and

Radical History Review
Issue 97 (Winter 2007) DOI 10.1215/01636545-2006-012

philosophical interpretations of reconciliation made the political task of reconciliation inherently conflictive, a seemingly insurmountable challenge for policy makers. What was to be done?

The period from 1959 to 1990 was not the first time that civil wars and political violence afflicted Central and South America. Indeed, most stereotypes of Latin America include mention of political violence and instability. If these societies had previously experienced civil wars, political violence, and human rights violations, how were those conflicts resolved? How was governability reestablished? What efforts were made to shape social memory and create official histories regarding political violence and civil wars? In short, was there a past history of political reconciliation in Latin America that perhaps informed the events of the 1980s and 1990s? Were there national or regional styles of political reconciliation after major conflicts? Did different meanings for, and styles and modalities of, political reconciliation have identifiable consequences for national politics?

We seek here to provide an abbreviated answer to these questions only for Chile as a contribution to the more general historical problem of political violence and reconciliation. We identify the major political crises in Chile from 1818 to 2006 and a distinct Chilean way of political reconciliation, *la vía chilena de reconciliación política*.[3]

This *vía chilena* includes modalities of conflict resolution and peacemaking that date to the Athenian constitution and the Roman Empire, if not before, and much of it is shared with Catholic Europe and the rest of Latin America.[4] But it is also, in some respects, particularly Chilean. It includes both impunity and resistance to impunity; a quest for truth and justice and a pragmatic resort to amnesties and pardons in the name of social peace and governability. It includes appeals to memory and the punishment of the guilty (*ni perdón ni olvido*) and also appeals to Christian forgiveness and the concept of turning the page to start anew. It also includes a particularly Chilean combination of political reconfiguration and institutional reform accompanied by discursive, cultural, and even literary appeals to reconciliation following internal warfare or even episodic intense internal violence. Along the way, in the construction and maintenance of this *vía chilena*, different forums and institutions served as arenas for seeking the truth and for contesting, often unsuccessfully, social and legal impunity.

Almost always, the *vía chilena* resulted in political compromises that tempered the findings and the politico-legal application of the law in the name of social peace. This tension between truth, justice, criminal punishment, and "forgetting" (in colloquial Chilean *echándole tierra*, a cover up, or *corriendo el velo del olvido*, drawing the veil of oblivion) with pardons or amnesties, and for the sake of political regrouping, *is* the Chilean story and constitutes, in many ways, the abbreviated political history of Chile itself. In this sense, the Chilean National Commission on Truth and Reconciliation (1990–91) discussed later in this article was only a recent chapter in a still (2006) ongoing story of a battle between truth, justice, impunity, political pragmatism, and oblivion.

La Vía Chilena

In the nineteenth century, there developed a recognizable Chilean way of political reconciliation as a response to major political conflicts and internal wars. Gradually evolving from the time of independence into the 1920s, this *vía chilena* included discursive, institutional, and policy responses to civil war and political violence in order to achieve political reconciliation. From 1924 to 1932, this *vía chilena* found itself called into question—but eventually reaffirmed. From the 1930s to the 1970s, the modalities of political reconciliation that subordinated concerns for justice to "looking forward rather than backward" became routinized aspects of everyday politics. After 1932, these modalities prevented another major breakdown of the political system—until 1973. Indeed, those who carried out the 1973 military coup viewed their actions as a response to a long-standing siege of *la patria* (the homeland) by international Marxism, a struggle between antagonistic forces with irreconcilable discourses and social utopias.

By 1932, the elements of the *vía chilena* had become so routinized and ritualized that they formed core elements of Chilean politics. For better *and* for worse, they buffered the country against political rupture from 1932 to 1973, making Chile the only Latin American country during that period to experience no illegal turnover in government and no unconstitutional presidential succession. According to this version of Chilean history, the final, but inevitable, battle had been postponed for four decades.[5]

A less dramatic interpretation would locate the political rupture of 1973 on the list of internal conflicts and civil wars in Chile from the early 1820s, especially the civil wars of 1829–30, 1851, 1859, 1891, and the severe political crisis (including several successful military coups) of 1924–32. Such an interpretation would not label what occurred from 1973 to 1989 as the "final battle." It would also anticipate future crises unless the cycle of political rupture and political reconciliation that has characterized Chilean politics since 1818 is broken.

Debates in Chile over political reconciliation in the 1980s and 1990s unconsciously echoed the newspapers, congressional debates, political parties, church leaders, and military officers of the nineteenth and early twentieth centuries. The modes (and limits) of political reconciliation of the 1980s and 1990s also mirrored, in important ways, the *vía chilena* constructed in the nineteenth century.[6]

Political Violence, Civil War, and Reconciliation

An essential frame for viewing nineteenth-century Chilean politics is the sequence of political ruptures and reconciliations that occurred in establishing and modifying the political regime institutionalized in the 1833 constitution: 1823, 1826–31,

1850–51, 1857–61, and 1890–91. Each of these political ruptures involved civil war, not only in the sense of internal wars but also of divisions within families, social groups, the church, and military institutions. These conflicts were literally fratricidal—in biological as well as social senses (as occurred again in 1973). Whatever the underlying class and even racial implications, each rupture involved conflicts over constitutional norms, election laws, presidential-legislative relations, judicial autonomy, cabinet selection, and presidential succession. Though embedded in particular socioeconomic circumstances (the final two in deep economic recessions and labor disputes in northern mining centers), regionalism, resentment against the Santiago elite, and disputes within and among government and opposition factions, each major political rupture was justified by reference to supposed violations of the constitution and electoral irregularities (whether in regard to registering voters, the actual voting, government intervention and manipulation of the elections, or corruption and violence during the electoral process). In each case, the opposition claimed that the president (or the government and Congress) had acted illegally, suppressed the political opposition and media, and intervened in elections to assure victory for government-supported candidates—or that the government intended to do all these things in upcoming elections in order to gain or maintain control of the congress. In the final three instances, the threat that such electoral intervention would occur in upcoming congressional and presidential elections made for an important precipitant of revolt. Always, there were charges of dictatorship and tyranny. And whichever side emerged victorious in these political ruptures, the winning side claimed that victory meant the restoration of constitutional rule—even if it was followed by significant constitutional and political reforms. Chileans spilled blood in the name of legitimacy and constitutionalism, whatever other motives underlay the conflicts.

Finally, all contenders for control of the state (and its growing resources and patronage opportunities) claimed that their actions were taken to save the homeland (*salvar la patria*) from the crimes and abuses of their adversaries. Soldiers, militia, and civilians died on all sides for *la patria*; no one fought against it. But the contending factions, parties, and interests did have different visions of, and dreams for, *la patria*. Antagonistic dreams for the homeland justified for those in power various modes of political repression: the preventive detention of political opponents, extrajudicial executions (assassination), the abuse of prisoners, torture, so-called internal exile (*relegación*), political exile, the confiscation of property, and sundry other forms of political persecution. For those opposing the incumbent government, claims of tyranny and despotism, unlawful acts, and of other political abuses justified street demonstrations, attacks on government property, efforts to subvert military and police forces, urban insurrection and, ultimately, internal war in efforts to oust the government. These conflicts left in their wake thousands dead, thousands more injured, extensive damage and loss of property, families divided, and bitter social polarization. And after each conflict, calls for reconciliation rang out.

How did Chilean political leaders reconstruct the political system and provide for governability after the various conflicts mentioned above? How did they treat political trauma? How did these experiences carry over to the two major twentieth-century political ruptures—1924–32 and 1973–89—and to intervening violent confrontations (for example, the massacres at Ranquil, in 1934, and at the Caja de Seguro Obrero, in 1938)?[7]

Crafting the *Vía Chilena de Reconciliación Política*: Impunity, Memory, and Governability

A schematic historical reconstruction of these events reveals that recurrent debates over how to construct and reconstruct a supposed unified Chilean family, that is, a shared identity within a legitimate Chilean nation-state and political system, occurred after each major nineteenth-century conflict and again after the 1924–32 political rupture that framed Chilean politics until 1970–73.[8] These debates, and the seemingly consistent Chilean approach to political reconciliation from the 1820s until World War I, shed light on the dilemmas facing Chile in the 1990s as a result of the most recent and most prolonged internal war in Chile's history: 1973–90.[9]

Underlying all these historical efforts at political reconciliation after political cataclysm and political trauma was the concern by Chilean political elites with formal restoration of a shared legitimacy and with the practical matter of governability (usually translated in the nineteenth century as *paz social* and *orden*). The social construction of, and appeals to, nationalism—encapsulated in the sacred invocation of *la patria* and *la familia chilena*—constituted the symbolic foundations for iterated national reconciliations. Both consciously and by a seemingly autonomic application of culturally devised and inherited habits, the political elites gradually developed a recognizable approach to political reconciliation, based partly on (1) the premises of a shared Ibero-Catholic culture and values, with little tolerance for religious or cultural pluralism; (2) adaptations of Spanish colonial traditions, especially the use of (*a*) amnesties, pardons, and reparations; (*b*) the concession of pensions, jobs, and other economic opportunities; and (*c*) legalistic formalities (*resquicios legales*) including the often-cited principle "I obey but cannot comply" (*se acata pero no se cumple*); and (3) pragmatism and elite political repacting. The premises of this model are inherently incompatible when applied simultaneously, but they do not come into conflict directly when applied alternately and unevenly. The typical modalities of the *vía chilena* are arrayed below.

Policies

1. commutation of prison sentences, pardons, and amnesties (*conmutaciones de penas, indultos, amnistías*) for political crimes and crimes committed by the military, police, and government officials during the period leading up to, during, and up to the end of the political trauma

2. return of political exiles, with or without restitution of government posts, with or without pensions or other forms of reparation

3. concession by general law or special laws (*leyes de gracia*) of pensions, subventions, or one-time payments to military and police personnel, and family members, on both sides of the conflict

4. special laws for named individuals passed with the explicit purpose of reparation for injuries during the conflict

5. miscellaneous symbolic measures (monuments, public acknowledgments, inviting family members to participate in government or public ceremonies, social invitations to high-visibility events)

Political Reconfiguration

6. creation of new political coalitions in which some of the losers in the conflict are included

7. redefinition of key actors (political parties, church leaders, military elites, entrepreneurs, and, later, workers organizations) in the conflict of doctrinal positions and programs to permit governability

8. reincorporation of losers in the conflict into cabinet posts, the foreign service, the military, Congress, as well as into bureaucracy, university, and teaching positions in secondary and primary schools

9. constitutional, electoral, and legal reforms to ratify and formalize the reestablished "union of the Chilean family"[10]

In every case from 1818 to the early twentieth century, political reconciliation in Chile also included efforts to suppress and reconstruct the social memory to facilitate impunity (from the perspective of the victims) and political absolution (from the perspective of the perpetrators) for political crimes committed during the political cataclysm. This social-memory or official-story aspect of political reconciliation demanded long-term commitment and was expressed in the rewriting of government-approved history texts, in public ceremonies, and in numerous subtle acts of symbolic reconciliation. Reparation, as part of political reconciliation, routinely included the reincorporation of losers into presidential cabinets, the legislature, and judiciary, and of ousted functionaries (*exonerados*) into positions within the military, universities, public schools, and government bureaucracies. By the 1860s and 1870s, for example, the most revolutionary liberals, even the leaders of the 1851 and 1859 civil wars, occupied ministerial positions, made Chilean foreign policy, controlled university and secondary school faculties, and exercised leadership in the congress. Chilean presidents, presidential candidates, congressmen, and policy makers from the 1860s to the 1880s had been persecuted by the governments of the 1840s and 1850s, had found themselves jailed, exiled, and, ultimately, amnestied. Lesser political dissidents, former army personnel, and bureaucrats (along with their families) received pensions or other benefits as a result of political reparation. This process was gradual and careful regarding the inclusion and exclusion of beneficiaries, and demonstrated both the skilled pragmatism and the petty vengefulness of Chile's political elite. Stitch by stitch, the political fabric's torn parts were patched and rewoven. As with any repair job, unseen weaknesses and perceptible (to the careful observer) flaws remained, but the fabric was again usable and publicly presentable.

Chilean political elites in the nineteenth century thus crafted an implicit set of procedures for political reconciliation after political cataclysm. There was never a formal political accord on the meaning of reconciliation or the political-psychological requirements for its achievement. But such an accord accreted as part of elite political culture. These implicit procedures did not go uncontested in their particulars, nor were they applied uniformly, but the essential elements of the *vía chilena* for political reconciliation are apparent in the late 1820s and recur after 1836–41, 1851–59, and 1891–96.

In every case, even in the general amnesty proclaimed by José Joaquín Pérez in 1861 to cover all political crimes from 1851 to 1861, reconciliation policies were piecemeal, igniting debates over coverage, inclusion, and exclusion.[11] The incremental negotiation of reconciliation policies in private meetings and in the congress precluded immediate omnibus laws of reconciliation. For example, the political trauma of the 1823–30 civil wars, the repression of the liberals after the Battle of Lircay (1830) and the adoption of the 1833 constitution, and the political conflicts of the 1830s elicited fragmented and partial reconciliatory legislation into the 1860s. Only in 1842 could Congress agree on the restoration of honors and reparations for the leaders of the Southern Cone independence movements, Bernardo O'Higgins and José de San Martín. In 1844, Congress agreed to erect a statue of O'Higgins, place his portrait in the Sala de Gobierno, and send a delegation representing each house of the legislature and the armed forces on a warship to Peru to bring back his ashes for internment in Santiago.[12] It was almost three decades after independence before opposing factions from the independence era could agree that the "Chilean George Washington" was a shared symbol for *la familia chilena* above, and despite, the factionalism, family feuds, bloodshed, exiles, and bitter memories from 1814–23.

With contextual variations, similar reconciliation policies and processes followed the ruptures of 1828–30, 1836–41, and the civil wars in 1851 and 1859.[13] The spirit of this evolving *vía chilena* is well captured in Francisco Encina's description of the general amnesty promulgated by President José Joaquín Pérez on October 18, 1861, to overcome the hatred and wounds stemming from the 1859 civil war and associated political repression: "President Pérez had assumed the Presidency in the name of concord between the political bands, separated by violent hatred that came from long ago and had culminated in the repressive measures that made the revolution of 1859 inevitable. The first measure of his political program was *an ample amnesty that, if possible would erase even the memory of these past convulsions*."[14]

Chile's political class did not believe that such forgetting (*olvido*) was literally possible, but its members insisted, periodically, on the necessity for legal, political, and symbolic "starting over." This did not mean reconciliation of persons at an emotional or psychological level, nor of parties and movements at an ideological or programmatic level. Such reconciliation was neither possible nor expected. Political reconciliation meant that certain issues were not discussed, or, if they were, that policies on "sensitive" matters did not exceed certain limits endangering the newly reconstructed unity (*concordia*). Such reconciliation required moderation, prudence, and common sense (*cordura*). It demanded pretense and public masks. It meant *fictive* harmony and the pragmatic toleration of differences, an end to violent conflict, a reaccomodation to the rule of law (whatever that law was at the moment), and governability. Above all else, political reconciliation was the art of the possible, political pragmatism at its best—and worst. For reconciliation to translate into governability, it required effective leadership by the president and key cabinet members; it also required thick skins, long-term political perspectives, and a sense of humor—men like President Pérez (1861–71) and Manuel Antonio Tocornal, rather than righteous, crusading leadership of whatever doctrinal or ideological persuasion (e.g., Diego Portales, José Victorino Lastarria, Pedro Félix Vicuña, José Manuel Balmaceda, and Arturo Alessandri).

1861 and 1990: Political Transition and Official Memory

Any understanding of the dilemmas, processes, and methods of political reconciliation in Chile after 1990 must begin, as we have outlined above, with the reconstruction and iteration of social memory (and memory loss) regarding other analogous moments in Chile's past. Chileans in the 1980s and 1990s almost automatically (if only partially consciously) drew on this *vía chilena* to reinvent a possible political reconciliation.[15]

Nineteenth-century Chilean political elites recognized how difficult it was to erase the memory (*borrarse hasta el recuerdo*) of political violence, hatred, and abuses. They thus invented and adapted methods for political reconciliation that were less exacting than those required for personal, moral, religious, and strict legal (criminal law) principles. After independence in 1818, there were rarely demands for confession, recantation, or penitence, only for abiding by the rules of the game imposed and/or negotiated by the victors.[16] Those who benefited from amnesties and pardons were free to engage in legal political activities and to struggle for political reform. They could also seek to (re)define social memory. The "real truth" (*verdadera verdad*) could be disputed, but only to the extent that such activities did not threaten governability, challenge the victors' version of the political system (the 1833 constitution, and the parliamentary spin on the 1833 constitution, which evolved by the 1870s and was reaffirmed after 1891), or meant reprisals against the victors.

Clarifying this historically crafted *vía chilena* for overcoming political trauma and political cataclysm makes evident that the demands made by many groups after 1989 for truth, the prosecution of victimizers (or heroes, for some), and social justice far exceed the pragmatism of the historical pattern. In contrast, the reincorporation of the losers into the political system, renewed efforts at political reform, and diverse forms of reparation for victims (subversives or terrorists, for some) are consistent with the historical emphasis on relegitimizing political order and assuring governability. Thus former socialists and even *Miristas* (members or ex-members of the MIR [Left Revolutionary Movement], a small, radical political movement that advocated armed struggle and maintained itself outside the Allende government coalition from 1970–73, and a target of severe repression by the military government) in the *Concertación* governments (1990–2006) followed in the footsteps of nineteenth-century subversives such as President Federico Errázuriz Zañartu (1876–81), a liberal militant in 1848 and a revolutionary in 1851; Benjamín Vicuña Mackenna, the director of the constitutional assembly (*asamblea constituyente*), a rabid enemy of the Manuel Montt government (1851–61), a political exile after the 1859 civil war, *intendente* (regional administrator) of Santiago in the Federico Errázuriz government, and later an unsuccessful presidential candidate; and Manuel Antonio Matta, sentenced to death for rebellion, then exiled to England, then the beneficiary of the 1861 amnesty, a founder of the Radical Party after his 1861 return, many times a deputy (a member of the Chamber of Deputies) and senator, and the minister of foreign relations in the 1891 *junta del gobierno* (government junta). Since the 1820s, political subversives, political exiles, political prisoners, and antiregime revolutionary leaders have routinely returned to public life and public office in Chile during periods of political reconciliation. Statues to honor their contributions to *la patria* adorn Santiago and provincial capitals.

Resistance to Reconciliation and Impunity: Creating and Contesting the Official Story

Resistance to reconciliation has also been a recurrent aspect of Chilean history, both by the victors and the vanquished. Debates over who should benefit from pensions, *leyes de gracia*, and reincorporation into the public administration after 1990 are also consistent with previous experience. Both victors and losers in incidents of internal war and political violence harbor resentments and hatreds that express themselves in lingering legislative and administrative subtleties. In these respects, the events after 1990 have followed the *vía chilena de reconciliación* fairly closely (but with important departures, see below), to the regret of many victims and opponents of the military regime, but also to the regret of many of the regime's *supporters*. This is particularly evident in the determined effort of some Chileans to create an official history documenting the crimes of the dictatorship (with the added twist of recourse to international norms for the prosecution of ex-government officials, as well as of military and police officers). Such an official history serves to legitimize private and collective social memories that contest the view of the military and their civilian allies: that the policies of the military regime, including any human rights abuses, were necessary to save *la patria* and that the legacy is a brilliant *misión cumplida* (mission accomplished).[17] Moreover, the extent to which some members of the military and the police during the military regime have been tried and punished for human rights violations goes far beyond (though not enough to satisfy human rights and victims' organizations) the traditional pattern. Sixteen years after the transition from military to elected civilian government, some important elements of the Chilean *vía de reconciliación política* have been pushed beyond their previous limits. Both the National Truth and Reconciliation Commission (1990–91) and the National Commission on Political Prisoners and Torture (2003–5), which we discuss below, somewhat extended the meaning of political reconciliation beyond the historical pattern—notwithstanding recurrent efforts to negotiate a *punto final* (final settlement) from 1990–91 until 2001, and proposals in September 2005 for pardons for members of the military and the police who had violated human rights during the dictatorship.[18]

Along with its pragmatism and the concession of juridical impunity, the Chilean *vía de reconciliación política* also exhibits a persistent and parallel tendency to resist social and historical impunity. In addition to the array of private and opposition media efforts to reveal the not-so-secret methods of repression, government investigations, administrative hearings, impeachment proceedings, and trials seek to establish an official truth to counteract the seeming impunity of the powerful. This undercurrent pervades Chilean politics and resurfaces periodically—a legacy from colonial times, the first years of independence, and the struggles of the liberals against the Portalian regime in the nineteenth century.

One important mode for establishing public accountability has been the constitutional procedures of *acusación constitucional*—a constitutional procedure similar to, but not exactly equivalent to, impeachment in the U.S. constitutional system, with elements of Spanish colonial accountability procedures such as the *residencia*—against incumbents and ex-government officials, including ex-presidents. The debates occasioned by the *acusación constitucional* procedure are frequently fierce, full of savage imagery, graphic denunciation, and moral discourse. The attacks on incumbent officials and even on ex-presidents (denounced as brutal dictators, responsible for crimes against the constitution and humanity) are merciless. Defenders of the incumbent government, or of the previous regime, also offer impassioned arguments and historical justifications for the actions that critics now deem unconstitutional and criminal.[19]

Above all else, truth seeking and efforts to construct an official historical story are *political and politicized*. They reflect the current correlation of forces of diverse social and political interests, but also the need to reconfigure the political map—and to provide relative social peace after periods of extreme violence and polarization. Ad hoc commissions and constitutional procedures (like the *acusación constitucional*) are inherently constrained by temporary political considerations at the same time that they claim to work according to universal religious, moral, and legal principles. They attempt to reconcile the immediate (and sometimes not-so-immediate) past with hopes for a better future—while enmeshed in the constraints and tensions of the present. In reading the debates over most of these *acusaciones*, it becomes clear that not only the fate of individuals is at stake but also the nature of official memory as filtered by the political and ideological antagonisms of the moment. Both history and the future are debated: what "really happened" and what ought to be.

Each of the *acusación constitucional* proceedings offers dramatic examples of resistance to impunity and demands for accountability—a plea for an alternative future based on the revelation of the truth about the present or the past. Most also offer vigorous defenses of repression and persecution when necessary to "save" *la patria*. In the present context, the *acusación constitucional* against the ex-ministers of President Balmaceda after the 1891 civil war and the first such proceeding after adoption of the 1925 constitution prove revealing. For illustrative purposes, we examine each of these, briefly, in what follows.

Acusación Constitucional 1891

In 1891, Chile experienced nine months of bloody civil war. President José Manuel Balmaceda had angered the congressional majority, refused to comply with constitutional restrictions on his authority, and was accused of being dictatorial. He also wished to impose his choice of successor in the upcoming elections—a pattern familiar to Chilean politicians, though one often resisted. Conflicts among British investors in the nitrate industry, a nascent labor movement in the nitrate fields and the ports, church-state conflicts, and a host of other issues had contributed to the breakdown of the Chilean political system and the onset of civil war.[20] Ultimately, defeated and alone, Balmaceda committed suicide in the Argentine embassy weeks after the war's end, as would President Salvador Allende, in the heat of battle in the presidential palace, during the military coup of 1973.

In December 1891 an *acusación constitucional* was presented in the Chamber of Deputies (Cámara de Diputados) against ministers in Balmaceda's last cabinet. They were accused of violating the constitution in numerous ways, ranging from corruption to the repression and torture of adversaries. According to the deputies who presented the *acusación*, they wished the truth to be made public, the guilty to be punished, and impunity not to be permitted. The accused cabinet ministers had escaped from the country; they resided in other Latin American countries or in Europe, where diplomats advised them of the charges brought against them. Some of their responses were published in Chile, but none dared return to the country under the reigning political circumstances. Nevertheless, the wives of several ex-ministers read their defenses to the congress.

The Chamber of Deputies found merit in the charges and sent them for consideration to the senate in accord with the provisions of the 1833 constitution. In the official letter to the senate, the Chamber of Deputies listed sixteen wide-ranging charges against the ministers, beginning with "seeking to overturn the constitutional order, creating an arbitrary and tyrannical dictatorship, attempting to alter the constitution and form of government, and promoting and carrying out a civil war."[21] After listing all the charges in detail, the letter continued: "[All] these facts are in the memory of the entire country; no one will deny their veracity nor fail to recognize their significance and the offense they give to the Republic."[22] The purpose of the proceedings according to the letter was to make sure that the truth be known to all, that the extent of constitutional rights violations be publicized, that the guilty be identified, and that impunity not prevail.

After listening to the report of its investigatory committee, the senate found all the ministers guilty of some or all of the charges against them in September 1893.[23] The senate committee called witnesses to testify regarding the crimes of the Balmaceda government; newspapers denounced the repression, robbery, corruption, and other crimes committed by the defeated Balmacedistas. Each of the testimonies began with the words: "The witnesses who appear here declare whether it is true that. . . ." Truth, declared the congressmen, was the primary concern. Then came that of impeding impunity.

The stories recounted in the testimonies provide ample evidence of crimes by both the Balmacedistas and their adversaries, the victors in the war. But it was Balmaceda's unwillingness to abide by the law, his efforts to impose a dictatorship, that had, according to the victors, taken the country down the road to civil war. And, of course, his cabinet ministers bore responsibility for their actions, as did the army officers who had remained loyal to the president and the public officials who had served in his administration. Hundreds of military personnel and civil servants populated the jails; purges in the public administration separated Balmacedistas from their employment. Political cartoons depicted the torture of prisoners by Balmaceda's police and military. Editorials in the country's newspapers railed against the tyranny that had afflicted the country. Public calls for justice clearly referred to the punishment of the defeated Balmacedistas for the crimes committed and the violation of the sacred constitution.

In the meantime, however, the political elite sought to put the political system back together, to reconfigure government coalitions, and to reunite the great Chilean family by seeking reconciliation. Beginning with a first amnesty law in 1891, as the deputy Enrique Montt explained, the elite worked to "forget" the crimes and suffering in the name of national unity: "The country is one family; it cannot live eternally divided. The battles have passed, victory was achieved; that is what is important. Now we must reconstitute the country. Oblivion, pardon, and peace. We must live again united and contented."[24]

Between late 1891 and 1894, even as the *acusación constitucional* against Balmaceda's ministers slowly worked its way through the senate, Congress approved several gradually more generous and far-reaching amnesty laws. In addition, some legislation provided for reparations—and this legislation would continue to be expanded in the first decade of the twentieth century.[25] By 1895, amnesties covered all the political crimes committed by military and civilian officials in the Balmaceda government and by members of the victorious congressional opposition—a self-amnesty that would be emulated by the military junta headed by Augusto Pinochet in 1978. In 1895, only four years after the civil war, members of Balmaceda's Liberal Democratic Party joined a governing coalition. The Liberal Democratic Party became a key element in tipping congressional majorities during the next decades; in 1919, a Balmacedista, Juan Luis Sanfuentes, was elected president.

The *acusacion constitucional* against the Balmacedista cabinet members was largely forgotten, though the trauma of the civil war and its hatreds long persisted among some families.[26] The *vía chilena*—the tension between truth, justice, punishment, and forgetting—persisted. It would continue to develop more complexity as the social and political system opened to new actors and as ideological polarization and class conflict became more obvious in the years after World War I.

Acusación Constitucional 1926

A military coup in September 1924 disrupted the Chilean parliamentary regime that had dominated politics since the end of the 1891 civil war. Although a new constitution was approved in 1925, and promulgated along with a general amnesty for all political and social crimes committed since the coup, it could not be fully implemented until 1932, following years of political instability, dictatorship (1927–31), and transition to constitutional rule.[27]

The amnesty that accompanied the 1925 constitution returned to their posts those purged from government jobs by the coup and interim governments. The constitution, like its 1833 predecessor, included provisions for *acusación constitucional* against certain government authorities. In 1926 the minister of the interior was accused of illegally ordering the arrest of a political agitator. The minister's legal defense claimed that the police had arrested the subject as part of their duties to maintain public order. Moreover, the minister argued that the *acusación constitu-*

cional was a politically inspired effort by the opposition to circumvent the provisions in the new constitution that eliminated legislative censure and control over presidential ministerial appointments.

The commission hearing the case in the Chamber of Deputies was divided, which resulted in a minority and a majority report: "Disagreement existing as to whether the Minister is responsible for the matters [*hechos*] attributed to him."[28] After debating the difference between "taking responsibility" for the actions of subordinates and "criminal responsibility," several deputies made clear that in addition to the narrow legal issues, the overall political context had to be considered. Thus the deputy Luis Urrutia Ibáñez (an ex-Balmacedista) argued that his political party was most concerned with "strengthening the principle of authority and with the maintenance of order and social peace, [like the majority of Chileans] who wish to repress the revolutionary, anarchist efforts of agitators who incite the masses to violence." According to this deputy, the minister had acted properly to uphold the constitutional order under attack by subversives, anarchists and leftists (572). Urrutia Ibáñez added that it was a "bloody irony [for those victims of communist terrorism], farmers, merchants, industrialists, workers, and especially the Army and police, that see that this poison is putting flashes of hatred in many eyes, the precursors of the fire to come" (576). The communist deputy José Santos Córdoba responded that it "was not possible to listen to so many lies without contesting them," and his colleague, the deputy Ramón Sepúlveda Leal (Communist Party; expelled in 1927, he became a Trotskyist, and later a leader in various socialist factions), proclaimed that no workers wanted to destroy the means of production and that in any case none of this had anything to do with the *acusación constitucional* under consideration (578). But Deputy Ismael Edwards Matte (Liberal Party) insisted that "the country clamors for the end of anarchy, the enemy of all progress" (584). Deputy Rudecindo Ortega, from the Radical Party, remarked that "upholding the principle of authority was inconsistent with ministerial abuse of authority in the name of upholding it," while the deputy Alfredo Bravo (Radical Party) argued forcefully that the *acusación constitucional* constituted the appropriate sanction against arbitrary absolutism (586). The debate went back and forth between constitutional and legal principles and the threat to social order, the danger of political agitation, the evils of capitalism, the legacy of the French Revolution, the horrors of Leninism and communist plans for world domination, and the abuses of the recent military junta—in short, it considered the course of world history and the nature of the republic and its future.

In this first *acusación constitucional* after the adoption of the 1925 constitution, all the political and ideological divisions that would eventually lead to the military coup of 1973 (*golpe* for supporters of the Unidad Popular government in 1973; *pronunciamiento* for those who supported the military coup—even the name of the event continued to divide the adversaries fifteen years later) were present. So, too, were the fears and hatreds that would produce the savagery of the post-1973 military regime.[29] Central to this debate were the nature of the political and social system itself, the issue of impunity for the powerful, government lawlessness, the abuse of authority, and the violation of citizens' civil liberties and rights. The minister Maximiliano Ibáñez did not have the constitutional authority to order the arrest of a citizen, yet he acknowledged that he had done so. But the debates over his actions allowed the recounting of past abuses and future aspirations as part of the *acusación constitucional* proceedings. This was the first of many twentieth-century rehearsals for the Rettig Commission of 1990–91 and the *acusación constitucional* against General Augusto Pinochet by a small group of deputies in 1998.[30]

During the 1926 debates, congressmen declared that they wished to "rescue from oblivion" the memory of the recent military coups (1924–25), and to battle against the impunity of the guilty. They also wished to debate the *future* of the country, the struggle between order and anarchy, among capitalism, socialism, and anarchism. But in practice, these debates reflected the historical antagonisms and current ideological and political cleavages that divided Chilean society. And always, the truth and justice were juxtaposed to forgetting, impunity, and political necessity. In the end, the Chamber of Deputies rejected the *acusación* against Minister Ibáñez. Temporary congressional majorities would determine the outcome of this proceeding, as they would of *acusaciones constitucionales* into the 1990s, including the 1998 *acusación* against the ex-dictator Pinochet. Yet debates over these *acusaciones constitucionales*, as *modes of resistance to impunity*, were never limited to contemporary constitutional and political issues. In 1926 and into the future, individual deputies justified their votes in such proceedings by reference to events as far back as the civil wars of 1830, 1851, 1859, and 1891, and they appealed to principled reasons for their votes, reflecting the moral, political, and ideological cleavages in Chilean national life.

The Ibáñez Government (1927–31) and the Commission to Investigate the Acts of the Dictatorship

Carlos Ibáñez governed Chile as president from 1927 to 1931 after ousting an interim president and orchestrating elections in which he won over 90 percent of the vote. In 1930, Ibáñez, in collaboration with representatives of most of the political parties, organized a congressional election in which each electoral district had only one candidate—allowing, by Chilean law at the time, all these congressmen and senators to be "elected" without challenge. For all practical purposes Ibáñez governed as a dictator; political opponents were arrested, harshly interrogated and tortured, sent into exile, and sometimes killed. The government censored the press, arrested labor and community leaders who dissented in public, deported political opponents, and sent many persons into internal exile (*relegación*), including those sent to prison camps on the islands Isla Más Afuera, Isla de Pascua, Chiloé, and further south.[31]

A secret police force infiltrated community and labor meetings, followed and monitored the activities of prominent politicians and minor dissidents, and transcribed telephone conversations on tapped phone lines. In short, Ibáñez established a police state, though not as thoroughgoing or as systematically repressive as those in Spain and Italy — models for some of his supporters.

After four years in office, Ibáñez fell victim to the Great Depression and to strikes by student and professional organizations that brought the capital to a standstill. Even while governing with congressionally granted dictatorial authority (*facultades extraordinarias*) since January 1931, he could not pacify the opposition without deploying the army — which he refused to do. He left for exile in Buenos Aires, delegating the executive authority to the president of the senate.[32]

As indicated above, though he donned the mantle of legitimacy conveyed by presidential elections in May 1927 and the congressional elections of 1930, Ibáñez governed as a dictator. Working-class organizations and the Communist Party, formally established in 1922, received particularly harsh treatment, but elite families, political leaders, and dissident army officers also suffered repression. Ventura Maturana, the chief of the secret police, put it this way: "Student and political meetings were signs that liberty was being abused . . . I received orders to deport a bushel [*un lote*] of politicians."[33]

With the fall of Ibáñez and the return of hundreds of exiles, demands surfaced for a complete investigation into the operations of the dictatorship. Opponents called for the truth and punishment for the crimes of the dictatorship.[34] A week after Ibáñez had left Santiago for Buenos Aires, the minister of the interior and future president, Juan E. Montero, decreed the creation of a commission to investigate the operations of the previous government.[35] The minister of justice, and political exile, Luis Gutiérrez Alliende also signed the decree. Montero appointed four former Supreme Court judges (ousted by Ibáñez) and high-profile political opponents from the main political parties to the commission. On its own, the commission changed its name from Comisión para Investigar la Gestión Gubernativa (Commission to Investigate Government Activities) to Comisión Investigadora de los Actos de la Dictadura (Commission to Investigate the Acts of the Dictatorship).[36]

The 1931 commission compiled twenty-one volumes of documents including police and military records, transcribed telephone tapping, detailed reports on the surveillance of opponents and the censorship of newspapers, and testimonies of the victims of illegal detention, arrest, torture, and exile. It also investigated cases of alleged disappearances (*fondeos*) and deaths (mostly in public political protests against the government) and documented corruption in the public administration. At the same time, it delivered information it considered relevant to the congress for *acusación* proceedings against Ibáñez, both as president and as the minister of the interior, and against various of his cabinet ministers. Congress carried out these proceedings against Ibáñez and some of his ministers; others were absolved in an increasingly politicized setting between September and December 1931 — a period during which there occurred extensive political realignment punctuated by a naval uprising, a presidential election, and an armed attack on Christmas eve 1931 against a small army post in Copiapó, followed by a massacre of workers and supposedly communist activists in Vallenar (a town to the south, between Copiapó and La Serena).

At first the 1931 commission received widespread and favorable press coverage. Then the treatment became less favorable in some of the partisan press as it called into question the legitimacy of the congress itself (constituted without elections in 1930) and became a thorn in the side of President Montero. In any case, Montero had more than enough problems to deal with, including massive unemployment caused by the economic crisis, a naval uprising (September 1931), threats of military coups, a possible return by Ibáñez, and the fierce political challenges of ex-president Arturo Alessandri, who would contest the presidency with Montero in late 1931.

The commission explicitly defined its work as an effort to discover the truth, send criminal cases to the courts, proffer information that would warrant *acusaciones constitucionales* against Ibáñez and his ministers to the congress, and provide evidence to the courts that would allow punishment of officials guilty of crimes during the dictatorship. It resisted forgetting the past and impunity. However, political conditions made the commission's activities increasingly inconvenient. Moreover, in 1931 and 1932, Congress approved numerous amnesties in efforts to pacify the country and restore governability.[37]

In November 1931, members of the commission resigned in protest over the senate's failure to approve the *acusaciones* against some of the ex-ministers of the Ibáñez government. The government initially refused to accept the resignations. Yet at the end of December, the commission insisted on resigning; the government thanked its members for their efforts and decreed its dissolution.

The commission did not finish its work, nor did it issue a final report. Twenty-one volumes of material in a Santiago archive document its essentially unsuccessful efforts to impede impunity. Most Chileans do not know the commission ever existed. Meanwhile, Ibáñez had written to the people to defend his patriotic leadership in difficult times. He rejected the campaigns of slander and falsehoods against him, denounced the *acusación constitucional* brought against him, and reminded the public that members of Congress who had gladly collaborated with his government, giving him "extraordinary authority" to confront the economic crisis, now rose to denounce him. He had done everything "for *la patria*."[38] Ibáñez eventually returned to Chile, the beneficiary of several of the amnesties decreed by the interim governments. He became an inveterate plotter and participant in failed coups. In 1952, Chileans, tired of "politics," elected Carlos Ibáñez as president by a wide margin. He came to office with a broom as a symbol: he promised to sweep clean the corruption of the political parties and the politicians.[39]

La Vía Chilena Continues

From 1932 to 1969 the Chilean modalities for political reconciliation became integral ingredients of everyday politics. To avoid political breakdown and restore governability in moments of crisis, pardons, amnesties, and other methods of political pacification conceded juridical impunity to government officials, military and police personnel, party and labor leaders, and miscreants of all sorts. Amnesties and self-amnesties became routine — ever more frequent, ever more institutionalized — for political matters, failed coups, bureaucratic malfeasance, violations of the electoral law, the failure to comply with the obligatory military service law, and for common crimes. The state internal security laws and labor laws made participation in so-called illegal strikes serious crimes — and a common rationale for pardons and amnesties to resolve immediate political conflicts. All governments from 1932 to 1973 used pardons and amnesties in this fashion; eventual impunity, or relative impunity (pardons, reduced prison sentences, and expunging criminal records) became routine. This did not mean that no one went to prison, that no one went into exile, or that no one suffered. But for political crimes, including illegal strikes and electoral violence, those who survived the initial repression, or avoided being the unlucky chance victims of the street clashes, were likely eventually to gain juridical impunity.[40]

As in the past, impunity reigned but was also resisted, both for moral and pragmatic reasons, as evidenced in the congressional debates and in the press.[41] In the 1950s, respite from amnesty debates in the legislature remained scarce. Those debates, in which Salvador Allende, Raúl Rettig, Eduardo Frei, and many of the leaders in the 1960s and 1970s participated, constituted a forum for the antagonistic discourses that framed Chilean politics of the era.

The 1973 Coup

In 1973, Chile experienced its most brutal political rupture in the twentieth century. At this time, the amnesties, pardons, and other institutional constraints could no longer postpone the cataclysmic confrontation announced repeatedly from 1926 until 1970. This was also the first political crisis in Chile televised globally via satellite. It occurred in a historical era framed by World War II, the Holocaust, the Universal Declaration of Human Rights, the Cold War (which was never *cold* in the third world), and the Cuban Revolution. And of course there was no debate over whether wars had actually occurred in 1828–30, 1850–51, 1858–59, and 1891, nor whether there had been an authoritarian regime in power from 1927 to 1931.

For the 1973–90 period, while the rhetoric of war was adopted by all contending factions, only the military, their close civilian supporters, and small factions of the revolutionary Left claimed that a "real war" existed in Chile. No matter. Whether the war was "real" or a juridical fiction, the dead had still died; the vanquished suffered in prison and in exile. The victors created a new political regime and formalized it with a new constitution in 1980. They characterized their deeds as a glorious *misión cumplida*, a salvation of *la patria*. They echoed Diego Portales, Joaquín Prieto, Manuel Montt, the victors in 1891, and Carlos Ibáñez, the self-proclaimed savior of *la patria* in 1931. The vanquished, as in the past, resisted this effort with an alternative history: in art, the theater, literature, the press, congressional debates, and in the politics and policies of reconciliation. And with the end of the military dictatorship, like the *pipiolos* (the liberal opposition from the 1830s to the 1860s) and the ex-Balmacedistas, the defeated supporters of the Allende government coalition sought government jobs, restitution of pension benefits, reparations, and an opportunity to again compete for political power. They also sought to establish the truth about the crimes committed, the abuses perpetrated, and they sought to impede impunity for those who had governed the country from 1973 to 1990.

The Rettig Commission, 1990–91

After almost seventeen years of dictatorship and the massive, systematic violation of human rights, Chile returned to an elected civilian government in 1990. President Patricio Aylwin named a commission,[42] headed by the longtime Radical Party politician Raúl Rettig, with the following four principal objectives:

> To establish as complete a picture as possible of those grave events, as well as their antecedents and circumstances;
> To gather evidence that might make it possible to identify the victims by name and determine their fate or whereabouts;
> To recommend such measures of reparation and the restoration of people's good name as it regarded as just; and
> To recommend the legal and administrative measures which in its judgment should be adopted in order to prevent further grave human rights violations from being committed.[43]

As the commission met, the ex-dictator Pinochet remained as commander of the army. His supporters in the rightist parties maintained enough votes in the senate to veto constitutional amendments and to impede social and economic reforms proposed by the *Concertación* coalition government. The Rettig Commission had no police or judicial authority. It was not permitted to publish the names of those it discovered had committed crimes. Its primary duty was to determine what had "really" happened ("the truth") in every case in which human rights had been seriously violated (but not including torture without death). It would identify the victims, the circumstances of their deaths or disappearances, and recommend measures that might be taken for reparation and to prevent the recurrence of such actions.

The decree creating the commission limited the scope of its investigation to only the most serious crimes, such as the disappearances of people arrested, executions, torture leading to death when committed by agents of the government or people in its service, and those kidnappings and attempts on peoples' lives committed by private citizens for political purposes. The decree also specified that those events leading to death or disappearance should be brought to the commission only if committed between September 11, 1973, and March 11, 1990. Events outside the country could be considered if they were connected to the Chilean government or to the nation's political life. The thousands of cases of torture victims who had survived (the vast majority) were excluded from the Rettig Commission's jurisdiction; at the time it was believed that there were simply too many of them, and the government desired a relatively quick investigation and report in order to close the book on the dictatorship and begin the process of political reconciliation.

The commission included highly regarded ex-government officials (including a minister and a judge during the dictatorship), lawyers, intellectuals, and social activists.[44] They were chosen carefully to represent most of the main political parties and to create the sort of balance that would give whatever report it eventually issued some credibility. However, it had no members from the leftist political parties or from organizations representing victims or their families. Thus both its charge and the extent to which it represented the victimized were much narrower than had been those of the 1931 commission appointed to investigate the acts of the dictatorship from 1927 to 1931.

According to the lawyer, human rights activist, and commission member José Zalaquett, the Rettig Commission faced the following dilemma: "How can a country overcome a legacy of dictatorial rule and massive human rights violations if the new government is subject to significant institutional and political constraints? How, in those circumstances, can the equally necessary but often conflicting objectives of justice and social peace be harmonized? What are the moral tenets which should guide the politician's actions in such ambiguous situations?"[45] Zalaquett also pointed to the political circumstances in Chile and Latin America more generally as transitions occurred from military to civilian rule: "The sobering lesson they taught was that the political stakes involved in settling accounts with the past are extraordinarily high, that a fully satisfactory outcome can hardly be expected, and that the social tensions brought about by the legacy of human rights violations linger on for a long time."[46]

What Zalaquett and other members of the commission did not consider as a group, or even discuss, was that Chile had faced this dilemma in the past, if admittedly not in the context of such a long-lasting, brutal dictatorship, nor with such a massive and systematic record of human rights violations. They did not review previous truth commissions, nor did they examine the pattern of amnesties and pardons of the past. They defined their main mission as establishing the truth regarding the particular human rights violations in question, almost in the sense of a criminal investigation, and then suggesting possible forms of reparation. Zalaquett himself gradually came to favor what he called "truth and justice with mercy" (essentially pardons, applying the statute of limitations where appropriate, and accepting the application of the military's 1978 amnesty decree for most cases). Pardons (*indultos*) meant acknowledging that the crimes had been committed, sentencing the guilty, and then reducing the sentences or waiving them. Applying the amnesty law—until the late 1990s the routine generally followed—meant accepting juridical impunity. In Chile, the meaning of an amnesty, unlike that of a pardon, was that for legal purposes, the events (the murders, torture, illegal detentions, exile, etc.) had not occurred at all (*como si no hubieran ocurrido*). An amnesty (*amnistía*) meant full legal impunity, though not social impunity or impunity from questions by family members, friends, and associates about the human rights violations documented by the Rettig Commission. In contrast, a pardon involved reducing a jail term or a release from prison, but not legal impunity or the elimination of a formal record (*prontuario*) of the crime. Amnesty meant legal *olvido*; pardon required acknowledging the crime (a criminal court conviction) before obtaining mercy, understood as a reduced sentence or the application of a statute of limitation legislation (*prescripción*) for particular types of crimes.

The Rettig Commission met under extremely tense political conditions; its report created a short-term furor in Chile, validating the victims' claims of abuse and state terrorism in agonizing detail and providing the rationale for policies dedicated to reparations. During its deliberations, in June 1990, a mass grave with victims was uncovered in Pisagua. The anguished faces of mummified disappeared persons (*desaparecidos*) stared from the country's newspapers and television channels at a stunned Chilean public. No further doubt could exist about the fate of many of the *desaparecidos*. They had been detained, tortured, murdered, and buried. (As it later turned out, some had been buried, disinterred, and thrown into the sea or had their remains otherwise disappeared for a second time to prevent evidence of the crimes being discovered.) President Aylwin apologized publicly to the victims on behalf of all Chileans and offered moral and economic reparations (legislated in law 19.123 of 1992).

General Pinochet referred to the commission as a "sewer" and declared that there was nothing to ask pardon for because the armed forces had saved the country from terrorism and international communism and should be proud of the mission they had successfully carried out. Leaders of all the armed forces and the national police (*Carabineros*) denounced the commission report, as did the Supreme Court—which the commission had criticized for its laxity in defending the constitutional rights and liberties of the citizenry during the dictatorship. On the other side of the political spectrum, the Communist Party newspaper, *El Siglo*, headlined: "Crimes without Punishment?" while the Agrupación de Familiares de

Detenidos-Desaparecidos (Association of Family Members of the Detained and Disappeared) lamented that the commission had not considered the cases of thousands of torture victims and exiles.[47]

Overall, the Rettig Commission had achieved limited but important success in investigating some of the human rights violations, documenting them, and providing a foundation for what would become a rather extensive politics of reparation over the following fifteen years.[48] But it had its critics from across the political spectrum. In some ways it conformed to the traditional Chilean pattern: it could not fully reveal its findings; it could not guarantee punishment of those who had violated human rights and the Chilean constitution; it could not overcome the apparent guarantee of impunity contained in the amnesty decreed by the military government in 1978. It seemed, at the time, that—like the senate *acusación constitucional* in 1891 and the 1931 commission that had investigated the activities of the Ibáñez dictatorship—the Rettig Commission would form a bridge from public outrage to political reconciliation based on the 1978 amnesty and political reconfiguration. And, as in 1931, the constitution imposed after a military coup (1925, then 1980) would remain in place to frame national politics.

In the short term, the Rettig Commission report was buried in semioblivion when assassins killed Senator Jaime Guzmán, a principal author of the 1980 constitution and the founder of the Unión Demócrata Independiente (UDI) party, the principal civilian prop of the dictatorship. The report passed from front-page news as the headlines focused on the war on terrorism and violent crime. Periodically, the human rights issues resurfaced, but everyday politics and the Pinochet supporters' resistance to constitutional reform took priority for the *Concertación* leadership still fearing the possibility of a military coup that might overturn the transition to civilian government.[49]

Acusación Constitucional 1998

Notwithstanding the painfully slow pace of implementation of the *Concertación* political and constitutional reforms, an unrelenting struggle to impede impunity for human rights violations and continuous court challenges to the validity of the 1978 amnesty decree proceeded. In March 1998, Pinochet stepped down as the army commander and assumed his senatorial seat as a lifetime senator (*vitalicio*) as stipulated in the 1980 constitution. For human rights activists, victims and their family members, and the political Left, Pinochet's investiture in the senate served as an intolerable reminder of his (and the military government's) impunity for crimes against humanity. In response, a group of *Concertación* legislators presented an *acusación constitucional* against Pinochet for "gravely compromising the honor and security of the nation"—one of the reasons specified in the constitution as a cause for an *acusación constitucional*. As had been the case with Manuel Montt in 1868, the *acusación* had more to do with Pinochet's role as dictator and president than with any technical violation of the constitution during his tenure as commander of the army during the Aylwin and the Eduardo Frei Ruiz-Tagle presidencies (1990–2000).

In accord with the constitution, if the Chamber of Deputies approved the *acusación* and the senate ratified it, Pinochet would lose his congressional immunity (*fuero*), exposing him to civil and criminal prosecution in numerous pending cases. Fearful that such an outcome would destabilize the political system, the Eduardo Frei Ruiz-Tagle government (1994–2000) opposed the approval of the *acusación*, despite its sponsorship by parties of the coalition and some members of Frei's own party.

The nearly month-long debates on the *acusación* proved acrimonious. In the end, the Chamber of Deputies rejected the charges; the congress also eliminated September 11 (the date of the 1973 coup) as a national holiday—to be replaced by a "day of national unity." Some groups on the political Left characterized the new holiday as a "day of national shame." Later the day-of-national-unity holiday was also eliminated. In the meantime, the month of debates on Pinochet's *acusación constitucional* had served to rake him and his government over the coals of public opinion and provide widespread coverage of the events in the national and international press. Pinochet won the legal battle, keeping his senate seat and *fuero*—but in the battle against impunity, it was a pyrrhic victory. Few in Chile had imagined, eight years earlier, that an *acusación constitucional* against Pinochet could be carried forward, that fierce debates could occur, and that he could be charged with crimes against humanity in the Chilean press and the congress—without provoking a radical military response. Nevertheless, the rejection of the *acusación* had its precedent in the *acusación* against President Montt in 1868. In 1998, President Eduardo Frei Ruiz-Tagle (and, indirectly, the ex-president Patricio Aylwin), fearful of a destabilization of the transition, worked to convince members of the Christian Democratic Party to reject the *acusación*.[50]

Several months later, even more shocking events would dent the impunity of Augusto Pinochet Ugarte. He was detained and arrested in London on October 16, 1998, on a warrant from a Spanish judge for extradition to Spain. His subsequent trial by the British legal system made clear that the historical battle between justice and impunity, truth versus forgetting the past in the name of governability, had been somewhat restructured: enter international human rights law, the claim to universal jurisdiction, and the rejection of statutes of limitations in the case of crimes against humanity. The Pinochet case would become emblematic for international human rights law and also mark a turning point in the routine application of the *vía chilena de reconciliación política*.[51] After Pinochet's return to Chile, he would find himself constantly barraged with criminal cases and have his immunity taken away, but he was never tried (to mid-2006)—for health reasons. According to medical exams, he had a slight but progressive dementia that made him incapable of standing trial.

The Valech Commission

Despite the gradual erosion of Pinochet's public standing and place in history, and with periodic public eruptions of moral outrage and ongoing resistance of the human rights organizations and some political parties to impunity, the transition from military government to elected civilian rule continued within the constraints of the 1980 constitution. No major constitutional reforms occurred from 1990 to 2001. Elections occurred as scheduled, and the *Concertación* coalition maintained control of the government. The political Right maintained its veto power in the senate and resisted changes to the electoral law that might erode this veto.

After assuming office in 2000, as the first socialist president since Salvador Allende (1970–73), Ricardo Lagos promoted a quiet judicialization of the human rights issue, after the meetings and report of the armed forces in accord with the agreements reached in the Mesa de Diálogo, a special group created by President Frei to incorporate the armed forces directly into the debates on human rights issues.[52] Special judges investigated the cases; a slow, grinding, and, for the military and the political Right, *annoying* process kept alive the possibility that some cases would be prosecuted and that the 1978 amnesty might not be applied. No *punto final* could be negotiated, though halfhearted proposals of one sort or another surfaced from time to time, as they had between 1990 and 2001.

In November 2003, President Lagos established a commission headed by Monseñor Sergio Valech (the Comisión Nacional sobre Prisión Política y Tortura [National Commission on Torture and Political Imprisonment]) to find appropriate means to include torture victims as beneficiaries of reparation policies.[53] As indicated above, torture victims, except those killed, had been excluded from the Rettig Commission charge and recommendations, though some had received health care, including mental health services, under a program called PRAIS.[54] As in the case of the Rettig Commission and Raúl Rettig, it became common to refer to this new commission as the Valech Commission. The commission took testimony from over thirty-six thousand persons who claimed that they, or family members who had died, had been tortured during the military government. The commission reported that it was able verify over twenty-eight thousand of these claims and acknowledged that it had no way of knowing how many more torture victims there might have been. Nevertheless, the claim made by military officers and civilian allies of the dictatorship that torture had resulted from individual excesses rather than a systematic and routine policy of state terrorism was discarded.

The commission documented 1,132 sites used as detention and torture centers during the military dictatorship, including almost every military base and police station in the country. The report lists these centers, provides pictures of some, and describes graphically the horrible tortures suffered by the victims from Chile's far north to the tip of Patagonia. The commission report includes a list of those persons (more than twenty-eight thousand, after reconsidering some cases initially not "verified" as torture victims). Approximately 94 percent of those who testified before the commission claimed that they had suffered torture.

Unlike the 1931 commission, the Valech Commission's published report circulated in Chile and on the Internet. The truth, this time, would be heard. Or at least part of it. The commission was not allowed to reveal the names of the perpetrators, nor could it release the testimony of the victims for fifty years. Even if this provision were to be amended to reduce the period during which the documents would remain unavailable, as is likely, the struggle for truth certainly did not prove altogether successful, to say the least. Likewise, since torture is a crime with a clear statute of limitations in Chile (unless certain cases are treated as human rights violations under international law, with no statute of limitations), the commission report did not contribute directly to justice understood as criminal prosecution for crimes committed.[55] In contrast, the commission's work did provide the political foundation for a quickly passed (and much criticized for its stinginess—approximately $200 per month) law providing reparations to torture victims identified in its report.

From the political Left, and the ex-armed opposition against the dictatorship, the Rodriguistas (Frente Patriótico Manuel Rodríguez [Manuel Rodríguez Patriotic Front] FPMR), came the criticism that judicializing the human rights issue provided even more impunity for the victimizers. The amnesty law had not been repealed, the armed forces and police had not been purged of criminals, and the courts continued to uphold the 1978 amnesty decree. From the Association of Retired Naval Officers (Asociación de Oficiales de la Armada en Retiro, ASOFAR) came the same old justification of "individual excesses" made necessary by the fight against terrorism and subversion. Significantly, the ex-military officers recognized that the ongoing struggle included the way in which historical memory would shape the future. Just as the battle over the depiction of Diego Portales and Manuel Montt in history textbooks in the nineteenth and early twentieth centuries helped define political contestation in the period between 1919 and 1932, the battle over characterization of the military government (1973–90) would help to define current political outcomes. Both the Rettig Commission and, now, the Valech Commission had contributed to the increasingly negative image of the Pinochet regime among Chile's new generation. Aided by international human rights organizations, diffusion of information on the Internet, and an increasingly globalized human rights movement, the *vía chilena de reconciliación política* had been transformed but not altogether overcome. Simultaneously, the battle in Chile of truth, justice, and reparations against oblivion and impunity had become emblematic of the global struggle between the norms of universal human rights and the policies of sovereign governments to fight a war against subversion and terrorism—as each government defined these evils. The Valech Commission contributed to both the Chilean and international struggles to gain support for international law in the battle against torture. But it also left questions unanswered and formed part of the ambiguous *vía chilena* — resistance to impunity and its reaffirmation; the quest for the "whole" truth and its partial negation.

Reconciliation without Conciliation?

The Chilean *vía de reconciliación política* had (and has) its advantages and its costs — some still to pay in the future. The modalities of the nineteenth century have been adapted, largely unconsciously, by personalities, factions, political parties, the church, and the armed forces to the post-1990 context. But *la familia chilena* is more diverse, more inclusive, more informed, and more demanding than at any time in the past. The intra-elite pacts that made reconciliation possible before 1925, and political accommodation feasible before 1964, face the challenge of scrutiny by the international community, the national media, and a tenacious minority that rejects reconciliation without truth and justice, if not repentance.

In the short term (1990–2000), the legacy of fear, the desire for social peace, and a growing economy precluded an immediate crisis. But the veil of forgetfulness, the deliberate repression of social memory, the presumption of impunity, and the inattention to the underlying social and political issues that provoked political rupture had periodically induced political breakdown from 1818 until 1973. When the temporary coalitions that made possible so-called transitions weakened, when the initial policies of reconciliation were exhausted, the underlying conflicts remained or were worsened by the trauma of the past rupture. The routinization of impunity and pacification as a political style, combined with some unique institutional aspects of the Chilean constitutional and party systems impeded breakdown from 1932 to 1970. But at the same time this postponement of treatment made the eventual trauma more severe. Thus the political conflict of 1970–90 proved fiercer and longer lasting than any previous conflict in Chilean history.

After 1990, many Chileans and their friends celebrated the gradual consolidation of a more democratic political system. Yet many legacies of the military-imposed regime remained in place, notwithstanding important reforms that modified the 1980 constitution, the penal code, and the highly repressive national security and antiterrorism legislation. Likewise, to a great extent, the *vía chilena de reconciliación política* also perdures. Impunity has not been complete, but it has been the rule. A partial truth about human rights violations has been achieved, and the results of the Rettig and the Valech Commissions have been widely publicized. Still, the limitations on naming the guilty, on releasing the testimony given to the Valech Commission, and on the prosecution of torturers remain in place. The historical tensions between pragmatic and legal oblivion achieved with pardons, amnesties, and justice persist. So, too, do the tensions between political reconciliation based on the need for governability and social peace and a policy of the principled implementation of domestic and international law regarding human rights. As the country approached presidential and legislative elections in December 2005, President Ricardo Lagos reminded Chileans of the need for reconciliation, saying that the quest for justice in cases of human rights violations during the dictatorship could not go on forever. As usual, resistance to this message came forth immediately from the human rights organizations, some of the political parties, and the associations (*agrupaciones*) of victims and family members.[56]

Of course, long-term insistence on *ni perdón ni olvido* would perpetuate social and political hatred across generations. On the other hand, a replication of the same old *vía chilena* would mean impunity even for crimes against humanity. Since 1990 Chileans have been caught in this bind, seeking once again to reconcile governability and social peace with a historical, social, and legal accounting for the conflicts and crimes of the past.

Epilogue

Chileans went to the polls to elect a new president on December 11, 2005. The governing *Concertación* coalition presented Michelle Bachelet, a member of the Socialist Party, as its candidate. Bachelet was the daughter of an air force general who had opposed the coup in 1973. The military junta ordered his arrest; he died in prison after being brutally tortured. Bachelet, as well as her mother, were also detained and mistreated in a notorious torture center. Freed from prison, Bachelet went with her mother to Australia, then into exile in East Germany, returning to Chile in 1979. During Lagos's presidency she had served as both the minister of health and the minister of defense. No woman had ever served as the minister of defense, nor had one ever been elected the president of Chile.

The political Right, split between the UDI and the Renovación Nacional (RN [National Renovation]) parties, presented two candidates: Joaquín Lavín (UDI), who had lost closely to Lagos in 2000, and Sebastián Piñera (RN), a multimillionaire entrepreneur who sought to wrest centrist, especially Christian Democratic, votes from the *Concertación*. Piñera had the flash, charm, money, and political experience to mount a serious challenge to a continued Concertación control of the presidency. Facing a socialist, and female, candidate with a nontraditional family life, whom he sought to identify with the bitter divisions of the past (that is, the Popular Unity government), Piñera pulled out all the stops in a campaign that promised to fight crime, create a million new jobs, improve the health care system, and commit itself to Christian humanist ideals.

Bachelet won approximately 46 percent of the vote in December; since no candidate received 50 percent of the vote, a runoff election between Bachelet and Piñera (coming second in the original election, with 25 percent) took place on January 15, 2006. As the election approached and Piñera seemed to be gaining ground on Bachelet, newspaper articles appeared "remembering" a proposal that Piñera had offered in the senate in 1995. Suddenly the battle between impunity, memory, and justice emerged once again as a critical issue, for Piñera, in the name of national reconciliation, had proposed an amnesty law for all persons ("authors, accomplices, and those who 'obstructed justice' [*encubridores*]") who had committed crimes from March 11, 1978, to March 11, 1990. He tied his proposed legislation directly to the 1978 amnesty decreed by the military regime, demanding that the "parade of officers before judges end" and amnesty be declared for all crimes covered by the 1978 decree law. Piñera's proposal had been rejected in 1995 and seemingly passed into oblivion along with various other proposals for "turning the page" and "not allowing the past to destroy the future."[57]

With memories of the findings of the Valech Commission fresh and renewed coverage of prosecutions of human rights violations in the media, Piñera could not successfully defend his 1995 call for impunity. Though not the only reason for his defeat, the resurgent battle between impunity and justice played an important role in the election of Chile's first female president. Ironically, but consistent with the historical tension between truth and forgetting, between reconciliation *a la chilena* and the resistance to impunity, Bachelet herself was seen as "a symbol of healing in a country long divided by ideology, class and competing versions of a tumultuous recent history."[58] Still, Bachelet's public remarks in an interview with German journalists represented a studied departure from the historical *vía chilena*:

> A country that has experienced such deep trauma as Chile can never be completely healed. I'm a doctor, so allow me to use a medical analogy to explain the problem: Only cleaned wounds can heal, otherwise they'll keep opening up again, and will likely become infected and begin to fester. It's clear to me that the truth must be brought to light. Of course, there are those—but they're a minority today—who just want to sweep everything under the rug. In a constitutional state, the government must take steps to ensure that the judiciary can operate without obstruction. The fact that I was elected shows that Chile has a mature society. And that's why most citizens insist that no one should be allowed to place themselves above the law and escape punishment.[59]

Of course, it remains to be seen whether Bachelet's efforts to cleanse the wounds so that they may heal will prove successful, as does whether *echándole tierra* over the human rights violations and the tradition of impunity will be replaced, in practice, with truth seeking and the rule of law. The *vía chilena de reconciliación política* has survived many changes in government since the early nineteenth century; the next four years of continued political transition from the military regime that began in 1990 likely will not see the end of this strongly embedded cultural pattern in Chilean politics.

Notes

1. See James Dunkerley, *The Pacification of Central America: Political Change in the Isthmus, 1987–1993* (London: Verso, 1994); Jack Child, *The Central American Peace Process, 1983–1991* (Boulder, CO: Lynne Rienner, 1992).
2. Jose Comblin, *The Church and the National Security State* (Maryknoll, NY: Orbis, 1979); Robert J. Schreiter, *Reconciliation: Mission and Ministry in a Changing Social Order* (Maryknoll, NY: Orbis, 1992); José Aldunate, S.J., *Derechos humanos: Camino de reconciliación* (Santiago: Ediciones Paulinas, 1988); Tony Misfud, "El rostro ético de la reconciliación," *Persona y sociedad* 1 (1987): 35–46. In English, see Harold Wells, "Theology for Reconciliation," in *The Reconciliation of Peoples: Challenge to the Churches*, ed. Gregory Baum and Harold Wells (Maryknoll, NY: Orbis, 1997), 1–15.
3. The brief overview provided in this article draws on ten years of research on political conflict and modes of political reconciliation in Chile. In particular, we draw here on two unpublished papers by Brian Loveman and Elizabeth Lira presented at the Conference on Legacies of Authoritarianism at the University of Wisconsin, Madison, April 3–5, 1998, "The Politics of Memory, Impunity, and Amnesty: The 'Chilean Road' to Reconciliation, 1818–1998," and "La política de la reconciliación: discursos, sacramentos y pragmatismo," and the following books by Brian Loveman and Elizabeth Lira: *Las suaves cenizas de olvido: Vía chilena de reconciliación política 1814–1932*, 2nd rev. and exp. ed. (Santiago: DIBAM/LOM, 2000); *Las acusaciones constitucionales en Chile: Una perspectiva histórica* (Santiago: FLACSO-LOM, 2000); *Las ardientes cenizas del olvido: Vía chilena de reconciliación política, 1932–1994* (Santiago: DIBAM-LOM, 2000); *Leyes de reconciliación en Chile: Amnistías, indultos y reparaciones 1819–1999* (Santiago: DIBAM/Centro de Investigaciones Diego Barros Arana, 2001); *Historia, política y ética de la verdad en Chile, 1891–2001: Reflexiones sobre la paz social y la impunidad* (Santiago: LOM/Universidad Alberto Hurtado, 2001); *Arquitectura política y seguridad interior del estado 1811–1999* (Santiago: DIBAM/Centro de Investigaciones Diego Barros Arana, 2002); *El espejismo de la reconciliación política: Chile 1990–2002* (Santiago: DIBAM-LOM, 2002); and Elizabeth Lira and Brian Loveman, *Políticas de reparación: Chile 1990–2004* (Santiago: LOM/DIBAM, 2004).
4. A general amnesty in the name of reconciliation is described in Aristotle, "The Athenian Constitution," part 39, available at classics.mit.edu/Aristotle/athenian_const.2.2.html (accessed August 3, 2006).
5. Luis Heinecke Scott, *Una larga amenaza que se cumple*, vol. 2 of *Chile: Crónica de un asedio* (Santiago: Sociedad Editora y Gráfica Santa Catalina, 1992). This is the military version of the history of international communism's attack on Chile since before World War I. It is extensively documented with extracts from leftist politicians and the revolutionary press.
6. We have limited ourselves in this article to describing the *vía chilena de reconciliación política* as a historical pattern for postconflict political reconfiguration and pacification in the search for political stability and governability and to describing and illustrating a parallel resistance to this pattern, that is, a resistance to political, legal, and moral impunity. We have not sought here to explain how this reiterated process contributed to the accumulation over more than half a century of unresolved conflicts or to the brutality and intensity of the repression after September 11, 1973. These themes we have addressed in several of the publications cited above (see note 3).

7. On the Ranquil uprising, see Brian Loveman, *Struggle in the Countryside: Politics and Rural Labor in Chile, 1919–1973* (Bloomington: Indiana University Press, 1976), 144–45; Consejo de Defensa Fiscal, N. 165, 4 mayo, 1933; Eduardo Téllez Lúgaro et al., "El levantamiento del Alto Biobío y el Soviet y la República Araucana de 1934," *Anales de la Universidad de Chile*, 6th ser., no. 13 (2001), www2.anales.uchile.cl/CDA/an_simple/0.1278,SCID%253D216%2526ISID%253D9%2526ACT%253D0%2526PRT%253D118,00.html. A more recent article in a Mapuche Indian magazine refers explicitly to the themes of *olvido* and *echándole tierra* with amnesties: Renato Reyes, "Levantamiento de Ranquil. A 70 años del olvido," *Mapuche Azkintuwe*, July 2004, www.mapuche-nation.org/espanol/html/articulos/art-59.htm. The most detailed account of the Ranquil incident in English is found in Thomas Klubock "Ranquil: Violence and Peasant Politics on Chile's Southern Frontier" (unpublished paper, September 2005). On the massacre at the Caja de Seguro Obligatorio (and for an anti-Alessandri frame for this event with graphic photos of the dead), see Ricardo Donoso, *Alessandri, agitador y demoledor: Cincuenta años de historia política de Chile*, vol. 2 (Mexico City: Fondo de Cultura Económica, 1954), chaps. 14, 15. For the Caja events, Congress created a joint fact-finding commission of senators and deputies to discover the truth about the massacre: "A investigar la forma en que fueron muertos los prisioneros tomados en la Universidad y a establecer quién impartió la orden de hacerlos volver, cuando eran llevados a la Sección de Investigaciones, al edificio de la Caja de Seguro Obligatorio" ("To investigate the manner in which the prisoners taken at the university were killed and to establish who gave the order for them to return to the Caja de Seguro building after being taken to secret police headquarters" (275). Donoso calls his chapter 15 "El escamoteo de la verdad" ("The Illusion of Truth").
8. Chilean historians and political elites have abundantly documented these battles from diverse political and ideological perspectives in nineteenth- and twentieth-century writing. Even the biographies of independence war leaders, early nineteenth-century politicians, military officers, and church officials are embedded in antagonistic historiographical traditions, identified roughly as "conservative," "liberal," "reformist," and "Marxist." An excellent example of this trend is the historiography on Diego Portales, surveyed in great detail in Enrique Brahm García, "Portales en la historiografía," in *Portales, el hombre y su obra: La consolidación del gobierno civil*, ed. Bernardino Bravo Lira (Santiago: Editorial Jurídica de Chile-Editorial Andrés Bello, 1989), 443–84.
9. Whether to accept the legitimacy of the notions of "internal war" or "civil war" (or "war" at all) from 1973 to 1990 is itself part of the discourse that frames this conflict and a tactic by opposing sides in its ongoing reinterpretation. For a fascinating interpretation of this issue, see Hernán Vidal, *FPMR: El tabú del conflicto armado en Chile* (Santiago: Mosquito Editores, 1995).
10. Thus new constitutions in 1828, 1833, 1825, and 1980; key electoral and legal reforms after political conflicts in 1837, 1851, 1859, 1860–61, and the early 1870s; and efforts to address the social question with decrees (1924) and a new labor code (1931) to overcome the political rupture of constitutional continuity (1924–32).
11. *Boletín de leyes* 29 (1861): 355–56, reprinted in Loveman and Lira, *Leyes de reconciliación*, 74.
12. "O'Higgins Bernardo—Se ordena la erección de la estatua de la Alameda, la colocacion de su retrato en la Sala de Gobierno i otros homenajes para honrar su memoria" (July 13, 1844). See Ricardo Anguita, *Leyes promulgadas en Chile, desde 1810 hasta el 1 de junio de 1912* (Santiago: Imprenta, Litografía i Encuadernación Barcelona, 1912), 1:435–36.

13. We have detailed these reconciliation policies after each political rupture in Loveman and Lira, *Las suaves cenizas del olvido*.
14. Francisco A. Encina, *Historia de Chile desde la prehistoria hasta 1891*, vol. 14 (Santiago: Editorial Nascimento, 1950), 199; emphasis added.
15. The authors have interviewed all the members of the Rettig Commission created by President Aylwin in 1990, as well as various functionaries of the Corporación de Reparación y Reconciliación (Corporation for Reparation and Reconciliation) that followed up on its work. Only one of the interviewees (a prominent Chilean historian) was aware of the *juicio de residencia* (an administrative "trial" for colonial administrators finishing their tenure in order to hold them accountable for any wrongdoing) of O'Higgins in 1823 and the *acusaciones constitucionales* against Manuel Montt in 1868, President Balmaceda's ministers from 1891–93, or against Carlos Ibáñez in 1931. None of them were aware of the history of pardons and amnesties in the nineteenth century in any detail, though the Rettig Commission and the Corporación de Reparación y Reconciliación did prepare a list (incomplete) of previous amnesties. Political exigencies of the moment prevented time and energy being dedicated to historical research on the context of previous amnesties. No attention was dedicated to discussing these precedents. Only Raúl Rettig had actually participated in previous amnesty debates, as a legislator in the 1950s.
16. There were exceptions. In 1827, Francisco Antonio Pinto insisted on a letter from the mutinous military personnel requesting pardon and promising future good behavior. From 1851 to 1857, President Montt, his ministers, and the Consejo de Estado (Council of State) also sought formal pardon requests, promises of good behavior, and conditioned pardons and commutations of sentences on political restraint, subject to application of the original sentence, whether capital punishment or incarceration. The authors have reviewed systematically the minutes of the sessions of the Consejo de Estado in which pardons were debated and the conditions placed on those pardons during the 1830s through the 1850s.
17. For a summary of this view, see Brian Loveman, "Human Rights, Antipolitics, and Protecting the Patria: An (Almost) Military Perspective," in *The Politics of Antipolitics: The Military in Latin America*, ed. Brian Loveman and Thomas M. Davies Jr. (Wilmington, DE: Scholarly Resources, 1997), 398–423.
18. In an effort to equate pardons for supposed terrorists (former MIR members and Socialists who carried out armed resistance against the dictatorship and sometimes engaged in violent crimes against innocent civilians) with pardons for military personnel who had served at least ten years in prison for human rights violations, several legislative proposals emerged in early September 2005. In the meantime, President Lagos pardoned Manuel Contreras Donaire, a noncommissioned officer who had participated in the murder of the labor leader Tucapel Jiménez in 1985, provoking outcries from human rights organizations and leftist parties. See "Lagos descarta más indultos," *El Mercurio*, September 14, 2005.
19. The brief summaries of each *acusación constitucional* that follow cannot do justice to the complexity of the social and political conditions telescoped when the events are considered in detail. Our objective here is only to reveal the patterns that developed and their persistence into the first decades of the twenty-first century.
20. Historiography on the 1891 civil war is rich. For varied interpretations of the Balmaceda era, see Julio Heise, *Historia de Chile: El período parlamentario 1861–1925* (Santiago: Editorial Andrés Bello, 1974); Luis Ortega, ed., *La guerra civil de 1891: Cien años hoy* (Santiago: Editorial Universitaria, 1991); Rafael Sagredo Baeza, *Vapor al norte, tren al*

sur: El viaje presidencial como práctica política en Chile (Santiago: DIBAM/Centro de Investigaciones Diego Barros Arana, 2001); Bernardo Subercaseaux, *Fin de siglo: La época de Balmaceda* (Santiago: CENECA/Editorial Aconcagua, 1988).

21. "Oficio de la Cámara de Diputados dirijido al Senado," December 16, 1891, reprinted in Loveman and Lira, eds., *Acusación constitucional contra el último ministerio del Presidente de la República don José Manuel Balmaceda, 1891–1893* (Santiago: DIBAM, 2004), 291.
22. Ibid., 295.
23. *Acusación al Ministerio Vicuña: Boletín de las sesiones especiales en 1893* (Santiago: Imprenta Nacional, 1893), reprinted in Loveman and Lira, *Acusación constitucional*, 489–493.
24. Cámara de Diputados, December 24, 1891, 403, Biblioteca del Congreso, Santiago.
25. For detailed discussion of the initial repression against the Balmacedistas, the debates over each of the amnesty laws from 1891–94, and other measures for political reconciliation from 1891 to 1919, see Loveman and Lira, *Las suaves cenizas del olvido*, 224–54.
26. In some cases the memories have been passed along among family members to the present. Thus ex-president Patricio Aylwin remarked that he remembers that his father and his father's mother had visited his grandfather in jail for having been a Balmacedista. To some extent this informed Aylwin's idea that reconciliation would only finally take place when the generations that experienced the conflict (whether 1891 or 1970–90) had passed from the scene. Patricio Aylwin, conversation with the authors at his home in Santiago after leaving the presidency.
27. Decreto Ley N. 535, *Diario Oficial* 14.278, 22, December 1925, reprinted in Loveman and Lira, *Leyes de reconciliación*, 96.
28. Cámara de Diputados, 15a sesión extraordinaria, October 26, 1926, 569, Biblioteca del Congreso, Santiago.
29. See Loveman and Lira, *Las acusaciones constitucionales en Chile*.
30. This is the "nickname" for the National Commission on Truth and Reconciliation created by Patricio Aylwin in 1990. The name comes from the surname of the commission's chair, Raúl Rettig, a longtime Radical Party politician. On the Pinochet *acusación constitucional*, see Cámara de Diputados, 9a sesión, April 9, 1998; excerpts are reproduced in Loveman and Lira, *Las acusaciones constitucionales en Chile*, 170–238.
31. On the Ibáñez regime, see Jorge Rojas Flores, *La dictadura de Ibáñez y los sindicatos (1927–1931)* (Santiago: DIBAM, Centro de Investigaciones Diego Barros Arana, 1993); Brian Loveman and Elizabeth Lira, *La Comisión Investigadora de los Actos de la Dictadura* (Santiago: DIBAM, forthcoming).
32. Pedro Opazo Letelier, the president of the senate, took over as interim president and then resigned the same day, July 27, 1931. He was succeeded by Juan Esteban Montero who had served as Ibáñez's minister of the interior until July 21, 1931, representing an effort to liberalize the regime, allow the return of some exiles, and restore relative freedom of the press. It was also a last-ditch effort to demobilize professional and student groups that had carried out strikes and street demonstrations against the government for several months.
33. Ventura Maturana R., *Mi ruta* (Buenos Aires: n.p., 1936), 124–25.
34. See Loveman and Lira, *Las acusaciones constitucionales en Chile*.
35. Ministerio de Justicia, Decreto 2676, August 4, 1931, Archivo Siglo XX, Santiago.
36. Comisión Investigadora de los Actos de la Dictadura, Acta de sesión 8a plenaria, August 18, 1931, Archivo Siglo XX, Santiago.

37. For details on the amnesties during this period, see Loveman and Lira, *Leyes de reconciliación en Chile*, 95–113.
38. Cámara de Diputados, 49a sesión ordinaria, August 31, 1931, 1765–67, Biblioteca del Congreso, Santiago.
39. During his second presidential administration (1952–58), Ibáñez was again subjected to the *acusación constitucional* procedure, making him the only president in Chilean history to face such proceedings twice during his term of office. See Loveman and Lira, *Las acusaciones constitucionales en Chile*, 118–69; Cámara de Diputados, 22a sesión, November 27, 1956, 1393–1414, Biblioteca del Congreso, Santiago.
40. It must be noted that amnesties benefited workers and peasants as well as military and police officials. After World War I, labor conflicts and violence periodically produced confrontations between miners, workers, peasants, and law enforcement officials or the army. Amnesties in 1925 (for the bloody events at Puerto Natales in 1919 and the nitrate camp at San Gregorio in 1921), in 1934 (for the events at Ranquil in 1934, and also for all workers and leftist politicians accused of crimes against the internal security of the state), and in 1936 (for striking railway workers, among others) all evidenced the expanding clientele for amnesties and pardons in the name of reconciliation.
41. The authors have documented these debates extensively in Loveman and Lira, *Las ardientes cenizas del olvido*. In the 1950s, pardons became so common that one congressman asked for a congressional investigation (more than five thousand pardons in less than three years—of course not all of them related to *political* crimes).
42. An English version of the commission's charge and its work can be found at www.usip.org/library/tc/doc/reports/chile/chile_1993_pt1_ch1.html (accessed September 4, 2005).
43. Ministerio de Interior, Decreto Supremo 355, *Diario Oficial*, May 9, 1990.
44. In the course of our research, we interviewed all members of the Rettig Commission regarding the commission's work, their perceptions of the limits on their activities, and the results of the commission report.
45. Quoted in the introduction to the English version of the report at www.usip.org/library/tc/doc/reports/chile/chile_1993_introeng.html (accessed August 3, 2006).
46. Ibid.
47. We rely here on Brian Loveman, *Chile: The Legacy of Hispanic Capitalism* (New York: Oxford University Press, 2001), 315–17.
48. This is a topic for another article. See Lira and Loveman, *Políticas de reparación*, for a detailed analysis of the various reparation policies during this period.
49. For a summary of major episodes and tension points in civil-military relations from 1990 to 2000, see Loveman, *Chile*, 331–35.
50. One of the authors, Elizabeth Lira, testified as a witness before a congressional committee designated to inform the Cámara de Diputados in the 1998 proceedings against Pinochet. For details and extracts from the proceedings, see Loveman and Lira, *Las acusaciones constitucionales en Chile*, 17–235.
51. On the Pinochet case, see Madeleine Davis, ed., *The Pinochet Case: Origins, Progress, and Implications* (London: Institute of Latin American Studies, 2003).
52. "Mesa de Diálogo" is a term used to describe a working group appointed to discuss a particular policy issue, for example, human rights, labor law, etc. It has no precise English translation. For reasons of space, and also because the Mesa de Diálogo does not neatly fall into the same patterns as the truth commissions and the *acusaciones constitucionales*, we do not include it further in this discussion. Elizabeth Lira participated as a member of this

group. For a summary of the agreement reached, see "Acuerdo de la Mesa de Diálogo," *La Nación*, June 23, 2003, www.lanacion.cl/p4_lanacion/antialone.html?page=http://www.lanacion.cl/prontus_noticias/site/artic/20030624/pags/20030624133756.html.

53. The Commission's list of over twenty-seven thousand persons recognized as torture victims can be found at www.comisiontortura.cl/inicio/Nomina.pdf (accessed September 4, 2005). The entire report is available at www.gobiernodechile.cl/comision_valech/index.asp (accessed September 4, 2005). The printed version is titled *Informe de la Comisión Nacional sobre Prisión Política y Tortura* (Santiago: La Nación, 2005). A note on the imprint page claims that thirty-three thousand copies were printed and would be distributed without charge.
54. This is an acronym for Programa de Reparación y Atención Integral de Salud (Program for Reparation and Integral Health Care). The program is described in Elizabeth Lira and Brian Loveman, *Políticas de reparación*.
55. Nevertheless, some new prosecutions were initiated as a result of the commission's report, including ones against Pinochet and Senator Sergio Fernández (UDI) who had served as minister of the interior in the military government and signed the 1978 amnesty decree. See Ana María Sanhueza, "Libelo fue presentado ayer en tribunales y se basa en antecedentes del informe Valechi Primera querella por torturas apunta a Pinochet y Sergio Fernandez," *La Tercera*, December 4, 2004, www.purochile.org/op. The new prosecutions initiated by victims and their legal representatives were based on international human rights law and a recent interpretation of the Chilean Supreme Court regarding the applicability of international law to human rights violations that occurred during the dictatorship.
56. For example, the Fundación de Ayuda Social de las Iglesias Cristianas (FASIC [Social Aid Foundation of Christian Churches]), an organization created in 1975 to support victims of the dictatorship, called for the application of international law regarding human rights violations (no pardons, no amnesties). See FASIC, "Declaración pública," August 19, 2005, www.fasic.org/doc/dec050819.htm.
57. For more on this, see Loveman and Lira, *El espejismo de la reconciliación política*.
58. Monte Reel, "Female, Agnostic, and the Next Presidente?" *Washington Post*, December 9, 2005, www.washingtonpost.com/wp-dyn/content/article/2005/12/09/AR2005120902040.html.
59. Michelle Bachelet, "Only Cleaned Wounds Can Heal," interview by Hans Hoyng and Helene Zuber, *Spiegel*, March 9, 2006, trans. Christopher Sultan, www.truthout.org/docs_2006/030906H.shtml (accessed August 3, 2006).

Educating Citizens in Postwar Guatemala: Historical Memory, Genocide, and the Culture of Peace

Elizabeth Oglesby

On February 25, 1999, the Guatemalan Commission for Historical Clarification presented its final report before a packed audience in Guatemala's National Theater. Most who attended the ceremony were surprised by the forcefulness of the report's conclusions, not because the content was unfamiliar, but because few had held high expectations for a commission whose mandate was circumscribed by the limits of Guatemala's dubious political transition. The head commissioner, Christian Tomushat, was interrupted numerous times by loud applause from the audience, which included victims of the crimes described by the report. The Guatemalan President Alvaro Arzú sat stone-faced alongside the army high command as Tomushat described the acts of genocide perpetrated by the state against the country's Mayan majority in the early 1980s, and the president declined to step to the podium to accept the commission's report.

Known by its Spanish abbreviation CEH (Comisión para el Esclarecimiento Histórico), the commission was created as part of Guatemala's multiyear peace process that culminated in a cease-fire in December 1996. The final peace accord put an end to a thirty-four-year armed confrontation in which an estimated two hundred thousand people lost their lives. Over 90 percent of the human rights violations tabulated by the commission were attributed to state forces, including the army, police, and army-organized so-called civil defense patrols.

Radical History Review
Issue 97 (Winter 2007) DOI 10.1215/01636545-2006-013

In addition to the massacres, forced disappearances, and other human rights violations chronicled by the commission, the CEH report dealt in surprising depth with the social and political context of the violence. This attention to the causes and origins of the armed conflict formed part of the commission's mandate, and it set the CEH apart from other Latin American truth commissions (Argentina in 1984, Chile in 1991, and El Salvador in 1993).[1] This part of the mandate was also an arena of contention during the commission's tenure, bringing to the fore the epistemological tensions between a strictly juridical framing of the violence and diverse social and historical understandings of the structural and processual dynamics that fed the conflict. The complexity of the CEH report produced through this melding of legal and contextual analysis makes it particularly important to investigate how the report's contents were and are transmitted to Guatemalan society.

Like most truth commissions, the CEH disbanded after presenting its twelve-volume report, *Memory of Silence*, to the public. The Guatemalan state did not take ownership of the report; on the contrary, three weeks after publication, President Arzú signed a full-page ad in the Guatemalan press repudiating many of the commission's recommendations, including the creation of a governmental office to provide follow-up to the commission's work. The United Nations office that had housed the commission produced several thousand copies of *Memory of Silence* and a very good summary of the report's conclusions and recommendations (some of which was reprinted in the Guatemalan press), but it did not conduct any formal follow-up in the communities in which testimonies had been gathered. Finally, despite the efforts of both the CEH and the Catholic Church's human rights office to document the atrocities of the counterinsurgency campaigns, at the close of 1999, the party of the former de facto head of state, General Efraín Rios Montt (1981–83), swept to power in presidential and congressional elections. Threats and attacks intensified against human rights leaders, researchers studying the histories of the conflict, and other activists.[2] Looking at things from these angles, it seems easy to assume that the CEH report had little impact on Guatemalan society.

Yet the report's influence can be felt in myriad ways. Many popular organizations in Guatemala have taken up the commission's recommendations as their own. Although the CEH report cannot be used as judicial evidence because of the restrictions of the original mandate, it has been used as contextual evidence in landmark human rights cases, such as the 2002 Myrna Mack murder trial.[3] Overall, there is a sense in which *Memory of Silence* is in the public domain, with the imprimatur of the United Nations and the official peace process, and this makes it harder to deny certain realities, whether in the press or in political discourse. The CEH report (as well as the Catholic Church's four-volume 1998 report, *Guatemala: Never Again*) helped create an opening to publicly discuss issues related to the armed conflict that until recently had been considered taboo.

At the same time, the actual use of the CEH report has been minimal. References to the report are almost always limited to the grim profiles of the violence, with little historical or social context to explain the conditions that gave rise to the armed conflict. In part this is due to the lack of formal follow-up to the commission, and the tentative nature of alternative projects that seek to publicize the report's findings. Yet the important issue is not the suppression of the report per se, but the ways in which certain portions of the report are repeated while others are muted, and how particular framings of historical memory are actively produced through these processes. These framings, in turn, have clear implications for the kinds of social and political reform projects that may emerge from the truth commission experience.

This essay examines the wake of the Guatemalan Commission for Historical Clarification in terms of a double movement. The existence of the report helps create space for a more public discussion of the war, which is important to the extent that Guatemalan society has yet to fully assimilate that experience. Yet this opening of space is accompanied by a narrowing of the range of narratives through which the past is understood. Current notions of historical memory are conflated to mean the individualized experiences of victims of human rights violations. This sort of discourse emphasizes that the war produced victims, but it does not elucidate that in the majority of cases, these victims also had identities as social actors, as members of organizations (some revolutionary, some not) involved in projects of social change. Such narrow framings of historical memory infrequently take into account broader histories of life that can give a fuller sense of identity to the victims, instead reducing the narratives to what I call "tales of death" (*relatos de la muerte*),[4] or what the Argentine sociologist Elizabeth Jelin called the "ritualized repetition of the traumatic and sinister story."[5] For example, the cover of a 2003 educational project proposal to the Guatemalan Ministry of Education shows a skeletal hand reaching up, under a caption reading "Historical Memory in the National Curriculum."

In many of the educational projects billed as efforts to disseminate the Guatemalan truth commission's findings, such as recent school textbooks and material produced by both human rights groups and international institutions, the inclusion of material on the war serves as a prelude to a much longer elaboration related to civic education and citizen formation. In the civic education framework, the history of the conflict is framed in two ways: either as an exposé of brutality or as the triumph of democracy. Indeed, the first framing is the hook that moves us along to the second. This is akin to what Tzvetan Todorov called "exemplary memory,"[6] or using the past as a guide for action in the present and future, in this case the creation of new subjectivities consistent with the goal of internalizing and institutionalizing limited notions of liberal democracy through culture-of-peace curricula. Historical memory in its circumscribed form serves to introduce new codes of conduct for the molding of postwar citizens. This lens helps us understand some developments that at first glance might seem paradoxical, for example, the fact that one of the best-funded efforts to disseminate material from the CEH report came from the U.S. Agency for International Development (USAID), through its peace and reconciliation program.

Charles Hale shows how neoliberal modes of governance in Guatemala have opened new political space in terms of a discourse of rights that in previous moments would have seemed out of reach. Yet, he argues, "these initiatives also come with clearly articulated limits, attempts to distinguish those rights that are acceptable from those that are not."[7] Liberal discourses of rights have always had this double nature, of course, at once emancipatory and disciplinary. As Wendy Brown makes clear, liberal constructions of personhood create a universalized, idealized subject, while at the same time obscuring concrete contexts of social, political, and economic subordination. Rights discourses may "[convert] social problems into matters of individualized dehistoricized injury and entitlement, into matters in which there is no harm if there is no agent and no tangibly violated subject."[8]

In Latin America, as Jelin writes, such decontextualization of historical memory has a particular genealogy linked to the rise of human rights movements that confronted authoritarian regimes in the 1980s and into the 1990s.[9] In the 1980s, the language of human rights helped create political space for victims' movements to emerge. Yet the positing of human rights language as a framework for understanding history is deeply problematic. Jelin writes: "For the interpretive framework of human rights violations, the polarity is between human rights violators on one side and victims on the other." In this discourse, a victim is depicted as a "passive being, harmed by the actions of others. The victim is never an active agent."[10]

In Latin America, conjoining the terms *history* and *memory* has meant privileging direct testimony by the victims of human rights violations.[11] In part, this is because of the perceived psychological benefit to victims of telling their story.[12] One of the obvious pitfalls of relying on testimony to reconstruct history, however, is that testimonies are highly subjective constructs. People are often reticent to talk about militancy or social activism, for instance. In Guatemala, as elsewhere in Latin America, social organizing was stigmatized through years of repression and the manipulation of language (even unarmed activists were often called "subversives"), producing both fear and "clandestine habits."[13] The failure of the revolutionary movements produced yet another layer of distress: given the psychological complexity of memory construction, it can be difficult for people to talk about their decisions or indecisions in a given moment that may have had serious consequences.

In Latin America, therefore, the depoliticization of historical memory over the past two decades has both political and psychological dimensions. By looking at the life of the Guatemalan truth commission report since 1999, this essay traces the points at which the human rights discourses converge with the instrumentalization of historical memory within projects of neoliberal governance. As part of this framework for postwar governance, the culture-of-peace narrative is very powerful in that it not only helps instill a highly individualized doctrine of rights but also draws explicit and implicit boundaries (by eradicating traces of collective or class mobilization, for example) for what is acceptable in the current context. I first look at how the arguments pertaining to the historical roots of the armed conflict were framed within the report. I then examine how teachers, human rights groups, and international institutions have taken up the report in educational projects. I end by critiquing the implications of the peace curricula initiatives for the construction of historical memory.

The CEH and the Debates over History

From 1997–98, I was a full-time member of the CEH support staff. Most of my work with the commission meant serving as a liaison between the CEH and a group of Guatemalan scholars known as the Historical Analysis Group.[14]

Some of the issues at stake in the historical analysis of the Guatemalan war included whether the war should be seen as primarily a Cold War conflict or whether the internal conditions in the country should be accorded preeminence. The Cold War framework, while obviously important and even determinate at key historical junctures, is also limiting, in that it allows powerful actors to assert that Guatemala had fallen victim to a global geopolitical struggle, making it easier for them to avoid responsibility for how things unfolded.

A related issue was whether the conflict should be framed as primarily a conflagration between two armed groups (the army and the insurgents), as uneven as that matchup was, or whether the historical analysis needed to be broadened to include other sectors (political parties, elites, social movements, etc.). The first interpretation is known in Latin America as the theory of the "two devils," or the "two fires," or simply the "theory of the sandwich," whereby the bulk of the population is caught rather passively in between.[15] At stake in the debates over how to frame this question is not only the fact that other social actors were involved in the conflict but also that people have an identity as historical actors beyond their identity as victims of human rights violations. It is not just that people suffered human rights atrocities, but that they were targeted in the majority of cases because they were members of social organizations, such as peasant leagues, progressive church groups, unions, student groups, and so on. The CEH report was very clear on these points:

> The CEH concludes that a full explanation of the Guatemalan confrontation cannot be reduced to the sole logic of the two armed parties. Such an interpretation fails to explain or establish the basis for the persistence and significance of the participation of the political parties and economic forces in the initiation, development and continuation of the violence; nor does it explain the repeated efforts at organization and the continuous mobilization of those sectors of the population struggling to achieve their economic, political and cultural demands.[16]

The historical analysis that the CEH put forward emphasizes multiple causes for the war: structural injustice, racism, and the closing of political space, particularly after the overthrow of the reformist president Jacobo Arbenz in 1954, and in the early 1960s. The report documents the "increasingly exclusionary and anti-democratic nature" of state institutions from the 1950s to the 1980s, as well as the "reluctance to implement substantive reforms that might have reduced the structural conflicts" (19, para. 12). The report also shows how Cold War policies such as the National Security Doctrine "fell on fertile ground in Guatemala" and "were first expressed as anti-reformist, then anti-democratic policies, culminating in criminal counterinsurgency" (19, para. 12). As new movements arose to counter the political and structural exclusions, the state's idea of an internal enemy, intrinsic to the National Security Doctrine, expanded to include just about every sector that opposed the government or pressed for change. Thus the CEH concluded that the state countered with a "disproportionately repressive response": "The inclusion of all opponents under one banner, democrat or otherwise, pacifist or guerrilla, legal or illegal, communist or non-communist, served to justify numerous and serious crimes. Faced with widespread political, social, economic and cultural opposition, the State resorted to military operations directed toward the physical annihilation or absolute intimidation of this opposition" (22, para. 25).

By focusing on the diverse movements for social change that arose in Guatemala from the 1960s through the 1990s, the CEH paints the conflict in broad yet grounded terms, trying to avoid both the sterile two-devils thesis and the equally useless slippery slope of "we were all responsible." The commission elaborates its historical analysis using material from many of the eight thousand testimonies collected, but also through interviews with key informants (*testigos claves*) triangulated with other primary sources and secondary materials.

How was this twelve-volume indictment received by Guatemalan society? Greg Grandin has provided an overview of responses printed in the press in the immediate wake of the report's presentation,[17] and the United Nations conducted a survey of perceptions of the report shortly afterward.[18] As an institution, the army did not respond to the commission's report, although several retired military officers expressed the opinion that the report was biased and reflected simply the perspective of the commission. Some members of the elite expressed similar sentiments, and the ruling on genocide struck a raw nerve.[19] On the other hand, popular organizations felt vindicated by the report's conclusions. The overwhelming attribution of human rights violations to state forces was important, but more than that, to the extent that the report's existence became known in communities, it helped people see that what they had faced in their localities formed part of a larger phenomenon.

Yet for all its importance, the CEH report remains inaccessible to most people. I return to the questions posed at the beginning of this essay: How is the report's content transmitted to Guatemalan society? Who are the report's brokers?

What relation do the secondary materials produced from *Memory of Silence* (popular and didactic versions, for example) have to the content of the original? How are these materials linked to particular sorts of postwar social and political reform projects? The following section details the efforts to incorporate the CEH report into school curricula and educational projects as one of the principle conduits for dissemination of the truth commission findings. In the absence of a national dissemination project, however, teachers and schools are developing ad hoc initiatives, while the best-funded efforts are coming from international agencies such as the US Agency for International Development.[20]

Teaching the Recent Past in Postwar Guatemala

The Guatemalan peace accords were supposed to improve the country's dismal educational system by raising government spending on education and mandating curricular reform to treat issues of ethnic diversity and multiculturalism.[21] The increased investment in education has not materialized, and Guatemala continues to have the lowest ratio of state spending on education of any Central American country.[22] Half of the school-age children in Guatemala do not attend school. The educational reform progressed as far as primary school, with new standards that mandate multiculturalism in these grades. As Kristel Foster notes, however, while the new standards were supposed to correct traditional depictions of indigenous cultures as relics of history (with lists of Mayan figures from the pre-Conquest period, for example), the new texts have gone far in the opposite direction and have removed history almost entirely, in favor of "social studies."[23] This is true for high school texts as well.

According to Gustavo Palma, a leading scholar of the Guatemalan educational system, the state is committed to public education only at the primary level. Roughly 80 percent of Guatemala's elementary schools are public, while only about one-third of high schools are.[24] The private high schools must also follow the national standards set out by the Ministry of Education, however.

There is no national project to address the teaching of historical memory. In some ways, of course, one could argue against the need for a national project. A state-approved textbook would likely emerge out of such levels of political compromise that it probably would not offer much improvement over what already exists. On the other hand, the obstacles to teaching about the recent past are formidable (lack of resources and guidelines, conservatism toward adopting new subjects, apprehension about the possible reaction of parents or other community members), and if national guidelines were set, it could be easier for teachers to introduce these sensitive topics into their program of study. Even if the national standards simply required a more rigorous examination of Guatemalan history, this would be an improvement over allowing history to be subsumed by social studies.

The development of national standards for teaching about historical memory had become an arena of struggle by the time I began this research, as consultants working within the Ministry of Education had attempted various proposals to teach the CEH report. In 2002, a textbook and a teacher-development guide based on the CEH report were produced under the auspices of the ministry; the text was called *Social-Historical Context of Guatemala and Educational Reality*, and it followed fairly closely the topics of the CEH report. It included an introduction called "Why Are We the Way We Are?" followed by a section on the multiple forms of exclusion that underlay the conflict, a section on racism called "Mayans as Enemies of the State," and a section drawing on cases documented by the CEH. Thousands of copies were printed, but a sector of the Guatemalan congress reacted vehemently against the books, so they were recalled.[25]

Several human rights groups have attempted, without much success, to develop proposals for the Ministry of Education to mandate historical memory as part of the national curricular standards. One Ministry of Education plan did gain currency, however. Called "Citizenship Formation in the National Curricula" and funded by UNESCO's Culture of Peace Project, the approved plan recommends that children study the conditions that led to political polarization in the past, as well as the "insurgent and counterinsurgent actions," along with the peace process, multiculturalism, and the dangers of drugs and alcohol.[26]

Textbooks Before and After the Peace Accords

Most teachers choose from about half a dozen common textbooks produced by private editorial houses in Guatemala City.[27] Textbooks prior to 1986, the year the country initiated a transition to civilian rule, made no mention of recent history at all. Textbooks produced after 1986 but before the culmination of the peace process offered a chronology of the military dictatorships of the early 1980s but did not discuss the armed conflict. Prior to the 1996 signing of the peace accords, none of the widely used textbooks mentioned the conflict, although some schools began to teach about the war even before the peace accords, especially after the Mayan activist Rigoberta Menchú won the Nobel Peace Prize in 1992. But teachers were on their own for curriculum development; there was no effort on the part of the Ministry of Education or any other organized sector to provide material.

Since the peace accords, all of the leading textbooks address the conflict to some degree. There is not much difference between elementary school textbooks and high school textbooks in terms of the topics presented to students, although a high school book will include units on international themes. Again, an important point is that with the exception of some of the very good private schools, Guatemalan students do not study history, even in high school. They have social studies, with texts that present a formulaic list of topics that varies little from one grade to the next. For example, the common high school textbooks will introduce post-colonial Guatemalan history with a few pages on nineteenth- and early twentieth-century military governments, continuing with a paragraph on the post–World War II reformist government of Jacobo Arbenz and a paragraph on the Cold War and the rise of the early guerrilla movements in the 1960s. Invariably, the texts then drop the historical narrative and continue with thematic entries, usually about one or two pages in length, such as ones on the peace accords, the culture of peace, human rights, and the rights of children. There is some variation from text to text—some texts are more sympathetic to Arbenz, for example—but the list of human rights themes that follows the brief historical timeline is nearly identical in all the books. The most recent textbooks include references to the report of the truth commission, although the references are brief and limited to the basic data of how many deaths and disappearances the CEH tabulated. Some textbooks include more visual elaboration, such as an image of Guatemalan refugees or a photo of Rigoberta Menchú.

Schools and the Agency of Teachers

As more material about the recent past hits the public consciousness, some teachers are motivated to develop alternative, autonomous curricular projects. Students in Santa María Tzejá, a returned refugee community in the northern part of the country, read supplementary materials about local history. Some teachers ask their students to write poems or conduct interviews with relatives or someone in the community who lived through the years of repression. In one upper middle-class school in Guatemala City, teachers developed an integrated lesson plan for which students in social studies read about the conflict, while reading testimonial literature, such as the memoir of Rigoberta Menchú and poetry from the 1960s and 1970s, in their Spanish classes.

There are more curricular initiatives going on than one might expect given the obstacles. In the capital, there is a strong network of private high schools, mainly Catholic, which organize debates on both international and national human rights topics; these attract students from many different schools, including the military high school. Universities provide resources, such as video libraries,[28] and popular organizations sometimes participate in these activities with the schools. Videos, novels, and theater productions that treat the violence also circulate throughout other parts of the country. Since there are no guidelines for teachers, it is the exception rather than the rule that high school teachers (especially in the rural areas) deal with topics not presented in the textbooks. Still, many exceptions do exist.

The individual teacher or school that assumes this sort of initiative takes on a certain risk. In rural areas, teachers might face students from communities that were at odds with each other during the war. Juana, a teacher in Santa María Tzejá, described dealing with parents from a neighboring village who complained about students reading books detailing the massacres that had occurred in the area, especially because many of the school's students came from neighboring communities where the fault lines of the conflict were still discernible. "But after a couple of years, they calmed down about it," she recounted. International solidarity support helped the Santa María Tzejá school develop a groundbreaking project commemorating the experience of the early 1980s: students there produced a play, and later a video, called *There Is Nothing Hidden That Will Not Be Revealed*, about the 1982 massacre in their community and the villagers' flight into Mexico. The play continues to be produced by successive generations of high school students in Santa María Tzejá, who tour the country performing in schools and municipal salons.[29]

Teachers at other schools have also found ways to respond to parents uneasy about their children studying topics related to the war. In the upper middle-class high school mentioned above, a teacher told me how the school deals with having students from military families:

> Maybe their grandparents were protagonists, and the mothers would come in and say, "I don't want my kid reading that, my father was Minister of Defense during that time." But the school administration didn't back down; they gave us the freedom to introduce what we wanted. We tried not to individualize the history; we tried to separate history from the person of the grandpa, to look at the army as an institution and how it responded in certain historical periods. We also told the family members they could come in and present an alternative viewpoint. No one did, but having the option seemed to satisfy them.[30]

Teachers recounted that sometimes students would ask why they were learning about the war, but said that in general there was significant interest. Often, students' interest stems from incredulousness, since, while some may have heard stories at home, many others have not. In southern El Quiché, when I attended a photo exhibit about the exhumations set up by a team of forensic anthropologists, one of the organizers told me that several teachers had come in with their students: "The kids were asking all sorts of questions, like how do the forensic anthropologists know how many bodies are in a pit, and what happened during the war. Many of them don't know anything about this. Maybe their parents have talked about it, but they can't believe it was real; they think it's like something that happened in a movie, somewhere else."[31] The forensic anthropologists I interviewed (from the Equipo de Antropología Forense de Guatemala [Guatemalan Forensic Anthropology Team]) explained that although they did not have a formal outreach program for students, at times they had to conduct exhumations near schools in the rural areas (the army often occupied these buildings during the war). In those cases, they have a psychologist on hand to work with the kids. In addition, especially in the capital, teachers often assign the forensic team's publications as supplementary reading material (for example, *Las masacres en Rabinal*) and invite the group to give presentations to classes.[32]

The Adolfo Hall Civic-Military Institute

The Adolfo Hall military high school in Guatemala City reveals both the recent openings for the educational system to treat topics related to the war and the limits of these processes. Located adjacent to the air force base in Guatemala City, with canons flanking the entrance and camouflaged cadets inside, the forty-five-year-old institute looks like the setting for a Mario Vargas Llosa novel. I was able to spend half a day there, talking with the vice director (a colonel), the head of academic programs (a captain, and a woman), several teachers, and a group of cadets. The school serves mostly middle- and lower middle-class students (co-ed in the past few years), and a shrinking percentage of these kids go on to join the military, since the army is no longer considered as attractive a vehicle for upward mobility as it once was. Although the institute is run by the army, it is still bound by the curricular standards set by the Ministry of Education. The curriculum at Adolfo Hall is more liberal now than it was before the peace accords. Teachers have wide discretion to choose their texts, and they use books common in other public and private high schools. Although the cadets are exposed to human rights material at every grade level, they do not read the CEH report. The academic director explained: "We're not ready for that. A few years ago, we couldn't talk at all about the war or the peace process. It's a gradual change. Now we talk a lot about the origins of human rights, the Geneva Conventions and their protocols, the peace accords in Guatemala. We deal with topics from the perspective of the peace accords [desde los acuerdos de paz se tocan los temas]."[33] The army major in charge of mandatory afternoon military classes at the institute (*iniciación militar*) insisted that the lack of attention to the pre–peace accord history was because "there isn't any documentation of the war, there isn't a book about the war."

> Well, there is the Church's book [the Catholic Church's 1998 multivolume report], but that is biased [*parcializado*]. The Clarification Commission's report is biased too. [The CEH report] isn't in the curriculum standards of the Ministry of Education, so we're not reading it. Maybe if there were more books from the Right as well as the Left to give a balanced view, maybe it would be a good idea to include this, but not now. We need a commission to evaluate this.[34]

When the origins of the conflict *are* addressed, it is within the context of the afternoon military classes, and the discussion is inevitably framed as a Cold War struggle in which the Left put itself on the side of attacking democracy, and the army on the side of saving it.

I was introduced to half a dozen cadets of different ages who astonished me with their command of the Geneva Conventions and all the major international human rights declarations and conventions. They knew the twists and turns of Guatemala's peace process and the content of the various peace accords, except the one that created the CEH. One sixteen-year-old, a distinguished student with plans to go on to medical school, told me he believed it was important to learn about the past because "in Guatemala, there is still a lot of fear, and it's important to know how the country got that way." Some of the cadets had just returned from a citywide high school debate on the concept of preemptive war, and according to this young man, other participants questioned the Adolfo Hall students aggressively: "They asked us, why was the army genocidal? And we reacted like, well, you can't blame us for the past, we're not responsible. And then we said, well, the army did what it did to defeat the insurgents. People get killed in wars; that's why wars are bad." He reiterated his belief in the importance of knowing the truth: "For example, a lot of people accuse Rios Montt of genocide, but there isn't any proof." I asked him if he had seen or heard of the CEH report, and he said he had not, although he knew about all the other peace accords.[35]

USAID and the Dissemination of the CEH Report

As part of its human rights and reconciliation program, USAID created a multimillion-dollar peace fund in Guatemala, channeling a large amount of aid to human rights groups around the country.[36] At times, the influx of USAID money into the countryside produces a sharp irony that even the agency's administrators joke about: every USAID-funded project has to display the agency's traditional logo (two clasped hands under a stars-and-stripes pattern), an image associated in many Guatemalans' minds with the sacks of U.S. food aid that went to the army-run "model villages" (strategic hamlets) during the 1980s: in other words, from the same folks who helped deliver counterinsurgency . . . now we have human rights and peace projects!

One of this program's largest new initiatives is a project to disseminate the CEH report. This includes running television ads in Guatemala City and the production, in 2002, of a *radionovela* (radio soap opera) broadcast in five regions of the country severely afflicted by the war. The television ads show a blindfolded man crossing a city street, as a voice-over pronounces, "We are all blind unless we know the truth."[37] The agency designed the TV ad to demonstrate to an audience in the capital that it was not just poor, rural Indians who were killed but urban professionals as well (professors, politicians, lawyers, students, etc.). "We want to reach those who aren't already convinced, to encourage them to pick up and read the report," USAID's program director told me.[38]

The *radionovela* is a thirty-one-chapter saga aimed at young people in the countryside. It takes place in the fictional community of El Trapiche and revolves around the story of an adolescent named Pablo. Pablo's father disappeared during the violence, and his mother is seeking an exhumation of a nearby clandestine cemetery to locate the body. The introductory segment notes that the residents of El Trapiche are highland peasants who used to plant sugarcane (*trapiche* means "sugar press") but who now plant nontraditional export crops such as broccoli (just the sort of rural economic transformation USAID has been promoting since the 1980s). As the story develops, Pablo and his friends receive lessons on various topics, such as the history of human rights, the rights of children, conflict resolution, tolerance and multiculturalism, the problem of lynchings, the Guatemalan peace process, the role of the army in a democracy, and the social importance of exhumations. When the *radionovela* hit the airwaves in early 2003, USAID says it reached 25 percent of the population in the five target departments. During the months of the broadcast, the program director told me, the office received letters from people in various parts of the country moved by the saga's content, who wrote: "This really happened; it's not fiction."

Although the *radionovela* delves into the consequences of the war as experienced by the child protagonist's family, the broadcasts contain very little historical content. The initial radio broadcast had no historical component; later, in response to comments, USAID produced a segment that included a brief mention of the structural causes of the war. The textbook that USAID produced as part of this revision to add historical content runs to one hundred pages, ten of which discuss structural issues, such as inequitable land tenure, a history of authoritarian governments, and racism. Another three pages discuss the reformist governments of Juan José Arévalo and Jacobo Arbenz in the 1940s and 1950s, and one page describes the rise of the first guerrilla movements in the early 1960s. The bottom of this page has a drawing of a soldier torturing a victim, while, next to it, a second drawing depicts a guerilla fighter torturing another victim; the only difference is that the guerrilla fighter has a beard and wears a beret. The text declares that the population was "caught between two armies," although it acknowledges the "army committed more violations." The text then moves immediately to the rights of children, violence within the family, international human rights, the peace agreements in Guatemala, and the need to promote a culture of peace.[39] USAID supervisors in Washington took out any mention of U.S. involvement in overthrowing the government of Arbenz in 1954, something the CEH report had pointed to as a watershed event for political violence in the country.[40] There are plans to reproduce several thousand copies of this text and to organize workshops with teachers.

The agency's materials are about "introducing the concept of rights into the countryside," the human rights and reconciliation program director explained. "AID is looking to foster a more peaceful, responsive democracy; they are not interested in accountability for past crimes." The program's director is a North American who came to Guatemala from a posting in Bosnia. He is both enthused and cynical about the peace curricula formula, believing the USAID administrators in Washington are attempting to instrumentalize these programs: "Before, aid was used to defeat communism; now the thrust is to promote a 'culture of peace,' to lay the groundwork for free trade in the region."[41] As a new project to win hearts and minds, a new framework for governance put forth by powerful political actors, what are the implications of the culture-of-peace discourse for constructions of historical memory?

The Limits of Peace Education

The phrase "culture of peace" is everywhere in Guatemala, from little supplements for children in the newspapers to school textbooks to the language of funding proposals by civil society groups to the Web site of one of the key private-sector development foundations. As a USAID administrator explained to me, the rights discourse and culture-of-peace lexicon has displaced *reconciliation* as the buzzword for new projects: "Even though we call our effort the human rights and reconciliation program, we did a survey and found out that 'reconciliation' had become a controversial term."[42] *Culture of peace*, on the other hand, seems to have general appeal.

It was UNESCO that launched this phrase when it declared 2000 to be the "Year of Culture of Peace" (now this has been stretched to a whole decade).[43] In Guatemala, UNESCO's culture-of-peace project is working to bring this framework into the educational system and civil society more broadly. The project produced booklets on various interrelated topics: culture of peace; democracy and citizen participation; interculturalism (a version of multiculturalism that emphasizes the interaction among cultural groups); conflict resolution; peace accords; and human rights and the rule of law. These booklets are just the right size to be inserted as a two- or three-page unit in school textbooks. Sprinkled throughout are references to the CEH report and to the culture of violence that led Guatemalans to commit "terrible and painful acts" during the war and which continues to plague the country.

One of the core problems with the culture-of-peace curricula framework is its giving the impression that the cause of the conflict in Guatemala was this culture of violence, a tautological interpretation that obscures more than it illuminates. For example, a sixth-grade textbook from 2001 gives this explanation of why the culture of peace should be practiced in Guatemala: "To avoid the violence that our society suffers. This violence occurred because during thirty-six years of civil war many people practiced a culture of violence."[44] While it might be argued that contemporary Guatemala has a violent culture, to posit this as the cause of the conflict ignores such central issues as how and why the armed movement began and how repressive practices evolved.

A second problem relates not to the teaching of rights per se but to the narrowing of possibilities for what else can be discussed. One can talk about the war now in Guatemala, but it is more difficult to address the specific conflicts that caused the war. What was it all about? The culture-of-peace materials frame the conflict as either limited to two opposing armed groups or as so broad as to be meaningless ("the culture of violence is responsible"). This redefines the conflict in ways that preclude any discussion of the broad social forces aligned on both sides, the deep social and political cleavages, and the diverse forms of social mobilization around particular political-economic visions that the two-fires paradigm cannot capture. As Inés Izaguierre argues,[45] the question we should be asking when we look at the politics of memory in Latin America is: What happened to the memory of politics?

The CEH and the Memory of Politics

In the case of Guatemala, the CEH report has helped open up social space for a discussion of the recent past. Although relatively few people read the multiple volumes of the CEH report, key parts of the report, such as the basic contours of the violence and the important recommendations, impacted public consciousness through a variety of mechanisms (press coverage, forums, educational initiatives) and became crucial touchstones for many different social organizations. The publication of both the CEH report and the Catholic Church's *Guatemala: Never Again* generated interest on the part of many teachers and schools to include material on the recent past in their program of study.

Some of the current struggles around the truth commission report in Guatemala concern the insertion of minimal information about the war into the school curricula and venues of popular education. This common-denominator vision of historical memory emphasizes that the war produced victims, yet a critical question is: what kind of victim figure is created through the equation of historical memory with histories of violence?

In Guatemala, this uncritical conflation of historical memory with histories of violence carries the danger of perpetrating racist stereotypes about the past—for example, that Mayan Indians were passive victims of violence, caught between two armies, or manipulated by outsiders. This is a powerful trope persisting to this day in Guatemala. For example, in July 2003, following riotous demonstrations in support of Rios Montt in Guatemala City, in which the ruling party bused in supporters from the countryside, a television anchorman asked the Nobel laureate Rigoberta Menchú her opinion on why Guatemala's Indians were always so prone to manipulation. In part, this trope is born of a legacy of racism in the country, but it is also reproduced by notions of historical memory that collapse and erase any sense of the history of collective politics.

Sibylle Fischer has detailed how in the wake of the Haitian Revolution narrative accounts were filled with the horrors of slavery while portraying the "fantasy of the submissive slave." This represented a Creole bargain: "In exchange for empathy and compassion in the face of unspeakable cruelty, the reader is offered the comforting image of a harmless, meek being that no one needs fear."[46] The terrible conditions of slavery were revealed, yet radical antislavery was disavowed.

What I have discussed in this essay could be called a sort of contemporary neoliberal bargain, whereby the horrors of the counterinsurgency war are revealed and the barbarism of the past is offered up as the very opposite of the current order (instead of an essential part of the birth of that order, as Grandin makes clear).[47] State violence is recognized, but ultimately reified, as its targets are drained of their identities as historical protagonists. In that sense, recognizing the state's atrocities may be less threatening to middle class and elite sensibilities in Guatemala than coming to grips with the histories of wide-spread indigenous mobilization. International agencies did not create this depoliticization of historical memory, but under the banner of projects to disseminate the CEH report, they are emerging as key brokers in sustaining it.

If the culture of violence is responsible for the death and destruction in Guatemala, then its corrective, the culture of peace, emerges as the solution. But just as the culture of peace didactic framework recognizes the individual as a victim of violence, it also throws back responsibility for society's failings onto that same individual, who must be instructed in new "peaceful" ways of being and acting. In the strains of *nunca más* (never again) that echo across Latin America, one might also hear efforts at a parallel refrain: never again to genocide, yes, but what about the simultaneous silencing of the histories of collective, contestatory politics?

The equation of historical memory in Guatemala with histories of death may seem to be an immutable narrative, for the political, psychological, and institutional reasons cited in this essay. Yet I have also seen instances of popular organizations returning to the text of the CEH report for alternative visions of history. In addition to the very strong summary the CEH produced of its conclusions and recommendations, the commission's report also included more than one hundred illustrative cases (*casos ilustrativos*) meant to show in greater detail the characteristics of the violence, as well as the different sorts of victims. These illustrative cases run five to ten pages in length each and are published in several appendices to the main report. They encapsulate the horrific patterns and consequences of the violence, but they also give insight into the life of the person or community and the context in which they lived and acted. An illustrative case of a kidnapped Coca-Cola worker, for instance, gives background on the labor movement, and illustrative cases of massacres in the highlands show the history of land struggles these communities faced, and how they organized. The illustrative cases also give some sense of the local histories of the war, and of the relationship between diverse local contexts and conflicts and the national scenario. These cases could, with relative ease, be integrated into school curricula, and one or two of the human rights groups I interviewed are turning toward this method. This would help do justice not only to the truth commission report but also to the lives that the report chronicles.

Notes

I thank the Carnegie Council on Ethics and International Affairs for support of this project, especially Lili Cole, the former head of the History and the Politics of Reconciliation Program. An earlier version of this essay was published online as a Carnegie Council working paper (see www.cceia.org). I am deeply indebted to the many people in Guatemala who generously shared their time and expertise with me, a number of whom requested to remain anonymous. A few friends went beyond the call of duty to give me much-appreciated intellectual, moral, and logistical support while I was in Guatemala; these are Diane Nelson, Marcie Mersky, Clara Arenas, and Gustavo Palma. I have benefited from conversations on the issues examined here with Greg Grandin, José García Noval, Beatriz Manz, Daniel Wilkinson, Carlota McAllister, Deborah Levenson, Brinton Lykes, Kully Kaur, Amy Ross, Carlos Beristain, Matilde González, Paula Worby, Luis Solano, Arturo Taracena, and, from 1986 until 1990, Myrna Mack. I presented the material in this article at the Carnegie Council, the 2004 meeting of the Latin American Studies Association (LASA), the 2005 meeting of the Association for the Advancement of the Social Sciences in Guatemala (AVANCSO), the University of British Columbia, the University of Georgia, Duke University, and Princeton University, and audiences at these venues provided useful critiques, as did *RHR*'s two anonymous reviewers. I am also grateful to Rachel Bengtson, a graduate student in law and Latin American studies at the University of Arizona, for excellent research assistance.

1. Greg Grandin, "Chronicles of a Guatemalan Genocide Foretold: Violence, Trauma, and the Limits of Historical Inquiry," *Nepantla* 1 (2000): 391–413; and Greg Grandin, "The Instruction of Great Catastrophe: Truth Commissions, National History, and State Formation in Argentina, Chile, and Guatemala," *American Historical Review*, no. 110 (2005): 46–67.
2. See Patrick Ball et al., "Democracy as Subterfuge? Researchers under Siege in Guatemala," *LASA Forum* 23 (2002): 6–10; and Rachel Sieder et al., *Who Governs? Five Years after the Peace Accords* (Cambridge, MA: Hemispheric Initiatives, 2002).
3. Myrna Mack was a Guatemalan anthropologist who studied the situation of the country's refugee and internally displaced populations. She was assassinated on September 11, 1990, by an army intelligence specialist, who was convicted in 1993 and sentenced to twenty-five years in jail. Myrna Mack's sister, Helen Mack, struggled for more than a decade to prosecute the high-ranking military officers who had ordered the murder, and the arduous legal process became one of Guatemala's most prominent human rights cases. In October 2002, Colonel Juan Valencia Osorio was convicted of ordering Myrna Mack's assassination; he later fled the country and remains at large. For a chronology of the Mack case, see Human Rights First (formerly the Lawyers Committee on Human Rights), www.humanrightsfirst.org (accessed August 10, 2006).
4. Elizabeth Oglesby, "Desde los cuadernos de Myrna Mack" ("From the Notebooks of Myrna Mack"), in *De la memoria a la reconstrucción histórica* (*From Memory to Historical Reconstruction*) (Guatemala City: Association for the Advancement of the Social Sciences [AVANCSO], 1999), 23–37.
5. Elizabeth Jelin, "The Politics of Memory: The Human Rights Movement and the Construction of Democracy in Argentina," *Latin American Perspectives* 21 (1994): 53.
6. Tzvetan Todorov, *Les abus de la mémoire* (*The Abuse of Memory*) (Paris: Arléa, 1998), quoted in Elizabeth Jelin, *State Repression and the Struggles for Memory*, trans. Judy Rein and Marcial Godoy-Anatavia (London: Latin America Bureau, 2003), 35.

7. Charles R. Hale, "Does Multicultural Governance Menace? Governance, Cultural Rights, and the Politics of Identity in Guatemala," *Journal of Latin American Studies*, no. 34 (2002): 490.
8. Wendy Brown, *States of Injury: Power and Freedom in Late Modernity* (Princeton, NJ: Princeton University Press, 1995), 124. Brown draws on Marx's criticism of bourgeois rights for creating an "illusory politics of equality, liberty and community" while disguising the workings of class. She also uses insights from Michel Foucault to argue that individuals are *produced* as subjects through the disciplinary mechanisms of rights discourses as they relate to the construction of liberal personhood.
9. Jelin, *State Repression*, 54–55, 140–41.
10. Ibid., 54.
11. Ibid.; Mauricio Gaborit, "Memoria histórica: Relato desde las víctimas" ("Historical Memory: Victims' Account"), *Estudios Centroamericanos* (*Central American Studies*), no. 57 (2002): 1021–32; Dora Schwarzstein, "Memoria e historia" ("Memory and History"), *Desarrollo económico* (*Economic Development*) 42 (2002): 471–82; María Sonderéreguer, "El debate sobre el pasado reciente en Argentina: Entre la voluntad de recordad y la voluntad de olvidar" ("The Debate Over the Recent Past in Argentina: Between the Will to Remember and the Will to Forget"), *Hispanamérica* 29 (2000), 3–15; Leigh Binford, *The Massacre at El Mozote: Anthropology and Human Rights* (Tucson: University of Arizona Press, 1996).
12. Gaborit, "Memoria histórica"; Marcie Mersky, "History as an Instrument of Social Reparation: Reflections on an Experience in Guatemala," *Just Word* 5 (2000): 1–4; Carlos Martín Beristain, *Reconstruir el tejido social* (*Reconstructing the Social Fabric*) (Barcelona: Icaria, 1999); Oficina de Derechos Humanos del Arzobispado de Guatemala (ODHAG, Human Rights Office of the Archdiocese of Guatemala), *Guatemala: Nunca Más* (Guatemala City: ODHAG, 1998); Igancio Martín Baró, *Psicología social de la guerra: Trauma y terapia* (*Social Psychology of War: Trauma and Therapy*) (San Salvador: Universidad Centroamericana, 1990).
13. Carlota McAllister, "Asking Too Much: Anthropological Manners and Clandestine Habits" (paper presented at the workshop "Revisiting Guatemala's Harvest of Violence," Duke University, Durham, NC, March 26–27, 2004); Daniel Wilkinson, *Silence on the Mountain: Stories of Terror, Betrayal, and Forgetting in Guatemala* (Boston: Houghton Mifflin, 2002); Mersky, "History as an Instrument of Social Reparation"; Oglesby, "Desde los cuadernos de Myrna Mack"; José García Noval, "Entre dos fuegos: Desde el mundo de los gatos pardos" ("Between Two Fires: From the World of the Dark Cats"), in *De la memoria a la reconstrucción histórica* (Guatemala City: Association for the Advancement of the Social Sciences [AVANCSO], 1999), 39–80; Beatriz Manz, "La importancia del contexto en la memoria" ("The Importance of Context in Memory"), in *De la memoria a la reconstrucción histórica*, 1–22; Linda Green, *Fear as a Way of Life: Mayan Widows in Rural Guatemala* (New York: Columbia University Press, 1999); Charles R. Hale, "Consciousness, Violence, and the Politics of Memory in Guatemala," *Current Anthropology* 38 (1997): 817–37; M. B. Lykes and M. Mersky, "Reparations and Mental Health: Psychosocial Interventions Towards Healing, Human Agency, and Rethreading Social Realities," in *The Handbook of Reparations*, ed. Pablo de Greiff (Oxford: Oxford University Press, 2006), 589–622.
14. The Grupo de Análisis Histórico was created by the head commissioner Christian Tomuschat, who invited all of Guatemala's universities and major research centers to appoint representatives to the group. At first, this was a mostly symbolic gesture meant to

show that the commission was receptive to input from Guatemalan society, yet it eventually coalesced into a twelve-person, multidisciplinary group that made recommendations to the commission and produced documentation and analysis used in the writing of the final report. Several members of the group participated directly in the writing of the historical volume of the report.

15. See Inés Izaguierre, "Recapturing the Memory of Politics," *NACLA Report on the Americas* 31 (1998): 30; and García Noval, "Entre dos fuegos." In the case of Guatemala, David Stoll expounds this thesis most famously. See his *Between Two Armies in the Ixil Towns of Guatemala* (New York: Columbia University Press, 1993). See also the responses to Stoll: Hale, "Consciousness, Violence, and the Politics of Memory in Guatemala"; García Noval, "Entre dos fuegos"; and Oglesby, "Desde los cuadernos de Myrna Mack," as well as many others.
16. Commission for Historical Clarification, *Guatemala: Memory of Silence; Report of the Commission for Historical Clarification, Conclusions and Recommendations*, 21, para. 23 (Guatemala City: United Nations Office of Project Services [UNOPS], 1999). The entire CEH report is available online at shr.aaas.org/guatemala/ceh/mds/spanish (accessed August 11, 2006). Subsequent references to the CEH report will occur parenthetically in the text.
17. Grandin, "Chronicles of a Guatemalan Genocide Foretold."
18. UNOPS, "The Operations of the Historical Clarification Commission in Guatemala," mimeograph document, n.d., 11–24.
19. The ruling on genocide was complicated in that it brought to the fore the inherent tensions between a strictly juridical perspective and a historical one. Did the army kill Mayans because they were Mayans or because they were organizing against the state? Based on a careful reading of cases, the report concluded that in *some* regions in particular periods, the violence had characteristics of genocide. Key here is the separation of motive and intent: the Guatemalan state intended to kill Mayans because it conflated these populations as part of the internal enemy, even though the ultimate motivation was to defeat the insurgency (see Grandin, "Chronicles of a Guatemalan Genocide Foretold"). The section of the CEH report that details the genocide argument is 3:249–423.
20. Research included a review of commonly used textbooks between 1986 and 2003, interviews with key informants at institutions involved in CEH dissemination projects, including policy makers in the Ministry of Education, representatives of international agencies involved in peace education programs (principally USAID and UNESCO), and Guatemalan human rights organizations involved in curriculum design (the Human Rights Office of the Archdiocese of Guatemala, the Guatemalan Human Rights Commission, the Instancia Multi-institucional por la Paz y la Concordancia (Multi-institutional Committee for Peace and Concordance), a coalition of civil society groups set up to provide follow-up to the CEH's recommendations, and academic representatives of the Convergencia Educativa (Educational Convergence), a council of research institutions set up to advise the Ministry of Education on curricular reform. Interviews were conducted in the summer of 2003. The core of the project involved interviews with teachers at six rural and urban high schools, including one upper middle-class private school in the capital, the military high school in the capital, two public schools in former conflict zones in El Quiché, one school in a less conflictive area of southern El Quiché, and one run by the private sector on the Pacific Coast. Although most Guatemalan students do not make it as far as high school, I chose high schools because students at this level are able to absorb more complicated material but are still subject to national curricular standards and programs of citizen formation.

21. Gustavo Palma and Alejandro Flores, eds., *Los contenidos de los cursos de estudios sociales en el contexto de la reforma educativa: Aportes para el debate* (*The Content of Social Studies Courses in the Context of Educational Reform: Notes for Debate*) (Guatemala City: Association for the Advancement of the Social Sciences [AVANCSO] and National Council for Mayan Education [CNEM], 1999).
22. Inforpress Centroamericana, "Guatemala: Entregan propuesta para educación" ("Guatemala: Education proposal submitted"), *Inforpress*, September 14, 2001, 12.
23. Kristel Foster, "A Tug of Post-war: History Education and the Politics of Reconciliation in Guatemala" (MA thesis, University of Arizona, Tucson, 2004).
24. Gustavo Palma, the research director at the Association for the Advancement of the Social Sciences, interviewed by the author, Guatemala City, August 1, 2003. According to Palma, the historic lack of attention to investment in education was rooted in the economic structure of the country, whereby rural labor was needed for the plantation economy (and thus there was not much need to educate the labor force). Now, with economic modernization, a functionally literate workforce is needed; hence the attention to primary education only. It is a functionalist analysis, but quite credible.
25. Interview with a Ministry of Education consultant, August 4, 2003, Guatemala City. Similarly, in 2002, the United Nations Development Program produced a popular version of its annual *Human Development Report* on Guatemala, designed for use in the classroom. The private sector raised a hue and cry, however, about the report's inclusion of land tenure data, and after an initial printing, the report was discontinued.
26. Raúl Zepeda, "Formulación de propuesta del area de formación ciudadana para la transformación curricular" ("Citizen Formation Proposal for Curricular Reform"), October 2002, mimeograph, Guatemala City, Ministry of Education and UNESCO.
27. According to Gustavo Palma, the most common school social science textbooks, all privately produced, are the Protagonistas (Protagonists) series, produced by Santillana (a Spanish publishing house franchised in Guatemala), and the Estudios Sociales (Social Studies) series, published by the Grupo Editorial Norma Guatemala (Palma, interview by author, August 1, 2003, Guatemala City). I surveyed texts in these two series from 1986, 1990, 1996, 1998, 2000, 2001, and 2002.
28. Guatemala has two masters-level programs related to political violence: a program in political violence and mental health at the national University of San Carlos, and a program in human rights at the Jesuit-run Landivar University.
29. Juana, interview by the author, July 26, 2003, Guatemala City. For a history of Santa María Tzejá and the surrounding region, see Beatriz Manz, *Paradise in Ashes: A Guatemalan Journey of Courage, Terror, and Hope* (Berkeley: University of California Press, 2003).
30. Interview with school teacher, August 6, 2003, Guatemala City.
31. Interview with organizer of forensic anthropology traveling photo exhibit, July 19, 2003, southern El Quiché.
32. See Equipo de Antropología Forense de Guatemala (EAFG, Guatemalan Forensic Anthropology Team), *Las massacres en Rabinal: Estudio histórico antropológico de las masacres de Plan de Sánchez, Chichupac and Río Negro* (*The Massacres in Rabinal: An Historical-Anthropological Study of the Massacres in Plan de Sánchez, Chichupac, and Río Negro*) (Guatemala City: EAFG, 1997).
33. Interview with academic director, Adolfo Hall Civic-Military Institute, July 24, 2003, Guatemala City.
34. Inteview with army major, July 24, 2003, Guatemala City.

35. Interview with student, July 24, 2003, Guatemala City.
36. Examples of these USAID-funded activities include an organization of formerly displaced refugees in Nebaj and a traveling photo exhibit of exhumations sponsored by one of Guatemala's forensic anthropology groups. In other parts of the country, USAID funds a Mayan organization that sponsors mental health programs for communities affected by the war, with programs directed specifically at young people. All of these are terribly important programs. The issue of whether to accept funding from USAID has been hotly debated by Guatemalan popular organizations. In some ways, this financing reflects the increasing dependence of popular organizations on international donors and a sort of governance through nongovernmental organizations. See, for example, Hale, "Does Multicultural Governance Menace?" In other ways, it reflects a deepening sophistication on the part of these organizations as they gain experience negotiating with state and international institutions. This program is implemented in Guatemala by a subcontractor, Creative Associates International (CAI). This group has done a lot of work with civil society groups, and in 1998 helped fund a forum for social organizations to make suggestions to the truth commission on the content of the report's recommendations.
37. This ad was in its final production stage when I was in Guatemala in the summer of 2003. USAID was looking for national organizations to cosponsor the campaign, but some groups declined, fearing the ad could be interpreted as an effort to sway the upcoming presidential election against Rios Montt.
38. Interview with director, USAID Human Rights and Reconciliation Program, July 23, 2003, Guatemala City.
39. Ignacio Santiago Urquijo, *El Trapiche: Donde la vida escribe sus historias* (*El Trapiche: Where Life Writes Its Histories*) (Guatemala City: Instituto Guatemalteco de Educación Radiofónica [Guatemalan Institute for Radio Education], 2003).
40. Interview with director, USAID Human Rights and Reconciliation Program, July 23, 2003, Guatemala City.
41. Ibid.
42. Ibid. See Hans Petter Buvollen, "National Reconciliation and Civil Society in Guatemala" (paper presented at the "Guatemala: Five Years after the Peace Accords" conference, Oslo, December 4–5, 2001), for the arguments about the use of the word *reconciliation* in Guatemala. This piece draws heavily from Marcie Mersky, *La reconciliación en Guatemala: Una propuesta de estrategia para la Fundación Soros en Guatemala* (*Reconciliation in Guatemala: A Strategy Proposal for the Soros Foundation in Guatemala*) (Guatemala City: UNOPS mimeograph, 2000). A common critique in Latin America is that *reconciliation* has been linked closely with church-infused ideas of pardon (see, for example, "La utopia cristiana de la reconciliación" ["The Christian Utopia of Reconciliation"], *Estudios Centroamericanos* [*Central American Studies*], no. 51 [1996]: 567–68; and Elizabeth Lira and Brian Loveman, "Reconciliación chilena: Entre el pragmatismo y la condena" ["Chilean Reconciliation: Between Pragmatism and Condemnation"], *Mensaje* [*Message*], no. 48 [1999]: 41–45). In Guatemala, some Mayan groups protested the use of *reconciliation*, saying the conflict in Guatemalan society was not a matter of the past forty years, but of the past five hundred; in other words, Guatemalan society has never had "conciliation," so it is difficult to talk about re-conciliation (Buvollen, "National Reconciliation and Civil Society in Guatemala," 7).
43. See the UNESCO Web site, www.ibe.unesco.org (accessed December 10, 2004) for information on other countries in which UNESCO has sponsored curricular reform in conflict societies.

44. Juan Francisco Sagüí Argueta, *Estudios Sociales*, vol. 6 (Guatemala City: Editorial Santillana, 2001), 185.
45. Izaguierre, "Recapturing the Memory of Politics," 28–34.
46. Sibylle Fischer, *Modernity Disavowed: Haiti and the Cultures of Slavery in the Age of Revolution* (Durham, NC: Duke University Press, 2004), 119.
47. Grandin, "The Instruction of Great Catastrophe," 58–67.

Introduction: A U.S. Truth Commission?

The United States, enjoying over two centuries of nearly uninterrupted institutional stability and constitutional rule, has never been forced to submit to a truth commission, at least in the way such bodies have generally functioned over the past two and a half decades: as an officially sanctioned inquiry into repressive acts on the part of the government or government allies with the goal of establishing the legal and moral legitimacy of a new, or at least reformed, state and social order. But there have been many investigations, authorized and unauthorized, into political violence, particularly of the kind that issued from racial domination at home and expansion abroad. Before the Civil War ended, the U.S. Congress began extensive and multiple inquiries into federal policy toward Native Americans, including a number of investigations into the 1864 Sand Creek Massacre, where seven hundred soldiers from the Third and First Colorado Regiments slaughtered and mutilated two hundred inhabitants of a Cheyenne village.[1] In the years following the Civil War, Congress launched a wide-ranging investigation into Ku Klux Klan violence, taking voluminous and harrowing testimony. But these investigations were carried out not in a dialect of contrition and confession, but with the full-throated self-confidence of an expanding, militarily triumphant state then consolidating an exceptional sense of national purpose. Even as it waged an eliminationist war against Native Americans, for instance, the U.S. government could claim that its investigation into the "brutal and cowardly acts" that took place in Sand Creek was "vindicating the cause of justice and upholding the honor of the nation."

. . . . .

By the second half of the twentieth century, though, in the wake of the civil rights movement, Vietnam, Watergate, and revelations about U.S. atrocities throughout the third world, such poise was hard to maintain as New Left critics rejected an

Radical History Review
Issue 97 (Winter 2007) DOI 10.1215/01636545-2006-014

interpretation of American history as a progressive unfolding of political freedom, instead focusing on the darker side of the United States' rise to world power, on the connection between domestic racial violence and overseas militarism and economic imperialism. The late 1960s kicked off a decade of notable official and unofficial inquiries into the misuses of U.S. power: from Bertrand Russell's 1967 International War Crimes Tribunal and the 1971 Winter Soldier Hearings to the 1975 Rockefeller Committee report into domestic covert activity—which found that the Central Intelligence Agency (CIA) had infiltrated political organizations, ran experiments with behavior-changing drugs on unknowing subjects, and carried out illegal surveillance of political activists—and the 1975–76 Church Committee investigation into covert government activities throughout the third world, which produced fourteen volumes dense with facts documenting the CIA's ties to the mafia, its involvement in coups, attempts to assassinate foreign leaders, and improper storage of toxic material. Similar to the phenomena of truth commissions in conflict-torn countries, these latter government inquiries were part of a broader attempt to restore government legitimacy following a period of sustained political crisis. The Rockefeller report was largely a whitewash, and the Church Committee, while more extensive, thorough, and damning, ultimately pardoned U.S. actions in the name of anticommunism, labeling the crimes it documented as an "aberration, explainable at least in part, but not justified, by the pressures of the time."[2]

. . . . .

The three reflections presented in this section, written by scholar-activists, consider unofficial inquiries into military atrocities, racial repression, and violence directed at civil and labor rights organizers. John Fitzgerald, a Vietnam veteran, an early member of Vietnam Veterans against the War, and a retired high school teacher discusses the Winter Soldier Hearings, convened in Detroit in early 1971 by the ad hoc Citizens Commission of Inquiry. Sally Bermanzohn, author of *Through Survivors' Eyes: From the Sixties to the Greensboro Massacre*, examines the Greensboro Truth and Reconciliation Project, an investigation into the November 3, 1979, Greensboro, North Carolina, massacre committed by the Ku Klux Klan and the American Nazi Party, with the complicity of the Greensboro police department, of community activists, labor organizers, and militants of the Communist Workers Party. Bermanzohn herself is a survivor of that massacre. Paul Ortiz, the author of the recently published *Emancipation Betrayed: The Hidden History of Black Organizing and White Violence in Florida from Reconstruction to the Bloody Election of 1920*, discusses his participation in the Behind the Veil project at Duke University's Center for Documentary Studies, an extensive oral history project that documented African American life in the post-Emancipation Jim Crow South.

—Greg Grandin and Thomas Miller Klubock

Note

1. *Condition of the Indian Tribes: Report of the Joint Special Committee Appointed under Joint Resolution of March 3, 1865* (Washington, DC: U.S. Government Printing Office, 1867) Joint Committee on the Conduct of the War, *Massacre of Cheyenne Indians*, 38th Cong., 2nd sess., January 10, 1865.
2. U.S. Senate Select Committee to Study Governmental Operations with Respect to Intelligence Activities, *Alleged Assassination Plots Involving Foreign Leaders* (Washington, DC: U.S. Government Printing Office, 1975), xiii.

A Massacre Survivor Reflects on the Greensboro Truth and Reconciliation Commission

Sally Avery Bermanzohn

The Greensboro Truth and Reconciliation Commission (GTRC), the first of its kind in the United States, published its report on May 25, 2006. Will this project succeed in establishing some basic truth about the 1979 Greensboro Massacre? Can it serve as a model for other such projects in the United States?

. . . . .

On November 3, 1979, Ku Klux Klansmen and American Nazis opened fire on union organizers and civil rights activists in Greensboro, North Carolina, killing five close friends of mine. We were black and white radical activists who had deep roots in the civil rights, Black Power, antiwar, and women's liberation movements. In the 1970s we became union organizers in textile mills and hospitals. Many of us, myself included, were members of the Communist Workers Party. On that fateful day, we wanted to protest the 1979 reemergence of the Ku Klux Klan (KKK) in areas of North Carolina in which union drives were in progress. We planned a spirited march through Greensboro, followed by a conference. Instead, the KKK and Nazis attacked us as we were gathering to march; they killed Jim Waller, Sandi Smith, Bill Sampson, Michael Nathan, and Cesar Cauce, who were all dynamic and dedicated leaders in their twenties and thirties. Gunshots wounded ten others,

Radical History Review
Issue 97 (Winter 2007) DOI 10.1215/01636545-2006-015

including my husband Paul Bermanzohn, who was shot in the head and the arm, permanently paralyzing his left side.

Twenty-six years later, a Greensboro Truth and Reconciliation Commission has reinvestigated these murders. Why a Greensboro truth commission? The basic answer is *government involvement* in the 1979 murders. Officials covered up the role of various state institutions in two criminal trials, leading to unanswered questions that have polarized the Greensboro community for a generation.

State Involvement and Cover-Up in the Greensboro Massacre

Trials, investigative reporting, government documents, and TV videotape have established the following facts concerning state responsibility for the massacre. The Greensboro Police Department (GPD) gave a copy of our police parade permit to the Klansman Edward Dawson, who was on the GPD payroll as an informant. Dawson had also been a Federal Bureau of Investigation (FBI) informant in the sixties and seventies, and he reported that armed Klansmen planned to come to Greensboro on November 3 to both his GPD supervisor and his former FBI agent supervisor. Under the direction of the GPD, Dawson recruited and organized the KKK to attack us. On November 3, 1979, using the information on our police permit, he led the Klan-Nazi caravan to where we were gathering. In addition, a federal agent of the Bureau of Alcohol, Tobacco, and Firearms (ATF) named Bernard Butkovich pushed the Nazis to join the Klan in the attack that day. As the Klan/Nazis gathered, formed a caravan, and drove toward us, two Greensboro plain-clothes officers observed them and repeatedly radioed headquarters, noting the KKK and Nazis' numerous guns. Instead of stopping the Klan and Nazis, or even warning us, the GPD headquarters pulled all officers out of the area, including those assigned to protect us, and sent them to an early lunch. In sum, the GPD instigated and facilitated the attack with the knowledge of federal agents in the FBI and the ATF.[1]

Yet in two out of the three trials that arose from November 3, the courts acquitted the Klan and Nazi gunmen. Both a state murder trial and a federal civil rights trial failed to investigate the role of police or federal agents. The government was more concerned with covering up its role than with prosecuting the gunmen. Prosecutors, as well as the Klan-Nazi defense lawyers, kept the truth buried, and the juries acquitted the murderers. Even the TV videotape of the murders failed to influence this outcome. In contrast, we victims brought a third trial, a civil one, where for the first time our own lawyers represented us in court. We focused our meager resources on revealing the government involvement and achieved a partial victory. A jury found three GPD employees jointly liable with the Klan and Nazis for one wrongful death. The city of Greensboro paid a $300,000 settlement for its police department, the Klan, and the Nazis. Despite these three trials, no Klansman or Nazi ever served prison time.

For decades the City of Greensboro has consistently denied any wrongdoing.

The powers that be continued to blame us, the victims, for the deaths of our friends. They scapegoated us as communists, as if we were despicable and subhuman. As the district attorney stated at a news conference one month after the murders, most people in Greensboro "feel the communists got . . . 'about what they deserved.' "[2]

Can a truth commission operate successfully in the context of Greensboro? A key factor in every truth-seeking project is the commission's relationship to the state. Usually a truth commission is established after a new government replaces a former regime, often following years of upheaval and state repression. The new regime tries to use the commission to help it consolidate public support. In the United States, however, there has been no change in state power. In Greensboro, as in the country as a whole, those who wield power are basically the next generation of the same group that exercised power twenty-five years ago. Some of the same individuals in power in 1979 continue to be influential today. Moreover, in Greensboro, all levels of government have consistently covered up their involvement in the events of November 3, 1979.

Seeking Justice

For survivors, a truth commission represents another chance for justice. People never forget the murder of their loved ones. In 1979, four women lost their husbands, a baby lost her father, two adolescents lost their stepfather, and we all lost close friends. For a generation, we survivors have sought ways to bring out the truth, holding commemorations, writing books, giving speeches, and encouraging reporters, playwrights, and documentary filmmakers to tell the story. We have built two long-term institutions. One is the Greensboro Justice Fund, directed for ten years by Dale Sampson, the widow of Bill Sampson, and for the past fifteen years by Marty Nathan, the widow of Michael Nathan. The other is the Beloved Community Center in Greensboro, directed by the Reverend Nelson Johnson, which organizes for decent education, housing, unionization, against police brutality, and keeps alive the memory of those killed in 1979. A leader in the African American community since the 1960s, Johnson was stabbed by a Klansman during the 1979 massacre.[3]

In 2000, we learned about the International Center for Transitional Justice (ICTJ), which advises truth-seeking projects around the world, based on the experience of South Africa and other nations.[4] The Greensboro Justice Fund and the Beloved Community Center invited the ICTJ to guide a truth-seeking project.

An Experiment in Grassroots Democracy

The Greensboro Truth and Reconciliation Commission took years to create. Before the commission was formed, broad-based community support needed to be organized to carry out the steps to build a commission process. Under the direction of the ICTJ's Lisa Magarrell, the Greensboro Truth and Community Reconciliation Project was founded in 2002, and called the "Project" to distinguish it from the

"Commission." A former Greensboro mayor, respected clergy both black and white, academics in local colleges and universities, African American city council representatives, labor unions, community activists, and survivors became actively involved in the project.

Through many community discussions in 2002–3, the project reached out to a wide variety of political, religious, and educational institutions, as well as community organizations. The project developed a mandate and selection process to name commissioners, and in early 2003 published this mandate in the Greensboro newspapers. The mandate stated that any resident of Greensboro or the surrounding Guilford County could nominate commissioners. The project invited seventeen groups to choose a representative to sit on the selection committee to participate in choosing who would serve as the seven commissioners among those nominated. Fourteen groups selected representatives including Greensboro's mayor, five college presidents, five college student governments, the Democratic Party, the Republican Party, the Central Labor Council, National Association for the Advancement of Colored People, African American churches, white churches, the Jewish community, the Muslim community, and community organizations. The three groups that refused to send representatives were the GPD, the Chamber of Commerce, and the Sons and Daughters of the Confederacy.[5]

The selection committee reviewed approximately seventy nominations, and in late spring 2004, selected seven people to serve as commissioners. Those chosen to be commissioners were Cynthia Brown, the consultant for nonprofit groups; Patricia Clark, the executive director of the Fellowship of Reconciliation; Muktha Jost, a professor at North Carolina Agricultural and Technical State University; Angela Lawrence, a counselor and community activist; Robert Peters, a retired corporate attorney; the Reverend Mark Sills, the director of Faith Action International House; and Barbara Walker, a retired corporate manager. These commissioners were diverse, including three African American women, two white men, one white woman, and one woman from India. Five were residents of Greensboro, one came from Durham, North Carolina, and one from Nyack, New York. They brought a wide variety of professional and life experiences to a challenging task. The commissioners worked on a part-time basis, volunteering their time. Funds from private donations and foundation grants allowed the commissioners to hire a small staff, including an executive director, a research director, a communications director, a public hearing coordinator, and an administrator.

On June 12, 2004, the Greensboro Truth and Reconciliation Commission was formally seated in a ceremony attended by five hundred people. The commissioners and staff put out a call for statements and received testimony from 150 people (55 of these individuals gave statements at public hearings, and 95 people gave statements to the commissioners privately, 12 of which were confidential). The commission also researched legal documents and historical materials.

The Greensboro process has focused locally, yet at the same time it has been part of an international phenomenon of truth-seeking. Archbishop Desmond Tutu, who headed up the pacesetting South African Truth and Reconciliation Commission, visited North Carolina in 2003 and 2005, meeting with both the project and the commissioners. The Reverend Bongani Finca, a commissioner on the South African truth commission, and Eduardo Gonzalez, a staff member of the Peru truth commission, have also visited Greensboro and given advice and support.

The Public Hearings

The commissioners held six days of hearings over a three-month period in 2005. The testimony came from every different viewpoint. Among the first speakers was the Ku Klux Klan leader Virgil Griffin, who rode in the caravan and denounced the hearings. The Klan leader's arguments sounded strangely like those of Greensboro's political elite. A few hours later, Gorrell Pierce, another Klansman, testified in a more folksy style, attempting to present the KKK as a benign group. Neither Griffin nor Pierce said anything much different than they had twenty-six years earlier. They did not offer any new information and seemed to come because of public pressure, indicating that the GTRC was having an impact. Asked why only anti-Klan activists had been killed, Griffin stated that "God guided the Klan's bullets." Griffin's statement was published in newspapers across the country, receiving more coverage than any other aspect of the GTRC to that point.

Other public testimony came from Judge James Long, who had presided over the 1980 state criminal trial that had acquitted the Klan and Nazis, as well as three Klan-Nazi defense lawyers. None of the commanding GPD commanding officers testified; three police officers, on duty on November 3, spoke at a public hearing, but all stated they were not officially representing the police department. Community people from the traumatized neighborhood where the massacre occurred bore witness to the impact of the events on their families and community. A wide variety of individuals from academic, civic, and community organizations shared what they knew.

Ten survivors were invited to speak, including three widows and three people who were wounded, including my husband Paul, who talked about living with bullet fragments still in his brain. Many survivors attended the hearings, and it was extremely emotional for us. Our spirits soared when the survivors spoke and dropped during the statements by those who had killed us or covered up the murders.

It became clear that the commissioners were under great pressure to continue the whitewash of November 3. At the first hearing, I felt the commissioners failed to ask serious questions of the Klansmen. I worried that the hearings would become just a "he said, she said" procedure, without the commissioners assessing the veracity of the statements. Fortunately in subsequent hearings, the commissioners played a stronger role.

In every hearing, the commissioners clearly recognized that five lives were lost that day. At the beginning and end of every day of hearings, there were eighty-eight seconds of silence, symbolizing the eighty-eight seconds of gunfire that had killed the five. In the first row of the audience, five chairs held roses, marking the presence of those who died.

Testifying

The commission asked me to testify on August 26, sandwiched between two other survivors: Floris Weston, whose husband Cesar Cauce had been killed in the massacre, and Nelson Johnson, who had been stabbed. We spoke at the end of a long day of testimony by those who opposed us, including the judge who acquitted the Klansmen and police officers who repeated the same cover-up we had heard for twenty-six years. Decades of anger welled up inside me.

As I sat down at the testimony table, I noticed the hundreds of people in the audience. I opened my mouth, and my memories of that day poured out, a flashback of the murders that I have relived countless times. I described seeing the caravan, hearing the racial epithets, hoping the Klansmen would just drive by, seeing the guns, hearing the shots, and then finding my dear friends bleeding to death. As I finished recounting my story, I was only vaguely aware of the commissioners and the audience. I noticed how quiet everyone was—they were listening to me. I have given many speeches, sharing this flashback with groups large and small. But for me, this was the greatest speaking experience ever. Speaking to a Greensboro audience of memories pent up for twenty-six years, my feelings soared. In contrast to the perpetrators, I had nothing to hide; I could only tell what I had seen and knew to be true. And with the Greensboro public, the commissioners were listening and taking the responsibility to sort through all the conflicting testimony and determine what happened. I was part of a process that would have an outcome.

My testimony focused on the role of the GPD in the massacre, and I concluded

> The Greensboro Massacre happened because of the behavior of top commanders in the police department. . . . There are many unanswered questions about other government agencies and officials on the federal, state, and local level. I do not think the police could have acted in isolation of other government officials. But regardless of whether these questions will ever be answered—there is *no doubt about the outrageous, illegal, criminal acts of the GPD commanders.*
>
> And where is the GPD in relationship to the Truth and Reconciliation Commission? Do the police brass think that by avoiding this process people will just ignore their role in the massacre? I believe their failure to come before the Commission points to them continuing to hide the truth.[6]

Although state political repression can involve many institutions, local police often prove central to the violence. The Greensboro Massacre is a case in point.

Greensboro Police Scandal, 2006

Lies covered up tend to grow. Hidden criminal acts by police officials festered inside the GPD for decades. In January 2006, they burst forth into a full-fledged police scandal that has divided the GPD, and the city of Greensboro, along racial lines. A black police officer found a listening and tracking device on his car in late 2005. A short time later, a black book with the names of 114 African American citizens of Greensboro, nineteen of them police officers, was found in the trunk of the assistant police chief's car. This occurred after the Truth Commission had concluded its hearings with no input from the GPD leadership, questions about the role of the police brass in the massacre still lingering. In January 2006, with vivid evidence of racist harassment against black officers and community members, the city council fired the chief of police and the assistant police chief, both white. The press talked about the chief and assistant chief being part of a "rogue group" in the department, but this was not just a rogue group—it was men at the top of the local chain of command. In April, forty black GPD officers (half of the African Americans on the city police force) filed a complaint with the Equal Employment Opportunity Commission as the first step in a civil lawsuit against the department.[7] There is evidence that this criminal element has existed for decades, back at least to 1979. It seems to be a longtime racist group that strove to control the GPD by preventing black police leadership from developing. A direct connection to the 1979 massacre appears likely; one officer implicated in the 1979 cover-up was the same man who owns the private detective agency that in 2005 attached the listening device to the black officer's car.[8] The police scandal is ongoing, with no end in sight.

The Greensboro Truth and Reconciliation Commission Report

On May 26, 2006, the GTRC released a 532-page report. Based on thorough research of all available sources, the report carefully weighs sharply-conflicting testimonies. It analyzes the events of November 3 in context of local history, including our involvement in the black liberation movement and labor organizing during the 1960s and 1970s. It discusses what is known about the preparation for that day by the GPD, the FBI, and the ATF. It also covers the aftermath of the murders, including the trials and the press coverage.

The commission's findings are comprehensive. Most important, they find the police culpable for failing to provide safety for the protesters or the residents of the community where the Klan attacked. In great detail, the report describes the GPD's awareness of the Klan caravan's movements, and their failure to take action to protect people. The report's conclusion states that a majority of the commissioners believe that "among *some* in the [Greensboro Police] department, there was intentionality to fail to provide adequate protection," and the commissioners name six officers who were decision makers that day.[9] The findings criticize the city's scapegoating of the victims and the failure of the court system to find the killers guilty. The commissioners also criticize us for violent language, a point with which many of the survivors agree.[10]

The Truth and Reconciliation Commission Report has made a significant impact in Greensboro. At a May 25 ceremony, eighty local community groups received copies of the report and promised to study it and to hold public meetings to discuss it. Greensboro's truth-seeking process can serve as a model for other similar projects in the country. Atrocities have occurred in many cities and communities across the nation—lynchings, race riots, police brutality, and other forms of political murders. People from a number of areas have visited Greensboro to investigate developing their own truth-seeking projects. There is great potential for such endeavors where there exists a dedicated core of people with deep roots in a community, who are willing to take on an intense and time-consuming effort.

Notes

1. For more details and a full documentation of sources of information, see Sally A. Bermanzohn, *Through Survivors' Eyes: From the Sixties to the Greensboro Massacre* (Nashville, TN: Vanderbilt University Press, 2003); and Signe Waller, *Love and Revolution: A Political Memoir* (Lanham, MD: Rowman Littlefield, 2002).
2. "District Attorney Says He Is Caught in the Middle of a No-Win Situation," *Greensboro Daily News*, December 12, 1979.
3. For more information on the Greensboro Justice Fund, see www.gjf.org (accessed August 10, 2006); and on the Beloved Community Center, see www.belovedcommunitycenter.org (accessed August 10, 2006).
4. For more on the International Center for Transitional Justice, see www.ictj.org (accessed August 10, 2006).
5. Greensboro Truth and Reconciliation Commission, pamphlet (2005), 8. For more information, see www.greensborotrc.org (accessed August 10, 2006).
6. All testimonies from the hearings can be found on the GTRC Public Hearings DVD, available at www.greensborotrc.org (accessed August 10, 2006).
7. See the *Greensboro News and Record*, January 9–April 22, 2006.
8. Nelson Johnson, letter to Mayor Keith Holliday and the Greensboro City Council, March 10, 2006.
9. GTRC, Final Report, May 25, 2006, 301; available at www.greensborotrc.org (accessed August 10, 2006).
10. Ibid., 375–76.

Behind the Veil

Paul Ortiz

The United States of America has never convened a truth commission to examine two centuries of racial brutality sanctioned by the state, although the Nobel Laureate Archbishop Desmond Tutu, the former head of the South African Truth and Reconciliation Commission, has repeatedly called on it to do so. The United States, Tutu said, "has not really faced up to the legacy of slavery or of the dispossession of Native Americans."[1] If such a commission met to consider the country's treatment of African Americans from Emancipation through the 1960s, it might come to the following conclusions: First, the human rights of African Americans were systematically violated during these years; second, segregation, like slavery, was a *labor system* designed to extract economic resources from African Americans in order to redistribute these assets to others. Segregation was maintained through terror (lynching, massacres, the destruction of black communities), fraud (ballot-box theft, tampering with election results, black disfranchisement), and a one-party rule that allowed the South to dominate American politics for decades.

Finally, white supremacy was marketed to the public through racial propaganda: Jim Crow postcards, films portraying African Americans as treacherous felons, and thousands of household products featuring caricatures of black women, children, and men that justified racial oppression. Underlying all of this was a distorted national history that depicted African Americans as the uncivilized wards of an enlightened white majority. The sanctity of white rule was promoted by universities, newspapers, employers, charitable foundations, and other institutions. These nongovernmental entities helped advertise, legitimize, and reproduce white busi-

Radical History Review
Issue 97 (Winter 2007) DOI 10.1215/01636545-2006-016

ness supremacy, not just within the United States but beyond. "Imperialism, the exploitation of colored labor throughout the world," as W. E. B. Du Bois noted in the 1930s, "thrives upon the approval of the United States, and the United States gives that approval because of the South."[2]

Segregation was a strategy of governance that implicated the entire nation. Stolen elections in the South were tacitly approved by the U.S. Congress and the North. The state-sanctioned convict lease system benefited northern firms, and cheap southern labor enriched outside investors. The cumulative legacies of segregation are all the more powerful because the system was so broadly participatory. Intellectuals, workers, middle-class suburbanites, rich people, unions, corporations, and government agencies such as the Federal Housing Administration helped build a separate-and-unequal nation. Jim Crow owed its extraordinary staying power in part to the massive transfer in wealth, governmental subsidies, educational resources, and political power away from black communities and into other communities that accepted these benefits largely without question.[3]

Segregation is difficult to grapple with because it cannot be relegated to the past. Indeed, Jim Crow is making a comeback. The resegregation of much of the nation's school system is now an accomplished fact. The disfranchisement of African American voters was the deciding element in the 2000 presidential election in Florida.[4] Five years later, the portrayal of African American flood victims in New Orleans owed much to stereotypes from the Jim Crow era. Cable television outlets and print media falsely depicted African American survivors of Hurricane Katrina as rapists, looters, and thugs and effectively pardoned the slow federal response to the crisis. This broadcasting of images that had no basis in reality was possible because most Americans have been taught a version of U.S. history in which African Americans either feature as dependent wards of the state or are predisposed to shoot down rescue helicopters. One of my students at the University of California, Santa Cruz, explained: "As a student of African heritage growing up in Santa Cruz, a predominately Caucasian town, the role my ancestors played in the development of the country was never revealed. Slavery was always downplayed in favor of glorifying Abraham Lincoln and the Emancipation Proclamation. How was I to regard my heritage with confidence while the environment I was raised in depicted Africans as nothing but slaves saved by a white man? Believe me no teacher ever let me forget that."[5]

But while the U.S. government has refused to convene a truth commission to investigate post-Emancipation segregation as a system of racial and labor exploitation, there have been a number of extragovernmental efforts, including by African American educators and activists, to create a popular historical memory that bolsters collective identities of struggle and black claims to equal rights. One of the most ambitious has been Behind the Veil: Documenting African America Life in the Jim Crow South, which began in the early 1990s and was based at Duke University's Center for Documentary Studies. Headed by the historians William H. Chafe, Raymond Gavins, and Robert Korstad, and initially funded by the National Endowment for the Humanities, Behind the Veil (BTV) included scholars and students not just from Duke but from historically black colleges and universities including North Carolina Central University, Clark-Atlanta, and Jackson State. In 2001, BTV generated a book, *Remembering Jim Crow: African Americans Tell about Life in the Jim Crow South*, with two audio CDs of oral history linked to a multimedia Web site and an NPR documentary.[6] The entire collection, consisting of approximately thirteen hundred interviews, family photographs, and other documents related to segregation is housed at the John Hope Franklin Research Center for African and African American Documentation at Duke's Perkins Library.

A sense of urgency animated the endeavor from the beginning. According to its first brochure, BTV's goal was to "recover the documentary base for understanding the experience of Jim Crow before this invaluable opportunity is lost." During de jure segregation, research universities amassed large collections of white-owned newspapers, manuscript collections, and other materials relating to segregation. Yet not unexpectedly, these institutions were not as rigorous when it came to collecting African American newspapers or black perspectives in general. "The historical amnesia that exists about the era of Jim Crow," BTV's brochure noted, "has resulted in a generation of young people, black and white, who know little about either the laws or institutions that separated the races, or the internal life of black communities."[7] The project's primary research method was to gather oral histories from survivors of the segregation era, a methodology that proved not only essential considering the lack of written sources but empowering as well. As one reviewer of *Remembering Jim Crow* noted, "oral histories offer an immediacy other historic tools don't have. In simple, powerful ways, they close the psychological distance between big words like 'disenfranchisement' and daily lived oppression."[8] Another wrote that for "some of the speakers, this is the first time they have been able to break their silence and speak out loud about the horrors they underwent growing up."[9]

Between 1993 and 1995, teams of graduate students fanned out across the South to interview black elders in scores of diverse rural, small-town, and urban communities of various sizes ranging from Fargo, Arkansas, to Memphis, Tennessee. Each summer, the graduate research directors Leslie Brown and Annie Valk (then history PhD students at Duke) coordinated oral history workshops and research seminars to ensure that the students were prepared to ask informed questions at each of the sites. I served as one of the graduate student interviewers and later as a research coordinator during BTV's archival phase. Ultimately, over thirteen hundred tape-recorded interviews were conducted with African American elders. The majority of these individuals were born before 1930. Fifty-eight percent of the informants were women. Twenty-five percent were educators, and the three next largest occupations held by interviewees were, respectively, basic manufacturing, agriculture, and domestic labor.[10]

Behind the Veil researchers carried important liabilities into the field. Student researchers were viewed with skepticism by African Americans wary of cooperating with Duke University, a historically white institution identified as a major bulwark of segregation. The multiracial character of the oral history teams at times created tensions between interviewers and interviewed, as well as between the field researchers themselves. Graduate interviewers were also saddled with the heavy baggage of two centuries of academic racism. It turns out it was not that easy to close the "distance between big words like 'disenfranchisement' and daily lived oppression." Ultimately, BTV owed its success to the forbearance of African American elders, historically black institutions (i.e., colleges, neighborhood associations, churches, secret societies, etc.) that guided us to interviews, and networks of community-based oral historians who helped us connect with local residents.

Conducting these interviews taught me many things. Many of the people I interviewed spoke of debt peonage, forced labor, lynching, schools with no resources, poverty wages, labor repression, and other mechanisms of domination as if these things had occurred only yesterday, suggesting that for many the transition from slavery to freedom in the United States has yet to be completed. African American elders spoke of relatives and loved ones lost or disappeared to racial terrorism. One series of these interviews conducted in Gadsden and Leon Counties in Florida allowed me to tell the story of the first ever statewide civil rights movement in U.S. history, and the mass murder of would-be African American voters in the presidential election of 1920.[11]

Women often focused on the everyday humiliations of Jim Crow. African American mothers had the nearly impossible task of explaining to their children why they were treated with such disrespect in public. Maintaining a child's sense of self and dignity in such an environment proved a Herculean task. Most white southerners refused to use courtesy titles when addressing black women or men no matter how old they were. Whites vowed never to "'Miss' a nigger," and preferred degrading titles such as "Suzie" or "Auntie" when addressing African American women. Even worse, African American women were considered fair targets of white men's sexual avarice. A fundamental premise of Jim Crow was that a white man could *never* be guilty of raping a black woman. Female domestic workers lived in a constant state of fear. Cleaster Mitchell of Brinkley, Arkansas, told me that when a black woman was attacked by a white man, "to go to the law didn't mean anything. There was no law [for] you to go to. And I'll tell you, one time in the South it's bad to say, white men was crazy about black women. They would come to your house. They would attack you. They took it for granted when they saw a black lady that they could just approach her, that it was not an insult to her for them to approach her."[12]

Malachia Andrews spoke with me in Tallahassee, Florida. He was intensely religious, a lifelong civil rights activist, and a supporter of the legendary Reverend C. K. Steele during the historic Tallahassee Bus Boycott in 1956. Andrews grew up in nearby Gadsden County, a place distinguished by rich tobacco farms and poor sharecroppers. "We were paid from fifty to seventy-five cents a day," Andrews recalled. His father challenged the landowner for a larger share of the profits during "settling-up" time, but resistance was costly. Andrews's family had to abruptly pack up all of their belongings and move on several occasions because they were identified as troublemakers by large growers. African Americans who challenged white economic domination in rural Florida too vigorously did so at the risk of their lives. Andrews noted: "This was dangerous. Black folks as far as they thought wasn't supposed to talk back, challenge the big boss, I'll say, about the harvesting, and sometimes it would cause house burning. Sometimes it would cause flogging, hanging and different things." When African American plantation workers in Gadsden attempted to purchase their own farms in order to escape white control, "the big farmers burnt them all out, burnt out the fields, set them afire, corn fields and all these types of things in order to break them down, to have them come back to the big farm."[13]

When I asked Andrews to reflect back on his life, he replied: "I can live, maybe not in full yet, but I'm proud of the distance that black people have come because I can't explain it all but it was, if you allow me, it was hell back then." Here was a man approaching the final years of his life who had every reason to be proud of the way he had lived. Andrews had fought for over a half century to end racial injustice, and he had been an organizer in some of the pivotal events of the modern civil rights movement. Yet he still *could not live a full life* because of racism. A reviewer of *Remembering Jim Crow* remarked that "these are stories that may bring a new and deeper level of understanding to those readers who don't understand cries for reparations or the lingering anger toward whites."[14]

The BTV archives contain a broad range of narratives that reveal a century's worth of hidden and open warfare against white supremacy. African Americans' political aspirations survived the defeat of Reconstruction, and black people resisted the onslaught of segregation in countless ways. African Americans fought Jim Crow on the streetcars, at the drinking fountains, and in the military. Black communities periodically took up arms to prevent lynching, and they organized underground NAACP chapters right under the eyes of the Ku Klux Klan. Lessons abound in the ways that oppressed peoples may organize to effect social change. The noted social-change educator Herbert Kohl includes *Remembering Jim Crow* in his suggested curriculum as a way to teach that the "struggle for civil rights and black liberation did not begin during the 1950s nor has it ended."[15]

Readers and audiences that have read or listened to interviews featured in *Remembering Jim Crow* sometimes frame the narratives within a human rights context. "Today," Rebecca Skloot writes, "in a post-terrorist-attack world quickly filling with prejudice against those of brown skin or Muslim faith, *Remembering Jim Crow* stands as a reminder of the dangers of racism."[16] Anushiya Sivanarayanan compares the BTV narratives to a report sponsored by Human Rights Watch titled "Broken People: Caste Violence against India's 'Untouchables.'" Contrasting the report's emphasis on the victimization and powerlessness of the Dalits with African Americans' narratives that speak of oppression *and* resistance, Sivanarayanan insists that black informants used a "consciously developed oral tradition" to "cast their stories within a framework of emancipatory politics, clearly aware that they are speaking to a multi-ethnic, multi-racial audience that has lived through the changes brought about by legislations of civil rights, voting rights and school desegregation."[17]

Sivanarayanan implies that oral narratives blending stories of suffering *and* struggle may ultimately help make audiences more receptive to histories of past atrocities that dominant societies have tried to silence. My experience of talking about the *Remembering Jim Crow* audio documentary with radio call-in audiences across the United States confirms this hypothesis. Needless to say, there are callers who deny that the Jim Crow era ever happened or who at least seek to minimize the impact its history exercises on contemporary society. However, I have also found that there are some listeners who are genuinely interested in engaging with the political content of the interviews. They want to understand *why* white southerners fought so hard to maintain their dominance, and they also want to understand the myriad ways that African Americans fought for dignity and social justice.

The political meaning of all documentary work is ultimately contested. After listening to people tell their stories of past suffering, we may offer our empathy, write up the results, and earn publication credits. In our roles as chroniclers of tragedy, however, neither oral historians nor truth commission members can guarantee that our societies will take our work seriously. Nor can we pretend that exposing injustices will move the United States to adopt policies that will repair the damages done by segregation to African American communities and to the American polity at large.

No one understands this better than the hundreds of African Americans who shared their time, family photographs, and memories with BTV. Emogene Wilson was born in Memphis, Tennessee, in 1924. She wrote for the *Tri-State Defender* in the early 1950s, where she met and fell in love with its editor, L. Alex Wilson. Wilson was a courageous reporter who had distinguished himself during the Emmett Till murder case in 1955. Two years later, he traveled to Little Rock, Arkansas, to cover the efforts of African Americans to integrate Central High School. Wilson's dramatic portrayal of those events played an important part in exposing the depths of bigotry in Little Rock. Wilson paid a price for his courage: he was beaten so severely by a group of whites seeking to halt desegregation at Central that he later died from his injuries.[18] In the course of her 1995 interview with BTV graduate students, Emogene Wilson paid homage to her husband. But she also wanted to impress on us that the fragile civil rights gains he had given his life for were under direct assault. "It started with Reagan," she noted, "and it progressed *backwards* with Bush and now with this — the Supreme Court now [is] just tearing everything apart."[19] Wilson reminds us that historical analysis *and* contemporary political activism are necessary tools in the struggle for human rights and social justice.

Notes

1. "Archbishop Tutu Speaks on NPR about GTRC," Greensboro Truth and Reconciliation Commission Web site, gtrc.blogspot.com/2006/01/archbishop-tutu-speaks-on-npr-about.html (accessed April 4, 2006).
2. W. E. B. Du Bois, *Black Reconstruction in America: An Essay toward a History of the Part Which Black Folk Played in the Attempt to Reconstruct Democracy in America, 1860–1880* (1935; New York: Meridian, 1965), 706.
3. Cheryl Harris, "Whiteness as Property," *Harvard Law Review* 106 (1993): 1709–91; William Darity Jr. and Melba J. Nicholson, "Racial Wealth Inequality and the Black Family," in *African American Family Life*, ed. Vonnie McLoyd, Nancy E. Hill, and Kenneth A. Dodge (New York: Guildford, 2005), 78–85; Melvin L. Oliver and Thomas Shapiro, *Black Wealth, White Wealth: A New Perspective on Racial Inequality* (New York: Routledge, 1995); Boris I. Bittker, *The Case for Black Reparations*, 2nd ed. (Boston: Beacon, 2003).
4. U.S. Commission on Civil Rights, *Voting Irregularities in Florida during the 2000 Presidential Election* (Washington, DC: Government Printing Office, 2001).
5. Jeremy Lamont Austin, "Black Liberation in the African Diaspora" (paper presented at University of California, Santa Cruz, April 24, 2006).
6. William Chafe et al., eds. *Remembering Jim Crow: African Americans Tell about Life in the Jim Crow South* (New York: New Press, 2001), including the oral history CDs as part of the hardcover edition. For the NPR documentary, see americanradioworks.publicradio.org/feathers/remembering (accessed April 4, 2006).
7. Behind the Veil: Documenting African American Life in the Jim Crow South project brochure, Center for Documentary Studies, Duke University (n.d.), in author's possession.
8. Lonnae O'Neal Parker, "Days of Jim Crow: An Oral History Project Fleshes Out the Meaning of the Segregation Era," *Washington Post*, February 9, 2002.
9. Anushiya Sivanarayanan, review of *Remembering Jim Crow*, *Callaloo* 26 (2003): 901–6.
10. These statistics were compiled by the project research coordinator Alexander X. Byrd after the interviewing phase of the project had been completed. Tabulated figures in the author's possession, n.d.
11. Paul Ortiz, *Emancipation Betrayed: The Hidden History of Black Organizing and White Violence in Florida from Reconstruction to the Bloody Election of 1920* (Berkeley: University of California Press, 2005).
12. Cleaster Mitchell, interview by the author, July 16, 1995, Brinkley, AR, available at Behind the Veil: Documenting African American Life in the Jim Crow South, John Hope Franklin Research Center for African and African American Documentation, Duke University. A more extensive version of this interview appears in *Remembering Jim Crow*.
13. Malachia Andrews, interview by the author, August 9, 1994, Leon County, FL, available at Behind the Veil: Documenting African American Life in the Jim Crow South.

14. Rebecca Skloot, review of *Remembering Jim Crow*, January 14, 2002, www.nasw.org/users/skloot/page6.html.
15. Herbert Kohl, "Good Stuff: The Journey to Freedom," *Rethinking Schools Online* 18 (2004), 1.
16. Skloot, review of *Remembering Jim Crow*.
17. Sivanarayanan, review of *Remembering Jim Crow*, 901–2.
18. Hank Klibanoff, "L. Alex Wilson: A Reporter Who Refused to Run," *Media Studies Journal* 14 (2000), available at www.freedomforum.org/publications/msj/courage.summer2000/contents.html (accessed April 3, 2006).
19. Emogene Wilson, interview by Mausiki Stacey Scales, July 5, 1995, Memphis, TN, available at Behind the Veil: Documenting African American Life in the Jim Crow South.

The Winter Soldier Hearings

John J. Fitzgerald

By the end of the 1960s, reports of U.S. atrocities committed in Vietnam had percolated into the mainstream media. The My Lai Massacre story broke in late 1969, followed shortly after by Simon and Schuster's publication of Mark Lane's *Conversations with Americans*, which told lurid tales of rape, murder, and torture of civilians in Vietnam at the hands of people who seemed more like homicidal maniacs than American soldiers.[1] While much (but not all) of what Lane presented in his book was revealed to be a fabrication by the investigative reporter Neil Sheehan in a December 1970 review that appeared in the *New York Times*, Sheehan nonetheless called for a

> sane and honest inquiry into the question of war crimes and atrocities in Vietnam by a body of knowledgeable and responsible men not beholden to the current military establishment. Who those men are and how that inquiry ought to be conducted are questions I do not have the space to discuss here, but the need for the inquiry is self-evident. Too large a segment of the citizenry believes that war crimes and atrocities have taken place for the question to be ignored.[2]

Even as Sheehan was writing his review, a year-long effort to convene such an inquiry by the ad hoc Citizens Commission of Inquiry—comprised mostly of Vietnam Veterans Against the War but also religious, labor, and celebrity antiwar activists such as the United Auto Workers secretary-treasurer Emil Mazey, Dick Gregory, Jeremy Rifkin, Jane Fonda, and Donald Sutherland—was coming to

Radical History Review
Issue 97 (Winter 2007) DOI 10.1215/01636545-2006-017

completion. Dubbed the Winter Soldier Hearings in reference to Thomas Paine's famous remark about "the summer soldier and the sunshine patriot" who "shrink from the service of their country," the inquiry took place over the course of three days in late January and early February of 1971 in Detroit, Michigan.[3] The proceedings, counseled by the Center for Constitutional Rights, went to great length both to verify the authenticity of the more than one hundred Veterans who gave testimony and to follow established legal doctrine, hoping to document that the kind of killing that took place at My Lai under Lieutenant William Calley's leadership was not an isolated incident but formed part of a larger, systematic breakdown of command and control within the military itself.[4] Only three branches of the Army and Marine Corps—the infantry, artillery, and armor—are considered combat arms, and most of those who testified were from the infantry, the branch that had the most interaction with the people of Vietnamese villages and suffered the highest fatality and casualty rates.

Despite the call issuing from the pages of no less than the *New York Times* for an inquiry into U.S. atrocities in Vietnam, the hearings were largely ignored by the press. The documentary made of the event, *Winter Soldier* (dir. Winterfilm Collective in association with Vietnam Veterans Against the War, 1972), likewise got limited play, yet watching it today, more than three decades later, I was reminded of the honesty and intensity the individual veterans brought to their testimony. Based on my own military experience in Vietnam in 1966, I believe that the film records truthful statements based on actual combat zone experiences. It strikingly reveals how war strips away the humanity of the participants. This forms part of the film's truth. With each day in the combat zone, one gradually becomes more callous, suspicious, apprehensive, and fearful. One learns to cope with the fear, but one pays a psychological price. One becomes cold, cynical, and inhumane. This is probably true for all wars, but in Vietnam, where one had not only the stress of combat but the uneasy notion that what one was told about the situation did not match the reality of events happening on the ground, intensified this effect.

Psychologists call this "cognitive dissonance." The official version of why we went to Vietnam was because the South Vietnamese government invited us to protect its people from attack by communists from the North. Harry S. Truman, Dwight D. Eisenhower, John F. Kennedy, and Lyndon B. Johnson had all promised help to the valiant people of Vietnam against communist aggression, telling us that our mission in Southeast Asia was the same as it was in Germany, Cuba, Iran, and Guatemala. This was the message of a Defense Department film shown to soldiers as part of their preparation for a tour of duty in Vietnam called *Why Vietnam?* (United States Department of Defense, 1965), a total distortion of the historical record of the U.S. role in French Indochina, the Cold War, and Vietnam.[5]

As captured in *Winter Soldier*, the reality of what a combat military unit encountered in Vietnam differed greatly from the official version. We were told we were "helping our friends" and "defending our allies," yet we experienced unrelenting hostility. When I served as a platoon leader with the Twenty-fifth Infantry Division, supplies for our base camp at Cu Chi in 1966 came in by air, or else by a heavily armed truck convoy. The roads to and from our camp were not secure, night travel was too dangerous to attempt, and convoys always had an armed helicopter escort. Snipers fired at our battalion headquarters nightly, from the village of Cu Chi, supposedly safe territory. In other words, we were not welcomed as friends, nor did we perceive the Vietnamese as friends. Twenty miles from Saigon, twenty miles from Cambodia, in a heavily fortified camp that was, prior to our arrival, in a strong National Liberation Front area, many concluded that no one was on our side and that their main goal now was not to help an ally but to simply survive their tour of duty.

Angry soldiers who have lost close friends can do illegal and immoral things. On the day I was wounded, and one of my men was killed, a sergeant who was the dead man's squad leader came up to me and told me that he had "taken care" of the prisoners that another squad had captured not far from where we were ambushed. At the time, I was not sure what he meant, but a month later, in a letter from another officer, after I had asked what happened to the prisoners, I learned that no prisoners were taken that day. The official body count for our action was nine enemy dead, a figure apparently plucked from thin air to balance the actual death of one of our soldiers (the sergeant who probably killed the prisoners was later killed in action, along with a number of other men caught in an enemy minefield).

Of the forty-three men of my platoon — First Platoon, B Company, Fourth Battalion, Ninth Infantry of the First Brigade, Twenty-fifth Infantry Division — who arrived with me in Vietnam from Hawaii in late April of 1966, everyone was either killed or wounded by the end of our year-long tour of duty. Of the survivors, all were psychologically wounded. The men in *Winter Soldier* talk to us in a manner far different from the way men talk in an American Legion club or a Veterans of Foreign Wars bar. They are not telling war stories but testimony that does not make them look good, offering serious commentary on the actual war on the ground, detailing what the war did to them and to the people of Vietnam. Theirs is not a pleasant world to view or to visit. It makes you think of insanity and psychopathology. Can these soft-spoken people actually be the killers that they claim to be? We have their words, but beyond that, there is no other evidence, except for what was left behind in South Vietnam.

The documentary, like the hearings, focuses primarily on the actions of individual infantry soldiers in the Army and the Marines. It does not include any testimony from B-52 pilots and crews who participated in carpet-bombing raids in North and South Vietnam. Raids typically included eighteen planes, each dropping about thirty tons of bombs filled with TNT on their target, which were called "enemy base camps" but were often villages of men, women, and children in free-fire zones. Nor does *Winter Soldier* include any testimony from the crews of destroyers and cruisers off the coast of Vietnam that were used to deliver naval artillery fire on Vietnam in support of land units. They were notoriously inaccurate and no doubt contributed to a large number of so-called friendly fire deaths. John F. Kerry appears briefly in the film, but he does not speak about his riverboat excursions and their infamous use of machine guns to do "reconnaissance by fire," which entailed firing into shoreline vegetation to see whether hostiles were concealed. Kerry later became the voice of the Vietnam Veterans against the War following his testimony before the Senate Foreign Relations Committee two months after the Winter Soldier hearings, but there, too, he declined to reveal his own swift-boat experience.

The power of the individual testimonies in the documentary in some way obstructs the hearings' objective of placing atrocities like My Lai in a larger chain of responsibility. *Winter Soldier* focuses on the actions of soldiers who did things considered illegal according to the military's own code of conduct, avoiding a larger critique of U.S. government policy. But what was official policy? It was to create free-fire zones in which anything that moved was presumed to be "enemy" and could be killed. It was to use so-called harassment and interdiction fire, usually from artillery, at preselected points on the ground. It was random, and the desired effect was terror. Policy was to use time-on-target barrages fired from long-range artillery to produce an airburst of fire over a potential target, blanketing the area with shrapnel. Policy was to deploy unmapped minefields, a violation of international law, which to this day injure and kill peasants. And it was policy to spray defoliants, such as Agent Orange, to kill off vegetation and crops in so-called enemy areas. But the documentary does not dwell on these issues, nor does it say much about the destruction wrought by the extremely powerful weapons deployed.

The men we see in *Winter Soldier* were the tools used to carry out this policy. They carry the mental and physical scars that come from being used as weapons of that war. The individual soldiers who raped and killed and tortured prisoners and civilians did violate the Uniform Code of Military Justice. These were crimes, even according to the military's own standards. But what of the greater crimes launched by Eisenhower, supported by Kennedy, escalated by Johnson, and continued by Richard M. Nixon? The film does not address the larger question of strategic war crimes in Vietnam. This is a serious fault, one akin to a film about Germany in World War II that only covered the felonies and misdemeanors of soldiers and never once mentioned the Nazi leadership—or of an inquiry into torture in Abu Ghraib that ignored the crimes of the Bush administration.

Notes

1. Mark Lane, *Conversations With Americans* (New York: Simon and Schuster, 1970).
2. Neil Sheehan, "Conversations With Americans," *New York Times Book Review*, December 27, 1970, 19. See also Neil Sheehan, "Should We Have War Crime Trials?" *New York Times Book Review*, March 28, 1971, 1–3, 30–34.

3. Thomas Paine, *Common Sense and Other Political Writings*, ed. Nelson Adkins (New York: Macmillan, 1953), 55.
4. Practically before the last witness finished testifying, defenders of the war launched a disinformation campaign designed to discredit the hearings, a campaign revived by the Swift Boat Veterans for Truth during John F. Kerry's 2004 presidential bid. Subsequent evidence, however, overwhelmingly supports the veracity of the Winter Solder Hearings revelations. See Nicholas Turse, "Swift Boat Swill: From the National Archives New Proof of Vietnam War Atrocities," *Village Voice*, September 21, 2004, available at www.fiatlux.info/archives/war (accessed August 8, 2006). See also the widely ignored *Toledo Blade*'s September 2004 series on war crimes committed by the elite U.S. Tiger Force.
5. For an excellent analysis of *Why Vietnam?*, see Henry Steele Commager, "On the Way to 1984," *Saturday Review*, April 15, 1967, 68–69, 80–82.

Dictatorship and Human Rights: The Politics of Memory

Felipe Agüero

I taught this course only once, in the fall of 2003. A course on the politics of memory was, for me, definitely stepping into new terrain, and closer to the domains of the historian and the social psychologist. In my research in political science, I had addressed issues in transitions to democracy, mostly in Latin America and southern Europe, and concerning democratization generally. I had also done work on military participation in politics. The courses I had been teaching included these themes in the broader framework of comparative politics, political regimes, and political change.

Naturally, issues related to memory had surfaced repeatedly, whether directly or indirectly, as themes both in my research and my courses. Democratic transitions, for instance, could not be considered completed unless claims from the victims of atrocities were adequately addressed. The reality of many of the cases I studied showed that organizations sympathetic to those claims had successfully prevented human rights issues from being suppressed and removed from public discourse and agenda, despite efforts by elites. Also, those issues were at the core of anything that had to do with the military both during authoritarianism and the successor democracies. Still, from within the disciplinary boundaries of a political science approach, those issues could be kept confined to the status of mere problems or hurdles in processes of democratic consolidation, or of sources of tension in civil-military relations. At best, one approached them as part of the dynamics of the invigoration of civil society and its demands.

Radical History Review
Issue 97 (Winter 2007) DOI 10.1215/01636545-2006-018

Nonetheless, the persevering work of the human rights organizations and movement managed to maintain demands for accountability alive enough to force them out of those boundaries. The massive character of human rights violations under the military regimes, the uncompromising nature of the fundamental claim at the basis of human rights mobilizations — finding the remains of the bodies of the victims, seeking explanations for their disappearance, demanding redress — and their gradual expansion to issues of imprisonment and torture kept them alive through the passage of time and against the desire of powerful sectors whose stance on questions of memory was simply to forget. Studying and teaching democratization in Latin America could therefore not ignore these specific questions about confronting the legacies of authoritarianism.[1]

In 2000, I was invited to a conference on constructing democratic governance in Latin America and to write a paper on the Chilean case.[2] A previous edited volume from a similar conference had addressed the early problems and dilemmas facing recently democratized countries. This new conference could now look at those problems with some distance from the transitions-period literature. What stood out in the Chilean case, however, was that actors there still wrestled with the very basic question of whether the transition had ended or not.

In my paper I wrote that since the resumption of democracy in 1990, Chile had been haunted by the specter of an unfinished political transition. The regime that emerged was hindered by lingering authoritarian enclaves imposing constraints on successor democratic administrations. However, unable to find congressional majorities for reform, those administrations focused during the 1990s on the agendas of growth and modernization, and were gradually led to act as if the authoritarian enclaves had been swept under the carpet. The overbearing self-imposed task of reassuring both the military and business elites led the leading elements in the ruling coalition essentially to give in to the idea that a consensual view toward a future benefiting all could ignore and easily suppress demands to reconcile with the past. They decreed the end of the transition and disseminated this impression to the rest of society. However, the obstinacy with which pending issues of the transition regularly surfaced, especially in the areas of human rights and civil-military relations, made them an inescapable feature of the new Chilean democracy.

The illusion of a completed transition and, with it, the burying of the problematic issues of the recent past, crashed against the inevitable resurgence of that past in the forms of a strengthened and hardened opposition from the Right,[3] followed shortly by the arrest of Augusto Pinochet in London in 1998 and the piling up of cases against him in Chilean courts.

The impact of Pinochet's arrest cannot be emphasized enough, especially its cathartic effect through which Chilean society rediscovered a language and retrieved the ability to utter the terms *dictator, dictatorship, torture, atrocities*, and other such expressions, and especially by having them articulated in the media, substituting for much milder terms such as *authoritarian regime* or the decidedly inaccurate *abuses* or *excesses*, which until then were the only ones that the politics of consensus and the ensuing social control had actually tolerated. The change in the scenario affected all forces. The Right began to distance itself from Pinochet, and the army gradually began the process of distancing itself from the military regime he had led. Then, the Mesa de Diálogo (Dialogue Roundtable) that brought together top military commanders and human rights lawyers for the first time under the auspices of the minister of defense, with the explicit purpose of debating ways of producing information on the remains of the disappeared, further changed the scenario in the direction of greater opening. The subsequent election of the socialist Ricardo Lagos to the presidency, with all the symbolism of having Salvador Allende's widow by his side on his victory celebration in January 2000, aided that process too. The terrain was ripe for a commemoration of the thirtieth anniversary of that other 9/11, the anniversary of the coup against Allende's government, which could for the first time open up the memories, as it tried to produce them, in ways that more fully encompassed those on the side of defeat in 1973, or those who had suffered social, economic, political, and physical repression under the military regime.

My course, it should be clear by now, was fully informed and inspired, or rather, I should say, urged, by that process. From following it closely and writing on it, the terrain, too, appeared to me to be ripe for a course on the politics of memory that took off from a focus on the Chilean experience.[4] The timing helped: the course program and the students would benefit from the commemorative events of "The Other 9/11" that took place at my institution, with guest speakers and videos, as well as from those taking place elsewhere in the United States, the world at large, and in Chile.

The course started with a general discussion of nondemocratic regimes, and their different types, in order to situate the features of violence, repression, and state terror. It specifically tried to locate the Latin American military regimes within those general regime types, debating the problematic associations found in the literature between regime type and terror. This section dealt with the diversity of forms of authoritarian governance in Latin America, despite their shared military feature, and differences in the scope and depth of their use of terror and repression. These regimes were presented in the context of their countries' structures of social, economic, political, and ideological conflict.

The course then directly focused on the Chilean case, and gave way to the questions that had most pressed me to think of organizing this course: How was it that the traumatic experience of repression under the Pinochet regime was to varying extents silenced during the successor democracy precisely when the ruling coalition had come from the victims' side? What were the particularities of this process, and how could it be compared with other experiences? What did the politics of the memory struggles exactly consist of? In a way, I wanted to be able to connect the implications of the politics of consensus with the politics of memory.[5] This required reflection about the contrast between the perceived imperatives of elite politics—reassurance, negotiation, stability—in the context of a powerful exiting military and a powerful business elite under well-institutionalized neoliberal policies, and, on the other hand, the basic demands for truth and justice from those seeking the remains of their loved ones, and, later, for recognition and redress from those victims that remained alive. At the bottom of the resolution of this tension between different positions in the politics of memory stood the persevering, indefatigable mobilization of the victims' organizations alongside human rights organizations and lawyers and in coordination with international networks and the activation of international human rights norms and institutions. How did the Chilean case compare with other contemporaneous cases? In many ways, those norms and institutions, available for Chileans and other contemporary cases, had not been available in previous experiences of trauma and atrocities in the twentieth century. How could the Chilean and other Latin American experiences be placed in the context of those other previous experiences? Of course, the questions were larger and broader than the course's (for me) tentative formulation could handle.

Especially useful for this section was the video material. *11 September 1973: The Last Stand of Salvador Allende* (dir. Patricio Henriquez, 1998) provides the indispensable visuals for what started it all—the brutal bombing of the government palace and the beginning of the repression. *Chile: Obstinate Memory* (dir. Patricio Guzmán, 1997) starkly presents the amnesia imposed on Chilean society during the successor democracy. With a remarkable device, the film captures the simultaneous surprise, aloofness, and disbelief in the facial expressions of pedestrians in Santiago as they watch a band (hired by the director Patricio Guzmán) marching down the street playing the official hymn of Salvador Allende's Popular Unity coalition, not heard since the early 1970s. Thomas Klubock (see the reference in the syllabus) views this documentary as expressive of the ways in which attempts at memory themselves form part of the changes that have weakened collective identities as the new economic regime emphasizes individualism. *The Pinochet Case* (2001), another documentary film by Guzmán, captures the drama of Pinochet's London arrest and contrasts it with the plight of the victims and their relatives.

The politicized nature of memory struggles are brought to light in Alex Wilde's depiction of the difficulties of expressive politics under what he calls the "conspiracy of consensus," and in Katherine Hite's description of the negotiations and concessions in Congress to obtain a monument for Allende. The use of material in Spanish would greatly expand the scope of references for the study and teaching of the politics of memory in Chile.[6]

The course then spent a couple of sessions on other Southern Cone (Argentina, Brazil, Uruguay) and Central American cases. There is always the need to balance the number of cases from different regions, as well as the sessions devoted to particular cases or to strictly conceptual or theoretical issues. However, it is clear to me that an iteration of this course should spend more time on Latin American cases, including, though also beyond, the Southern Cone countries. New developments have taken place during the Kirchner administration in Argentina—for example, the decision to annul the amnesty law, the purge in the military, the decision to inaugurate a museum of memory in the old naval facilities in Buenos Aires—and some movement has started in Uruguay, and with these developments, new material has been produced.[7] But more analytical depth can be reached by comparing these with the Central American cases, especially those of Guatemala and El Salvador, that evolved out of war and peace settlements. In hindsight, one should ask about the consequences of the manners of transition, the different kind of settlements, and the reports of the different commissions established to deal with the atrocities of the previous regimes. What was the impact of the different weight of international actors and institutions, of the varying domestic power configurations, of the strength of civil society organizations?[8] What have been the levels of truth and justice attained in these different countries, and what degree of commitment to sound human rights policies exists with the political actors in the new institutional settings? How have the politics of memory played out to influence these outcomes? Greater depth and scope would be reached by including the different experiences of, for instance, Peru and Mexico. The existence of different kinds of reports by ad hoc commissions in all these cases on the atrocities committed under the previous regimes would provide a sound starting point for comparison.

An interesting comparative question points to the degree of success of the different cases in the attainment of justice or the obtainment of truth in relation to the paths followed to reach those goals. A related question has to do with the extent to which society in general gets to share and participate in the indignation for the crimes of the previous regime as a basis for sustained and enduring policies of redress and defense and the promotion of human rights. How is relative success—since most cases fall well short of truly achieving those goals—related to the swiftness and frontal way in which past crimes are confronted by successor regimes? There is a difference here between cases that involved war and peace settlements, which always meant the establishment of truth commissions of some sort, those in which tribunals were established promptly after the democratic inauguration (as in Argentina), and those cases in which this establishment was developed more gradually. Mark Osiel offers useful insights for dealing with these questions by conveying the symbolic importance of either tribunals or commissions for their ability to generate debate and deliberation in society as a whole.

The rest of the course combined a view of the other cases for comparative purposes—South Africa, Spain—and a glimpse at the literature, and the debates, over memory issues as they have been constructed from the experience of the atrocities committed by the Nazi and the Stalinist regimes, as well as the issues of silence and collaboration that emerged from the Second World War.

DICTATORSHIP AND HUMAN RIGHTS: THE POLITICS OF MEMORY

Fall 2003

The British historian Eric Hobsbawm wrote about the twentieth century as the "Age of Extremes." The unprecedented magnitude of the atrocities and genocides that took place within its span gave it one of its distinctive features. Repressive regimes entrenched in the power of the state availed themselves with ever more sophisticated tools—technical, ideological, organizational—for the suppression of their peoples. However, the twentieth century also was marked by the defeat of colonialism, one of the sources of massive repression, the expansion of democratic regimes, and the emergence of an international human rights regime. Yet societies still were left with the task of confronting violent and traumatic pasts. How have societies coped with traumatic pasts, and how have they faced the tension between remembering and forgetting? How have memories been contested and constructed, and how have they aided the development of collective identities? How do memories and understandings of the past become institutionalized? In what ways have these tensions permeated political struggle? What consequences do the politics of memory have for the future? These are some of the questions that this course will explore with a view to various approaches and scenarios.

At the outset, the course will plunge into a case study of the politics of memory in Chile to take advantage of "The Other 9/11" symposium organized for September 10 and 11, 2003, that will reflect on the thirtieth anniversary of the coup d'état in that country. Following that, the course pauses to reflect on some general issues of history, politics, and memory, before addressing cases primarily in Latin America and Europe.

The following book is available for purchase in the University of Miami bookstore and at Book Horizons: Alexandra Barahona de Brito, Carmen González-Enríquez, and Paloma Aguilar, eds., *The Politics of Memory: Transitional Justice in Democratizing Societies* (Oxford: Oxford University Press, 2000).

Evaluation

The course will require active student participation, which in turn will demand that students come to class prepared by reading the assigned material for that particular session. Participation in class will count for 17.5 percent. The rest of the evaluation will be based on three written reports (ten pages each) that will develop views based on class readings and other materials. Specific guidelines will be provided. These reports are due October 8, November 12, and the final week of classes. Each will account for 27.5 percent.

TOPICS AND READING ASSIGNMENTS

August 27 Introduction

September 3 Memory as a Pressing Issue of the Present

Discussion of recent newspaper clips on memory-related issues.

September 8 Dictatorship and Human Rights
Paul Brooker, *Non-democratic Regimes: Theory, Government, and Politics* (New York: St. Martin's, 2000), ch. 1, "Theories of Non-democratic Government."

September 10 The Other 9/11: September 11, 1973
Pamela Constable and Arturo Valenzuela, *A Nation of Enemies: Chile under Pinochet* (New York: Norton, 1991), ch. 1, "The War"; ch. 6, "The Culture of Fear."

Video presentation and panel discussion, *11 September 1973: The Last Stand of Salvador Allende* (dir. Patricio Henriquez, 1998), Center for Latin American Studies, 9/10, Storer Auditorium, 7 pm.

"Reflections on the Thirtieth Anniversary of the Coup d'État in Chile," presentation by Paul Drake, dean of social sciences, University of California, San Diego, followed by panel discussion. 9/11, Learning Center 170, 5:30 pm.

September 15–17 Chile: The Politics of Memory
Patricio Silva, "Collective Memories, Fears, and Consensus: The Political Psychology of the Chilean Democratic Transition," in *Societies of Fear: The Legacy of Civil War, Violence, and Terror in Latin America*, ed. Kees Koonings and Dirk Kruijt (London: Zed, 1999), 171–96.

Felipe Agüero, "Chile: Unfinished Transition and Increased Political Competition," in *Constructing Democratic Governance in Latin America*, ed. Jorge Domínguez and Michael Shifter, 2nd ed. (Baltimore, MD: Johns Hopkins University Press, 2003), 292–303.

Luis Roniger and Mario Sznajder, *The Legacy of Human Rights Violations in the Southern Cone: Argentina, Chile, and Uruguay* (Oxford: Oxford University Press, 1999), ch. 1, "Repression and the Discourse of Human-Rights Violations in the Southern Cone."

Alan Angell, "Reflections on the International Reaction to the Coup in Chile," published as "La reacción internacional frente al golpe: La mirada de un historiador ingles," *El Mercurio* (Santiago), August 24, 2003.

Alan Angell, "The Pinochet Case," in *The Pinochet Case*, ed. Madeleine Davis (London: Institute of Latin American Studies, 2003).

Peter Kornbluh, "Opening Up the Files: Chile Declassified," *NACLA Report on the Americas* 37 (2003), 25–31.

September 22–24 Obstinate Memory and Expression
Video presentation, *Chile: Obstinate Memory* (dir. Patricio Guzmán, 1997).

Alexander Wilde, "Irruptions of Memory: Expressive Politics in Chile's Transition to Democracy," *Journal of Latin American Studies*, no. 31 (1999): 473–500.

Thomas Miller Klubock, "History and Memory in Neoliberal Chile: Patricio Guzman's Obstinate Memory and the Battle of Chile," *Radical History Review*, no. 85 (2003): 272–81.
Teresa A. Meade, "Holding the Junta Accountable: Chile's 'Sitios de Memoria' and the History of Torture, Disappearance, and Death," *Radical History Review*, no. 79 (2001): 123–39.

Katherine Hite, "Resurrecting Allende," *NACLA Report on the Americas* 37 (2003), 19–24.

September 29–October 1 The Southern Cone
Roniger and Sznajder, ch. 3: "National Reconciliation and the Disruptive Potential of the Legacy of Human-Rights Violations"; ch. 6, "Oblivion and Memory in the Redemocratized Southern Cone."

Alexandra Barahona de Brito, "Truth, Justice, Memory, and Democratization in the Southern Cone," in Barahona de Brito, González-Enríquez, and Aguilar, *The Politics of Memory*, 119–60.

Video presentation, *The Pinochet Case* (dir. Patricio Guzmán, 2001).

Report due October 8.

October 6–8 Concepts for Memory, History, and Politics
Paloma Aguilar, *Memory and Amnesia: The Role of the Spanish Civil War in the Transition to Democracy* (New York: Berghahn, 2002), ch. 1, "Regarding Memory, Learning, and Amnesia."

Michel-Rolph Trouillot, *Silencing the Past: Power and the Production of History* (Boston: Beacon, 1995), ch. 1, "The Power in the Story."

October 13–15 The Historical Context(s) of Memory
Charles S. Maier, "Consigning the Twentieth Century to History: Alternative Narratives for the Modern Era," *American Historical Review* 105 (2000): 807–31.

Charles S. Maier, "Hot Memory . . . Cold Memory: On the Political Half-Life of Fascist and Communist Memory," *Transit Europäische Revue, Tr@nsit-Virtuelles Forum*, no. 22 (2002), www.iwm.at/index.php?option=com_content&task=view&id=316&Itemid=481.

October 20–22 Law, Institutions, and Collective Memory
Martha Minow, *Between Vengeance and Forgiveness: Facing History after Genocide and Mass Violence* (Boston: Beacon, 1998), ch. 1, "Introduction."

Mark Osiel, "Ever Again: Legal Remembrance of Administrative Massacre," *University of Pennsylvania Law Review*, no. 144 (1995): 464–505.

October 27–29 Central America: Peace and Democratization
Video presentation: *Crimes against Humanity: The Search for Justice*, vol. 1 (Films for the Humanities and Sciences, BBC, and the Ford Foundation, 1998).

Rachel Sieder, "War, Peace, and Memory Politics in Central America," in Barahona de Brito, González-Enríquez, and Aguilar, *The Politics of Memory*, 161–89.

Priscilla B. Hayner, *Unspeakable Truths: Facing the Challenge of Truth Commissions* (New York: Routledge, 2002), ch. 1, "Introduction"; ch. 2, "Confronting Past Crimes."

November 3–5 South Africa: Apartheid, Transition, and the Truth Commission
Video presentation: *Crimes against Humanity: The Search for Justice*, vol. 2 (Films for the Humanities and Sciences, BBC, and the Ford Foundation, 1998).

Richard A. Wilson, "Justice and Legitimacy in the South African Transition," in Barahona de Brito, González-Enríquez, and Aguilar, *The Politics of Memory*, 190–217.

Hayner, *Unspeakable Truths*, ch. 3, "Why a Truth Commission?" ch. 4, "Five Illustrative Truth Commissions."

Report due November 12.

November 10–12 Spain: Transition and Memory of the Civil War
Video presentation: *The Spanish Civil War* (Films for the Humanities and Sciences, 2002).

Paloma Aguilar, "Justice, Politics, and Memory in the Spanish Transition," in Barahona de Brito, González-Enríquez, and Aguilar, *The Politics of Memory*, 92–118.

Paloma Aguilar, *Memory and Amnesia: The Role of the Spanish Civil War in the Transition to Democracy* (New York: Berghahn, 2002), Conclusion.

November 17–19 Confronting the Nazi Past and Its Memory
Video presentation: *Genocide in the First Half of the Twentieth Century* (dir. Robert J. Emery, 2002).

Norbert Frei, *Adenauer's Germany and the Nazi Past: The Politics of Amnesty and Integration* (New York: Columbia University Press, 2002), xi–4.

Osiel, "Ever Again," 691–99.

Alan Milchman and Alan Rosenberg, "Remembering and Forgetting: The Social

Construction of a Community of Memory of the Holocaust," in *Contemporary Portrayals of Auschwitz: Philosophical Challenges*, ed. Rosenberg, James R. Watson, and Detlef Linke (Amherst, MA: Humanity Books/Prometheus Books, 2000), 251–82.

November 24–26 Problems of History and Memory

Charles S. Maier, *The Unmasterable Past: History, Holocaust, and German National Identity* (Cambridge, MA: Harvard University Press, 1997), preface, 1997; preface to the original edition; introduction; ch. 1, "The Stakes of the Controversy"; ch. 3: "A Holocaust Like Others?"

Charles Maier, "A Surfeit of Memory? Reflections on History, Melancholy, and Denial," *History and Memory*, no. 5 (1992): 136–51.

Dominick LaCapra, *History and Memory after Auschwitz* (Ithaca, NY: Cornell University Press, 1998), ch. 1: "History and Memory: In the Shadow of the Holocaust."

Henry Rousso, *The Vichy Syndrome: History and Memory in France since 1944* (Cambridge, MA: Harvard University Press, 1991), foreword by Stanley Hoffmann; introduction.

December 1–3 Class Discussion of Reports Due This Week

. . . . .

I have spent many nights sleeping in the plazas of Buenos Aires with a bottle of wine, trying to forget . . . I am afraid to be alone with my thoughts.
—Argentine Captain Adolfo Scilingo, confessing to having thrown thirty people from a navy helicopter during the so-called Dirty War

Publicly coming forward to give such testimony is a way of returning to a horrible past that we are trying to forget.
—Argentine President Carlos Menem, responding to Scilingo's public confession

The struggle of man against power is the struggle of memory against forgetting.
—Milan Kundera

Notes

1. Katherine Hite and Paola Cesarini, eds., *Legacies of Authoritarianism in Southern Europe and Latin America* (Notre Dame, IN: University of Notre Dame Press, 2004).
2. Felipe Agüero, "Chile: Unfinished Transition and Increased Political Competition," in *Constructing Democratic Governance*, ed. Jorge Domínguez and Michael Shifter, 2nd ed. (Baltimore, MD: Johns Hopkins University Press, 2003), 292–320.
3. Felipe Agüero, "Chile's Lingering Authoritarian Legacy," *Current History* 97 (1998), 66–70.
4. I will say at the outset that I would much rather not have to bring up an even more personal

connection to all this, but I decided that it would be dishonest not to disclose it when writing about the context for this course. My own experience was an expression of the silences of the transition and the post-Pinochet period, as well as of the cathartic process started with the arrest of Pinochet. In February 2001, I wrote a letter to the director of the Institute of Political Science at the Universidad Católica in Santiago, Chile, in which I denounced a member of the faculty there as a former torturer—I had been one of his victims—at the national stadium in 1973, when he was a naval reserve officer. I had recognized him at a professional meeting in Santiago in the early 1990s. The letter became public, and this person filed a criminal libel suit (*calumnias e injurias graves*) against me. This made it one of the first cases involving torture to be dealt with in court, as well as in the media. After hearing several witnesses, the court ruled against the suit, dismissing it and freeing me of all charges. The court made its decision not on technical grounds, but with reference to the *exceptio veritatis* clause in the penal code, the master frame for all legal and judicial proceedings in the country. The case was reported and analyzed in Patricia Verdugo, ed., *De la tortura NO se habla: Agüero versus Meneses* (*Of Torture You Do NOT Speak: Agüero versus Meneses*) (Santiago: Editorial Catalonia, 2004).

5. Or "a conspiracy of consensus," as Alex Wilde has called it. See Alexander Wilde, "Irruptions of Memory: Expressive Politics in Chile's Transition to Democracy," *Journal of Latin American Studies*, no. 31 (1999): 473–500.
6. See, for instance, the series of books authored by Brian Loveman and Elizabeth Lira, and other works by Chilean historians. A recent addition to the literature in English is Steve J. Stern, *Remembering Pinochet's Chile: On the Eve of London, 1998* (Durham, NC: Duke University Press, 2004).
7. See Eric Hershberg and Felipe Agüero, eds., *Memorias militares sobre la represión en el Cono Sur: Visiones en disputa en dictadura y democracia* (*Military Memories of Repression in the Southern Cone: Contending Views under Dictatorship and Democracy*) (Madrid: Social Science Research Council, with Siglo XXI Editores, 2005).
8. See, for instance, Stephen C. Ropp and Kathryn Sikkink, "International Norms and Domestic Politics in Chile and Guatemala," in *The Power of Human Rights: International Norms and Domestic Change*, ed. Thomas Risse, Ropp, and Sikkink (Cambridge: Cambridge University Press, 1999), 172–204.

Teaching Truth Commissions

Charles F. Walker

My interest in human rights and history led me to teach an undergraduate history seminar on truth commissions. I had followed the Peruvian Truth and Reconciliation Commission's work closely, listening to a friend's stories of interviews with leaders of the Shining Path or of the interference put up by all political parties (as well as the military and the church) with rapt attention. I was fascinated by the process of compiling and publicizing the report, surprised (naively, no doubt) by the difficulties the commissioners faced. They confronted opposition from all fronts, including the Alejandro Toledo government (2001–6), who quickly shed his aura of a leader of the anti-Fujimori campaigns and caved in to the powerful groups wary of the report. Nonetheless, the commission released their twelve-volume report in August 2003, disseminating it via the Web (access is surprisingly widespread in Peru), in town meetings, and in different published versions (www.cverdad.org.pe).

The report is an astonishingly thorough and accessible account of political violence in Peru since 1980. In essence, it is a history of Peru in the final decades of the twentieth century. It does not elude race and social inequality, and it spreads the blame widely. It is a superb work of history that led me to wonder about the relevance of my current research on an eighteenth-century earthquake/tsunami in Peru. It also prompted me to want to know more about truth commissions, to compare their mandates, organization, and impact.

I had several objectives. I wanted the students to learn about specific cases of wide-scale violence, usually state-sponsored, and the struggles around justice and memory. The course stressed different national truth commissions—their emer-

Radical History Review
Issue 97 (Winter 2007) DOI 10.1215/01636545-2006-019

gence, development, and impact—more than theoretical issues regarding violence and memory. In other words, I wanted them to be able to discuss Argentina, Chile, Peru, Guatemala, and other countries with historical depth. This approach allowed the theoretical and methodological questions concerning violence, social divisions and stratification, justice, and memory to emerge from these discussions. We paid close attention to differences in how truth commissions surfaced, the obstacles they faced, and their significance. Students demonstrated the most interest in the questions of whether documenting violence can lead to social justice and some form of reconciliation. These issues, of course, touched on those of memory and the significance and endurance of violence. While this might seem like an overly traditional historical approach—allowing theory to trickle down from case studies—it worked well with a diverse group of undergraduates. We had many fine moments in the seminar when the students found themselves engaged in deep discussions about violence and reconciliation. Race and identity emerged as a recurrent topic that linked the different countries we studied but also found its way into exchanges about the United States.

Studying truth commissions requires close attention to international campaigns for truth and justice since World War II. The numbers of these commissions continue to expand (twenty-four as of May 2006), and a worldwide community of experts—and the concomitant literature, Web sites, and conferences—exist. Nonetheless, the reports themselves tend to be very national in focus; they rarely discuss international factors or make comparisons. The reasons are evident. The reports are created to explore a nation's violent past; examining the role of other countries is not part of their mandate. This is problematic in Latin America, where the United States has supported repressive regimes. Yet the truth commissions generally do not have the resources to move beyond the nation and examine murky transnational connections. Moreover, their findings could step on the toes of the United States, which many leaders want to avoid. On the other hand, a focus on another country could serve as an evasion, a potential form of exoneration for national participants through a more abstract blame on foreign powers. Yet the national approach by the commissions does not prevent illuminating comparisons, a goal of the class.

Selecting the focus and reading for the first class presented a challenge. I debated whether to read parts of a truth commission report, such as the Argentine *Nunca más* (*Never Again*), available in English and Spanish. Instead, I decided to use Priscilla Hayner's *Unspeakable Truths: Facing the Challenges of Truth Commissions*. It studies the reasons truth commissions were created and the challenges they confront, highlighting comparisons between different commissions and their limitations. Some students found it a bit overwhelming, but everyone judged it useful. In fact, most returned to it when preparing their final papers. I wish, however, that I had included some introductory texts about the concept of human rights and something on the Nuremberg War Crimes Trial. We all would have benefited from a historical and critical understanding of human rights and current debates about them. At times, our discussions returned to the age-old (yet no less repellant) justification of torture as a means to prevent violence. These should have been more grounded in debates about human rights. More specifically, many of the readings referred to World War II and the Nuremberg Trial. For these students born in the mid-1980s, that is distant history.

Another organizational question was the balance among books and articles, Web sources, and videos. In the end, I had a perhaps traditional division, using books and articles as the key homework, taking advantage of the Internet for bibliography and other information, and showing videos to illustrate some of the major issues and to delve into particular countries and periods. The Web pages from the United States Institute of Peace (www.usip.org/library/truth.html), the University of Colorado's Beyond Intractability (www.beyondintractability.org/essay/truth_commissions), and the Truth Commission Project (www.truthcommission.org) proved particularly helpful.

I used the film *Discovering Dominga* (dir. Patricia Flynn and Mary Jo McConahay, USA, 2002) in the first class in order to address questions of memory and reconciliation.[1] Throughout the seminar, students frequently returned to Dominga — Denise Becker — when debating whether reconciliation was ever possible for victims and their family members, and when discussing identity. Some of them looked farther into the Río Negro massacre and Maya resistance to a World Bank–funded dam. The documentary *Botín de guerra/Spoils of War* (dir. David Blaustien, Argentina, 1999) worked well with Marguerite Feitlowitz, *A Lexicon of Terror: Argentina and the Legacies of Torture*.[2] In conversations with students, Anglo and Latino, outside of class, I received the impression that the Argentine case had shown many of them that state violence could happen to anyone, not just "indigenous peasants." Their lives and identities felt much closer to those of the middle-class Argentine victims than those of the Mayas. *Estadio Nacional/National Stadium* (dir. Carmen Luz Parot, Chile, 1999), a film about Chile in the months after the Pinochet coup, showed both the mechanics of mass torture and the various ways that these practices are hidden and denied.[3] I wish that I could have shown *Long Night's Journey into Day* (dir. Frances Reid and Deborah Hoffman, South Africa, 2000) and *State of Fear* (dir. Pamela Yates, Peru, 2005). Of course, the list of pertinent documentaries is long. I benefited from an excellent Latin American film series that graduate students had organized the same quarter. Many of my students saw *Innocent Voices/Voces Inocentes* (dir. Luis Mandoki, Mexico, 2004) about El Salvador in this forum.

After discussing *Discovering Dominga* and *Unspeakable Truths*, we spent three weeks on specific truth commissions. In week three, we discussed Chile. One student had lived there the previous semester and had many insights. The discussion frequently moved to the role of the United States in the overthrow of Salvador Allende. The case of Argentina intrigued and appalled students. Many of them sought more information about the Madres de la Plaza de Mayo and the search by grandmothers for their kidnapped grandchildren, the children of detainees. Some students liked *Lexicon of Terror* very much; others said it was overwritten, or just difficult to penetrate. One suggested that we read more of the Argentine commission's *Nunca más*. If I repeat this seminar, I would include more excerpts from the reports themselves. The following week, we examined Peru's commission, using the report itself, as well as photographs from the period. The Shining Path fascinated students. They were struck by the fact that the truth commission charged this group with more than 50 percent of the killings, whereas in every other Latin American case, the state had been the culprit in the vast majority of cases. We also had an interesting discussion about race, an issue highlighted by the report.

In weeks six and seven, students presented reports about the organization and impact of other truth commissions. For some but not all, this represented the beginning of their final papers. I stressed the need for them to make lively presentations and link their arguments with the themes of the course. We also discussed Greg Grandin's essay, "Chronicle of a Guatemalan Genocide Foretold." Some also read his "The Instruction of Great Catastrophe: Truth Commissions, National History, and State Formation in Argentina, Chile, and Guatemala."[4] The richer moments of the discussion moved to the question of the relationship between state violence and the Cold War. Some students understood the horrors of Guatemala, Argentina, El Salvador, and Chile as a campaign by U.S.-backed right-wing regimes to exterminate the Left. Others questioned such a broad interpretation, using Peru to question whether the United States always had a prominent role in supporting the repression. The vast differences among the Shining Path, guerrilla groups in Central America, and the targets of repression in the Southern Cone (the Left, unions, students, the Jewish population, community workers, the list continues) confounded some students, but also led to great discussions and much learning.

One topic that came up frequently was why some truth commissions had so much impact or resonance (Chile and Argentina) and others much less (Haiti, El Salvador, and Guatemala). We discussed the comparative strength of the investigative state and civil society versus the repressors (the military is still omnipotent in Guatemala) and the class background of the victims. One student asked whether human rights efforts would have been more challenging in Argentina if the victims had been peasants, rather than primarily urban and middle-class. Everyone quickly said yes. There were several nice pedagogical moments when the students realized that they were posing the big, comparative questions that they had read about, but not necessarily understood, just weeks before. They showed much more interest in the meaning of "truth" and the search for reconciliation than in questions of memory.

Students presented their final papers in the final two classes. I requested that they address the course's big themes and not just summarize the truth commissions' missions or histories. Also, with seven presentations in three hours, they had to be engaging and clear.

The topics were:

- Children and Violence: The Uganda Truth Commission
- The Challenges of Reconciliation in South Africa
- Haiti's Troubled National Commission for Truth and Justice
- Death Squads in El Salvador
- Liberation Theology and Repression in El Salvador
- Land and the Guatemalan Truth Commission
- The United States and the Guatemalan Military
- Trauma and Truth in Guatemala
- The Genocide against Maya Women in Guatemala, 1978–83
- The Panamanian Truth Commission
- The Church and the Chilean Truth Commission
- The Organization of Terror in Pinochet's Chile
- Repression and Women's Bodies in Argentina
- The Disappeared in Argentina

I would have liked to squeeze in a session on international tribunals. These came up in our discussions about the challenges in countries in which the accused still hold a great deal of power, such as El Salvador, Haiti, and Guatemala. The role of the United States surfaced, and it would have been interesting to examine opposition in Washington to international tribunals. I also wish that I had planned for reading and discussion about human rights in the post-9/11 United States. This came up much less than I expected. I would like to believe that it reflected students' interest in Latin America (and Africa) and their immersion into their paper topics. I worry that it indicates a lack of reflection among students (and faculty) about homeland state repression. I do believe that these students will be much more informed when and if they confront these issues in the future.

TRUTH COMMISSIONS

Winter 2006

Course Description

This course examines truth commissions, "bodies established to research and report on human rights abuses over a certain period of time in a particular country or in relation to a particular conflict" (www.usip.org/library/truth.html). While focusing on the Latin American countries of Peru, Chile, Guatemala, and Argentina, we will also look at other cases such as South Africa and Sierra Leone. We will begin by reading about the emergence of truth commissions and some of their pitfalls or limitations. We will then look at specific cases. Students will develop a final project that focuses on a particular country and some aspect of the truth commission report or this country's human rights record. This final paper is essential to the class. Please start thinking about it and consult with me soon. I will provide two key Web articles that will lead you to larger issues and a bibliography.

The seminar allows for the substantial discussion of readings. Additionally, students write two short papers and one longer one (6–8 pages). Participation is essential.

Readings

Required readings, on sale at the bookstore:
Priscilla B. Hayner, *Unspeakable Truths: Facing the Challenge of Truth Commissions* (New York: Routledge, 2002).
Marguerite Feitlowitz, *A Lexicon of Terror: Argentina and the Legacies of Torture* (New York: Oxford University Press, 1998).
* There will also be readings for you to purchase at Classical Copies.

Classes (the readings should be done before the class)

January 9: Introduction to the course
Video: *Discovering Dominga* (dir. Patricia Flynn and Mary Jo McConahay, U.S., 2002)

January 16: Martin Luther King Holiday—no class

January 18: The Creation and Meaning of Truth Commissions
Hayner, *Unspeakable Truths*, preface, introduction, and chaps. 1–8. This is a long, detailed (and valuable) book—I will discuss reading strategies.
* I will hand out a question for Short Paper #1 due on January 23:

In *Unspeakable Truths*, Priscilla Hayner quotes a South African poll that stated, "two-thirds of the public believed that revelations resulting from the truth commission process had made South Africans angrier and led to a deterioration in relations between the races" (156). This could easily be interpreted as an argument against truth commissions. In a three-to-four–page double-spaced paper, you should refute this view, demonstrating why truth commissions have positive effects on nations and can lead to reconciliation, even if they increase rancor and tension on their reports' publication and dissemination. This is a broad question and there is no single "correct" answer. You have read about many benefits of truth commissions, as well as about potential problems. You may focus on one positive aspect or develop several of them. (If you single out one, you should probably refer to or list other lines of argument.) You may stress one country or bring in many. I want to see that you have understood the material presented by Hayner and contemplated it. I also want to see that you can present your arguments coherently. You might have your doubts about truth commissions. This is fine (if you do so with reasoned views), but I want you to stress the arguments for them. It is always valuable to understand the counterargument.

January 23: Truth Commissions, Past, Present, and Future and the Case of Chile
Video: *Estadio Nacional/National Stadium* (dir. Carmen Luz Paret, Chile, 2001)
*First paper due
Finish Hayner, *Unspeakable Truths.*

January 30: The Case of Argentina
Video: *Botín de Guerra/Spoils of War* (dir. David Blaustien, Argentina, 2001)

Feitlowitz, *A Lexicon of Terror*, introduction and chaps. 1–3 (three students will present chaps. 4–6)

February 6: Peru
Selections from Peruvian Truth and Reconciliation Committee Final Report, distributed by the professor

Peruvian Truth and Reconciliation Committee Final Report, available at www.cverdad.org.pe/ingles/ifinal/conclusiones.php.
You should hand in a one-paragraph summary of the topic for your final paper. This should include the truth commission that you will study and your emphasis or focus. I will e-mail you comments.

February 13: President's Day holiday

February 20: Other Truth Commissions, Part 1
Working in groups of two or three, you will present information about a truth commission. By now, you should have a clear idea of key questions. You should:

- Summarize the conflict and violence
- Provide an overview of the truth commission and its findings
- Present its contributions and limitations
- If possible, review its aftermath and impact

Visuals (PowerPoint or video clips) and handouts (maps, summary of findings, basic arguments, etc.) are useful. I recommend using them.

February 27: Other Truth Commissions, Part 2
*Turn in second paper
This should be a three-to-four-page proposal for your final paper. It should include

- Key information about the truth commission that you will study
- Your key issues (I will provide examples in class)
- Hypothesis
- Sources

March 6: Presentations

March 13: Presentations
*Final paper due in the history department by 4:00 p.m., March 20

Suggested Readings
Students are expected to develop their own bibliographies as they work on their final paper.

Argentina, Comisión Nacional, *Nunca Más (Never Again): A Report by Argentina's National Commission on Disappeared People* (London: Faber and Faber, 1986). This report is available in Spanish and English. See Web sites for other countries' reports. Make sure to include them in your papers.
Barahona de Brito, Alexandra, Carmen González-Enríquez, and Paloma Aguilar. *The Politics of Memory: Transitional Justice in Democratizing Societies.* Oxford: Oxford University Press, 2001.
Ignatieff, Michael. *Human Rights as Politics and Idolatry.* Princeton, NJ: Princeton University Press, 2001.
Jelin, Elizabeth. *State Repression and the Labors of Memory.* Trans. Judy Rein and Marcial Godoy-Anativia. Minneapolis: University of Minnesota Press, 2003.
Minow, Martha. *Between Vengeance and Forgiveness: Facing History after Genocide and Mass.* Boston: Beacon, 1998.
Phelps, Teresa Godwin. *Shattered Voices: Language, Violence, and the Work of Truth Commissions.* Philadelphia: University of Pennsylvania Press, 2004.
Robertson, Geoffrey. *Crimes against Humanity: The Struggle for Global Justice.* New York: New Press, 2000.
Sanford, Victoria. *Buried Secrets: Truth and Human Rights in Guatemala.* New York: Palgrave Macmillan, 2003.
Wilson, Richard A. *The Politics of Truth and Reconciliation in South Africa: Legitimizing the Post-apartheid State.* Cambridge: Cambridge University Press, 2001.

Also see these Web sites:
Truth Commission Project (Harvard Law School, Search for Common Ground, European Centre for Common Ground): www.truthcommission.org/about.php?lang=en.
The United States Institute of Peace: www.usip.org/library/truth.html.
The Beyond Intractability Project, University of Colorado: www.beyondintractability.org.

Notes

1. *Discovering Dominga* follows Denise Becker's return from Iowa to her native Guatemala in search of the truth about her family, killed in the 1982 Río Negro massacre. She had miraculously survived and two years later was adopted by an American family.
2. *Spoils of War* follows the search for the children of detainees during Argentina's Dirty War, kidnapped and then turned over to military families. It highlights the brave women, particularly grandmothers, who led this struggle.
3. For two months after the 1973 coup, the national stadium was used as a detention and torture center, holding up to twelve thousand prisoners. The documentary includes the testimony of over thirty survivors. I would like to thank Pablo Whipple and Michael Lazzara for help in selecting and obtaining these documentaries.
4. Greg Grandin, "Chronicle of a Guatemalan Genocide Foretold: Violence, Trauma, and the Limits of Historical Inquiry," *Nepantla: Views from the South* 1 (Spring 2000): 391–412; Greg Grandin, "The Instruction of Great Catastrophe: Truth Commissions, National History, and State Formation in Argentina, Chile, and Guatemala," *American Historical Review* 110 (2005): 46–67.

The Elusive Pursuit of Truth and Justice: A Review Essay

Mary Nolan

Annie E. Coombes, *History after Apartheid: Visual Culture and Public Memory in a Democratic South Africa*. Durham, NC: Duke University Press, 2003.

Antjie Krog, *Country of My Skull: Guilt, Sorrow, and the Limits of Forgiveness in the New South Africa*. New York: Three Rivers, 2000.

Teresa Godwin Phelps, *Shattered Voices: Language, Violence, and the Work of Truth Commissions*. Philadelphia: University of Pennsylvania Press, 2004.

Deborah Posel and Graeme Simpson, eds., *Commissioning the Past: Understanding South Africa's Truth and Reconciliation Commission*. Johannesburg: Witwatersrand University Press, 2002.

Fiona C. Ross, *Bearing Witness: Women and the Truth Commission in South Africa*. London: Pluto, 2003.

William A. Schabas and Shane Darcy, eds., *Truth Commissions and Courts: The Tension between Criminal Justice and the Search for Truth*. Dordrecht, Netherlands: Kluwer Academic, 2004.

Richard A. Wilson, *The Politics of Truth and Reconciliation in South Africa: Legitimizing the Post-apartheid State*. Cambridge: Cambridge University Press, 2001.

Radical History Review
Issue 97 (Winter 2007) DOI 10.1215/01636545-2006-020

How have and how should states and societies deal with histories of pervasive human rights violations, systemic violence, and structural racism? Since the end of World War II, three principle strategies have been deployed: trials, reparations, and truth commissions. (The fourth option, of course, and one regrettably widely practiced, is state refusal to acknowledge crimes and injustice in any legal or public forum.) Whereas the Nuremberg option of war crimes trials predominated after 1945 and reparations were put on the agenda for some but far from all victims of crimes against humanity in the 1950s, commissions of inquiry have come to the fore in the past two decades. Beginning with the Bolivian National Commission on the Disappeared and its Argentine counterpart in the early 1980s, over twenty countries have established truth commissions. These include Guatemala, Chile, El Salvador, Ghana, Nigeria, Sierra Leone, East Timor, and Bosnia.

What unites these disparate countries is that their movement away from regimes characterized by gross human rights violations, if not genocide, did not come from the victory of an internal opposition or external forces. Rather, the transition away from state violence and structural racism and toward democratic government, however partial it has often been, was negotiated among former opponents, between perpetrators and victims. Victor's justice via trials for war crimes and crimes against humanity of the sort implemented in Germany and Japan after World War II has not proven an option. This has encouraged a search for alternative means of publicly documenting the past, holding perpetrators accountable, giving voice to victims, and yet moving forward in societies still deeply divided about both the past and the future. Commissions of inquiry, or truth commissions, as they are more commonly called, take many forms in terms of their membership and mission, the evidence and testimony they evaluate, the publicity of their deliberations and conclusions, and the reports they produce. Some commissions were composed of only nationals, others had international members as well. Some, such as the one in Guatemala, saw their mandate as establishing a full and contextualized historical record; others, such as the one in South Africa, above all pursued the promotion of reconciliation. Some, such as the one Ghana, were fully insulated from the court system, while others, such as the ones in Argentina or East Timor, provided information useful for the prosecution of human rights violations. Some cast their investigations broadly, others, such as the one in Chile, focused more narrowly only on crimes leading to death; few have explored structural racism and socioeconomic violence, as opposed to specific criminal acts. Most took oral testimony, but few did so in well-publicized public hearings. Some focused on the witness of living victims and the fate of dead ones; others sought the voices and actions of perpetrators as well. Concluding reports varied greatly in focus, documentation, and recommendations. Most have been published, but that of Zimbabwe remains confidential.

The current popularity of truth commissions is twofold. Many consider truth commissions a practical necessity because many transitional societies could not pursue prosecution for political or economic reasons. In some societies, too many upholders of the old order survived in positions of judicial, police, and bureaucratic power, in others, state capacity was weak. In all, the cost of extensive trials was deemed prohibitive. For many others, however, necessity and desirability coincided. Truth commissions are viewed as morally superior to and politically more constructive than retributive forms of justice, even if the reality of their deliberations and effects has usually not lived up to the often exaggerated hopes invested in them. They are viewed as ways to promote human rights, even as they leave aside issues of social and economic rights.

The current infatuation with and optimism about truth commissions has been nowhere more evident than in the South African case. Yet the Truth and Reconciliation Commission (TRC) and the numerous analyses of it done at the time of its tenure and subsequently raise a host of contradictions and questions associated with all such truth commissions. Three broad themes emerge from the rich work on the TRC and the comparisons made between it and other such commissions, especially those in Latin America. The first involves the meaning(s) of and relationship among truth, justice, and reconciliation. What kind of truth do such commissions elicit or produce? What is the relationship between legal or forensic truth and narrative or historical or experiential truth? Is truth a form of justice, as some argue, or an alternative to justice defined as accountability by prosecution? And must a society choose between the Nuremberg and TRC options, or can the two be effectively combined? How are we to evaluate the complex meanings of revenge, retributive justice, restorative justice, and the claims made by those desiring these contending visions of settling accounts?

The second focus of concern and controversy involves issues of victims and voice. Which kinds of crimes and human rights violations do such commissions recognize, and which do they ignore or repress? How do such commissions weigh the injuries and needs of victims against the exigencies of nation building? Whose voices are heard, whose silenced or distorted to fit the evidentiary orientation of a given commission and the master historical narrative it seeks to produce? Does speaking heal? Can stories reconcile? Do truth commissions, as Teresa Phelps claims, "give something adequate back to victims" (39)?

The third area of debate involves history—not the history of these commissions, but the histories they produce. Do such commissions "construct an official and irrefutable history of the dark past," as Richard Goldstone, a judge on the South African Constitutional Court, the chief prosecutor at the UN Rwandan Genocide Tribunal, and the chairperson of the International Independent Inquiry on Kosovo, has claimed (quoted in Schabas and Darcy, *Truth Commissions and Courts*, 193)? Or do they produce only a partial and decontextualized record, as Greg Grandin, a historian who worked with the Guatemalan Commission for Historical Clarification, argues for most Latin American commissions?[1] Or is Michael Ignatieff's oft-cited claim that truth commissions merely reduce the number of the lies in circulation most accurate (quoted in Phelps, *Shattered Voices*, 66)? How does the emphasis on moving into the nation's future distort understandings of its past? Can and should such commissions put the past behind, or are they merely the opening round in a multifaceted and never-ending "coming to terms with the past," as the Germans label the difficult process in which they have been engaged—willingly or reluctantly—in the sixty years since the Third Reich was defeated?

Given the plethora of analyses of the South African TRC, where does one best begin exploring its accomplishments and failings, the hopes invested in it by many, and the disillusionment of many others? Antjie Krog's *Country of My Skull: Guilt, Sorrow, and the Limits of Forgiveness in the New South Africa* is one possible starting point. Krog, who headed the South African Broadcasting Company's coverage of the TRC hearings, is not only a journalist but a noted Afrikaans-language poet and a longtime opponent of apartheid. Far from producing a dispassionate chronicle of the TRC's proceedings, Krog provides an evocative and emotional narrative of its mission and methods, recording not only multiple voices of prominent South Africans but also the stories of those who testified and who heard their testimony. She chronicles her own wrenching reactions to the crimes uncovered, and her relationship to them as an Afrikaner. Krog's work, which mixes reporting, transcripts from the hearings, poetry, and personal reflections, captures the intensity and contingency of these years and compellingly portrays how much of the nation was swept up in the debates about the goals and procedures of the TRC. While she traces the opposition to the TRC, which at various points encompassed each and every major political party, she remains committed to its project of reconciliation and optimistic about its accomplishments. The views of politicians and the lives of ordinary South Africans have been changed by the revelations of the TRC, she argues. Of equal importance, "Against a flood crashing with the weight of a brutalizing past onto new usurping politics, the commission has kept alive the idea of a common humanity" (364).

But the strengths of Krog's work are also its weakness. If it recreates with a compelling immediacy the history of the TRC, it lacks analytical distance. It recreates the enormous hopes placed in the TRC as both an alternative to other roads to justice and as a path forward for a new South Africa, suggesting who did and did not share them. But there is too little critical discussion of the contradictory vision behind the TRC or its results. Much as Krog presents multiple voices, she is deeply, perhaps overly, involved in her own story. She understands Afrikaners in particular, and whites in general, better than blacks, which she herself admits. One wishes there were comparable black chronicles of the TRC that received as much international attention and promotion as did Krog's.

In the past few years, a host of more critical and scholarly assessments of the TRC have been produced. These center around the kinds of truth produced, the relationship of truth and justice, and the possibilities and limitations of satisfying local and individual needs, as well as national and political ones. An excellent introduction to these new debates is *Commissioning the Past: Understanding South Africa's Truth and Reconciliation Commission*, which brings together contributions by South Africans involved in the TRC and outsider evaluations of both the TRC and victims' stories. Insiders were as critical as outsiders. Piers Pigou, for example, who spent two years working in a regional investigation unit of the TRC in Johannesburg, offers a depressing catalogue of "False Promises and Wasted Opportunities," as he titled his essay. The TRC was mandated to investigate only gross human rights violations committed from political motivation, and this eliminated serious violations associated with discriminatory legislation, such as pass laws and forced removals. The amnesty provision, which required individual confession for amnesty, was controversial in and of itself, and failure to develop consistent criteria for granting amnesty and to investigate whether confessions leading to it were complete and accurate compounded the problem. There was ongoing tension between individual revelations and investigations and the TRC's focus on broad thematic areas. And key groups, such as the African National Congress (ANC) and the National Security Management System, were not adequately investigated.

Insiders and outsiders alike concurred that there was no agreed-on definition of truth or the methods by which it could be ascertained. The insider researchers Janet Cherry, John Daniel, and Madeleine Fullard stressed the conflicts between historical, legal, and quasi-psychological approaches to the production of knowledge. The TRC, they argue, came to see itself as "a state-directed investigative commission rather than an exercise in writing and rewriting history" (19). The emphasis was on empirical evidence more than on context and causality. The outsiders Deborah Posel and Graeme Simpson insist that this preference for factual and forensic evidence left "little room in legal proceedings for structural explanations of wrongdoing; from the perspective of the law, agency is first and foremost a question of individual accountability" (6). As Posel elaborates, the TRC report used this forensic conception of truth to claim objectivity. The report gestured toward other kinds of truth—personal and narrative, social and dialogic, healing and restorative—all of which are complex and subjective, but lapsed back into "a conventionally positivist stance on the source of its own authority as the official, objective version of the past" (156). Motive was severed from cause, cases were not integrated and synthesized, description predominated over analysis, and as a result, agency became delinked from structure and thus misunderstood. "Underlying the report's claims for the authority of its findings," Posel concluded, "is a self-effacing, circular process in terms of which the past is recorded only in so far as it is necessary to produce moral judgment; and the only basis for these judgments is the version of the past as it is written in the report" (161). The goal was a master narrative built around the perpetrator-victim binary that would provide a common memory and promote nation building.

The resulting history both acknowledged and cleansed liberation politics and state violence, as Simpson argues, but ignored the everyday and structural violence of apartheid.

In his concluding analysis, Simpson highlights both the enormous challenges that the TRC faced and the contradictory results it produced. The TRC's hybrid approach to truth and accountability put it between the German model, on the one hand, and the Chilean blanket amnesty, on the other. Truth recovery was to be "a restorative alternative to punitive justice" (221). Although this ideal was never fulfilled, the TRC did show "the fundamental clumsiness of criminal law as a means of doing substantive justice, of achieving reconciliation, and of meeting the needs of victims and survivors of human rights abuses for information and acknowledgment" (230). The alternative was far from perfect, for many disclosures were not full, and there was often neither forgiveness by victims nor contrition by perpetrators seeking amnesty. Nonetheless, he concludes, "The harsh reality is that the vast majority of apartheid's victims probably stood to gain more from the opportunity to tell their stories (coupled with the meager reparations promised by the TRC) than from the criminal justice system" (233). Simpson's bold assertion is followed by a warning of the disservice done by those who claim to speak for victims but who in effect silence them.

Did victims gain from telling their stories? Did they want punitive justice or reconciliation? Or were they simply silenced? Three works explore the tangled issue of voice and victims, of uncovered or constructed memories, of complex conceptions of justice. Teresa Godwin Phelps, *Shattered Voices: Language, Violence, and the Work of Truth Commissions*, offers an optimistic assessment of the benefits of storytelling in several truth commissions. Fiona C. Ross's *Bearing Witness: Women and the Truth and Reconciliation Commission in South Africa* explores the multiple ways in which women's voices and injuries were excluded from the hearings and the resultant history. Richard A. Wilson's *The Politics of Truth and Reconciliation in South Africa: Legitimizing the Post-apartheid State* examines the persistence and consequences of popular ideas of revenge and retribution in South Africa despite the nationally hegemonic discourse of redemptive reconciliation.

Phelps sees truth commissions, and especially the TRC, not as an alternative to justice, but as "a radically new kind of justice" (9). They should be judged, she insists, not in terms of international law, but rather in terms of the stories they enable to be told, for such stories are a vital part of justice as an ongoing process. Phelps enumerates several potential benefits of storytelling that can help transform victims into survivors, ones who see their suffering as part of a larger story. Making stories of our lives, she argues, is human and affirms our humanity. Reclaiming stolen or repressed or manipulated language is a way of balancing harm done. Stories uncover truth and refute false stores; they facilitate communication among groups who usually do not understand one another. Stories can provide a space to celebrate freedom, renarrate the social order in a way similar to M. Bakhtin's idea of carnival, and thereby restore dignity. The healing promoted by storytelling is of potential benefit not only to shattered selves but to families and societies as well. Finally, stories can provide a new history for emerging democracies.

Phelps draws on narrative theory to outline the positive power and potential of storytelling, but there is too little exploration of whether such potentiality was actualized. Her concluding chapters look at how the final reports of truth commissions in El Salvador, Chile, and Argentina, as well as in South Africa incorporated stories and used them to construct master narratives. Her analysis of the Argentine report, *Nunca Más*, for example, argues that the multitude of individual stories served to help construct a master narrative focusing on repression and those responsible for it, while at the same time disrupting and escaping this narrative; they demanded a hearing on their own terms. In South Africa, she asserts, the hearings, despite their imperfections, were empowering to individuals and healing for the nation. And the final report incorporated the many stories to tell a grand narrative of a nation moving beyond its past of horrendous violence and suffering to unity, reconciliation, and some, mainly symbolic, reparations for victims. But if stories were incorporated into national historical narratives, precisely whose stories, and with which distortions? Nowhere is there evidence of whether the individuals whose stories were incorporated into the reports felt that they had been heard correctly. Nowhere is there evidence that telling healed shattered selves and families or promoted understanding among formerly hostile or indifferent communities. Nowhere is there evidence about which individuals and groups saw storytelling as an alternative form of justice.

Fiona Ross, like many other critical voices, analyzes the TRC's limited "grammar of pain" (1), but she attends to the gendered implications of it. The TRC's focus was on "violence . . . construed as naturally gendered and . . . women's experiences of violence, rather than violence and its links to gender and power" (25). Both the everyday experiences and sufferings of women under apartheid and the particularities of women's activism and their understandings of it were marginalized. Although roughly equal numbers of men and women testified, women spoke more often of men's suffering and victimization than of their own. Within the reigning victim-perpetrator dichotomy, there was no room for those harmed by apartheid in their roles as wives, mothers, and sustainers of communities (just as there was no place for the beneficiaries of apartheid). Women came to be seen as a specific category, as "secondary witnesses" (17).

Yet the testimonies of ordinary women reveal richly layered experiences that say much about the everyday harms of apartheid: homes that failed to contain and protect, temporal disorientation, disrupted rituals and conventions, silences and secrets between the sexes and generations. They show that women organized in defense of family and of the ordinary against the onslaughts of apartheid, but it was a form of politics that received little recognition during the hearings or after. Finally, women's testimonies suggest that not all experiences can be put into words, that silences need to be explored.

Ross pays particular attention to activist women, whose testimonies highlight a distinctive set of themes: detention, gender-specific violence and vulnerabilities, charges of being "unnatural," and efforts to maintain social solidarity in the face of fractured relationships. Women such as Yvonne Khutwane, active in the ANC and civic organizations, gave a multifaceted testimony that discussed bodily harm in detention, the betrayal of relations, and experiences of collective struggle. The TRC and the media, however, highlighted only her sexual abuse, ignoring both the issues of agency and struggle and the local complexities of betrayed relations that were of vital importance to her. Because interpretation was contingent and reception uneven, not all forms of violence were recognized, and "individuals may feel isolated and vulnerable" (101). This problem was compounded by the TRC's "construing apartheid as a particular violence whose effect was to produce victims" (5). Activism and questions of agency and resistance were thereby elided. This led to both an undervaluing of women's activities and limited the assessment of harm. These erasures and elisions have contributed to the difficulties activist women have faced in reconstructing a sense of self during the transition to democracy. Overall, Ross concludes that "prevailing conceptions of voice—particularly the equation of speaking subject with healed subject—and the methodologies used to elicit it, do not do justice to the range of women's experiences of harm and the diversity of efforts to cope" (165).

Richard Wilson explores another group of marginalized voices, those local ones still advocating revenge or retributive justice in the face of the dominant discourse of reconciliation. In South Africa, Wilson argues, human rights became a discourse of restorative justice and forgiveness, whereas in the international context, human rights discourse supports the International Criminal Court (ICC) and the tribunals in former Yugoslavia and Rwanda. In South Africa, human rights discourse and the TRC have also been vehicles of legal centralization and nation building. Finally, he argues, "in the transitional era, reconciliation discourse mitigated the crisis of legitimacy caused by granting amnesty to torturers and entering into a power-sharing arrangement with former apartheid leaders" (97). Whether reconciliation and restorative justice were wrapped in the language of *ubuntu*, with its romanticized references to traditional African communities of reciprocity, respect, and cohesion, or in a Christian language of religious redemption, they have found uneven resonance on the local level. There, legal pluralism persists in terms of attitudes and even institutions. His own ethnographic research has convinced Wilson that "retributive understandings of justice are much more salient in South African society than versions emphasizing reconciliation as forgiveness" (27).

While *The Politics of Truth and Reconciliation in South Africa* offers a trenchant critique of the national TRC for decontextualization, scientism, and prioritization of the imperatives of nation building, the innovate heart of the book lies in Wilson's ethnographic studies of Johannesburg townships and their local cultures of justice. He uncovered three principle relationships to the TRC: adductive affinities, procedural pragmatism, and relational discontinuities. His interviews with TRC statement takers, many of whom were religious personnel, revealed that they both communicated religious values to the victims from whom they were taking testimony and integrated messages of reconciliation into those testimonies. For both individuals and communities, religious values and institutions proved formative in creating receptivity to the TRC's message of restorative justice. Others participated in the TRC for reasons of their own; they were not so much opposed to the language of human rights and reconciliation as unaware of or uninterested in it. The TRC, argues Wilson, was less successful at forging a consensus about human rights among the population than at "holding together a fragile elite coalition in the first years after apartheid" (153).

Still others in the townships rejected the TRC because it did not embrace their own punitive view of justice. "Protecting human rights requires a measure of retributive justice for offenders," argues Wilson, echoing an argument made by John Borneman in *Settling Accounts: Violence, Justice, and Accountability in Postsocialist Europe*.[2] The absence of retributive justice can "exacerbate an already existing situation of judicial impunity and a trend toward violent retribution" (161). Indeed, precisely that has happened in Sharpeville, where historic patterns of wild justice persisted, armed gangs practiced revenge, and local justice remained little touched by state authority or norms. "The greater the factionalism within a locale, and the more a social context approximates a Hobbesian moral universe," concludes Wilson, "the greater the resistance will be towards post conflict human rights talk" (186).

By contrast, if local community courts persist, they can provide a vehicle to channel desires for revenge. Boipatong, a township adjacent to Sharpeville, provides a suggestive but problematic and contested example of how local institutions "place checks on revenge and channel vengeance into a more mediated (although still violent) form of retribution" (199). These communal courts are strongly patriarchal and insist on the right to punish. They reject human rights talk and amnesty, insisting that suffering can only be canceled if punishment is meted out. Yet ironically, these courts "end up facilitating the kinds of solutions extolled by the TRC" (212). They have reduced revenge killings and have promoted peaceful coexistence. While some community members have criticized these local courts in the language of human rights and gender equality, Wilson notes that they have invoked these national discourses to legitimate a punitive conception of justice.

Wilson skims too lightly over the patriarchal character of these local courts, leading one to fear that here, as in the TRC, women's voices and views are once again marginalized. But his book does persuasively argue that without some measure of retributive justice, desires for revenge will fester and promote wild justice and criminality. Is there, then, a middle ground between prosecution and amnesty, blanket or limited?

Whereas Wilson suggests finding this in the collaboration of local and national institutions, the articles in *Truth Commissions and Courts: The Tension between Criminal Justice and the Search for Truth* explore a variety of ways in which truth or inquiry commissions and national legal systems have been combined. In the wake of bloody civil war and controversy about a full amnesty provision, Sierra Leone established both a truth and reconciliation commission and, via negotiations with the United Nations Security Council, a special court. The special court had jurisdiction over individuals accused of committing the most serious violations of international humanitarian law. William Schabas provides a detailed analysis of the workings of these two bodies, the conflicts over sharing testimony, and the difficulties arising from first granting full amnesty and then qualifying it. In Peru, as Eduardo González Cueva shows, the truth commission did not have jurisdictional power, but public opinion believed strongly (60 percent) that the punishment of criminals was the most important step toward reconciliation. The Peruvian truth commission came to facilitate such retributive justice not only through its final report but also by establishing a special investigation unit that cooperated with the attorney general's office. In Guatemala, Susan Kemp argues, the Commission for Historical Clarification was not accompanied by judicial proceedings through regular or special courts. However much this was advocated as a fast track to stability and integration into the global economy, avoiding prosecution, she insists, marginalized victims, harmed the establishment of the rule of law, and represents "a tangible barrier to healthy civil-military relations. . . . If the legal system cannot respond to the worst atrocities of the past and hold state agents accountable, then it is failing and that bodes ill for any emerging democracy" (101–2).

Finally, there is the international dimension. As the editor Schabas notes, "even if truth commissions fit within some acceptable domestic compromise, they cannot be insulated from prosecution in other jurisdictions, including international ones" (1–2). Augusto Pinochet has provided the most public example of this. Whether similar cases will be pursued in alternative national venues or the International Criminal Court remains to be seen. Some believe the ICC will intervene if a state fails to prosecute gross human rights violations; others think it will hesitate to act if a truth commission compromise is facilitating peace. At the international, as at the national, level, it will be difficult to achieve both truth and justice, to serve at one and the same time the international defense of human rights, national needs for peace and nation building, and local needs for justice and retribution.

If a mixture of truth commissions and retributive justice seems more promising than truth commissions alone, one should be wary of putting too much faith in prosecutions. The Nuremburg option proved much more limited and less conclusive than is often believed. It did lead to the conviction of a few dozen top Nazis and several hundred lesser ones, but denazification was quickly turned over to the Germans, who immediately dismissed over half of the pending cases, and convicted few of the remainder. It was precisely in the claimed interests of political stability, state rebuilding, and social reconciliation that such policies were followed. And no truth commission aired the crimes of perpetrators and the harms of victims, alive or dead. If this created a relatively quiet 1950s for West Germany, the past came back to haunt that country with a vengeance thereafter. There was the Adolf Eichmann trial and the Frankfurt Auschwitz trials in the 1960s, the television documentary *Holocaust* in the 1970s, the so-called historians' debate of the 1980s, the 1990s controversies around Daniel Goldhagen's *Hitler's Willing Executioners* and the photo exhibition War of Annihilation about the Wehrmacht on the Eastern Front,[3] and the current debate about Germans as victims of the Allied air war. Each trial and public debate aired more aspects of the crimes of the Third Reich, each uncovered more about the voices and fates of victims, each revealed more about how implicated bystanders and beneficiaries were. As Günter Grass so colorfully put it in his novel *Crabwalk*, "History, or to be more precise, the history we Germans have repeatedly mucked up, is a clogged toilet. We flush and flush, but the shit keeps rising."[4]

Countries that have had truth commissions are also finding that the past does not pass away. Far from being full and definitive, the history presented in final reports is uneven and incomplete. As Posel and Simpson conclude in *Commissioning the Past*, "The TRC did not settle the matter, close the debate and put paid to lingering questions and controversies about South Africa's troubled history" (13). This, they claim, is a good thing.

One place in which the open and contested nature of the TRC's master narrative is evident is in ongoing controversies about how to memorialize the past. In *History after Apartheid: Visual Culture and Public Memory in a Democratic South Africa*, Annie E. Coombes explores the multiple conflicts surrounding postapartheid South Africa's efforts to develop historical sites that recapture both the history of violence and structural racism and the multiple struggles against it. Her richly illustrated and provocative chapters on the Voortrekker Monument, Robben Island, and District Six in Cape Town lay out the contending political, historical, aesthetic, and economic forces fighting to shape these sites. Coombes explores how the Voortreeker Monument, a foundational icon of the apartheid state, has both retained its meanings for Afrikaners, eager to remember their 1838 march, and been reinterpreted or retranslated by antiapartheid groups. It has even been commercialized by advertisers. She pays particular attention to performances that both engage with the monument and its narrative of the past and disrupt them. If the Voortrekker Monument is not quite as it was under apartheid, it has no settled meanings; rather, it "has provided the stage upon which new identities and challenges have been launched" (53).

Robben Island, made famous by the decades-long imprisonment of Nelson Mandela and hundreds of other antiapartheid fighters, raised the issue of whether to preserve or destroy monuments to the previous regime's barbarity. Some wanted to make Robben Island a recreation site, others a museum focusing on past crimes, still others a place embodying a new South African future. Coombe's analysis shows how difficult it is to reconcile diverse ideas of public history, lived experience, and national heritage, as well as to accommodate the voices of the many different anti-apartheid constituencies whose history intersected with that of Robben Island. Should there be one narrative, and if so, whose? The ANC's? Mandela's? Those of the much less famous but more numerous and younger prisoners? And whose experiences are excluded from the dominant narrative of the liberation movement's heroic stoicism in the face of apartheid's brutal and isolating forms of imprisonment? (Women, as she shows, are once again the excluded.) How can a Robben Island museum simultaneously serve the interests of the local constituency of former prisoners, the desires of national proponents of a unified history, and the demands of international tourism?

Rather than providing answers, Coombes chronicles the unfolding of such struggles both around Robben Island and District Six, the site of forced removals under apartheid. She has particular praise for the District Six Museum, which resulted from long debate and negotiation. It is, she maintains, "one of those very rare institutions that is capable of supporting initiatives that are more likely to expose problems and contradictions than to smooth over dissent" (147–48). This is the sort of commemorative site and memory culture that all societies emerging from gross human rights violations, systemic state violence, extreme socioeconomic inequality, and structural racism need, for truth commissions only open questions about the past; they do not definitely answer them.

Notes

1. Greg Grandin, "The Instruction of Great Catastrophe: Truth Commissions, National History, and State Formation in Argentina, Chile, and Guatemala," *American Historical Review* 110 (2005): 46–67.
2. John Borneman, *Settling Accounts: Violence, Justice, and Accountability in Postsocialist Europe* (Princeton, NJ: Princeton University Press, 1997).
3. Daniel Jonah Goldhagen, *Hitler's Willing Executioners: Ordinary Germans and the Holocaust* (New York: Alfred A. Knopf, 1996).
4. Günter Grass, *Crabwalk*, trans. Krisha Winston (New York: Harcourt, 2002), 122.

Many Are Guilty, Few Are Indicted

Grant Farred

In My Country, directed by John Boorman. Sony Pictures Classics, 2004.

All truth and reconciliation commissions, from those in Bolivia to those in East Timor, from the ones in Chile and Argentina to the ones in South Africa, are governed by the logic of political temporality. These commissions want to determine the historical "truth" of the time before: the now represents its own epistemology, the time not possible before, the time that now makes possible a supposedly truthful rendering of the past, a rehabilitation of the past into a new political use. The eradication of the power of the past inscribes the present as an ethical time, or at the very least, a time open to ethical inquiry about the time before. The search for the postapartheid ethical is the project of Afrikaner writer Antjie Krog's *Country of My Skull*, a poetically journalistic account of the South African Truth and Reconciliation Commission (TRC) from 1996 to 1998.[1]

Adapted into a movie, *In My Country*, Krog's work "locates" (translates) the time of the past into a series of pastoral spaces: the family farm of the Afrikaner poet and radio journalist Anna Malan (Juliette Binoche), the film's lead female protagonist, in the Orange Free State, for centuries a bastion of an especially conservative Afrikanerdom; the environs of the various Truth and Reconciliation Commission (TRC) venues, from cramped classrooms in the South African hinterland to more spacious settings in the urban capitals, where the commissioners, journalists,

Radical History Review
Issue 97 (Winter 2007) DOI 10.1215/01636545-2006-021

victims, and perpetrators all create the opportunity for ministering into historical record the horrors of apartheid violence; and the crisscrossing of the South African landscape, where lush greenness alternates with starkly barren plateaus, always haunted by the specter of the too-recent apartheid past.

In *Country*'s terms, the Malan farm is symptomatic of the excesses of Afrikaner rule, and so it is necessary that Anna, one of the *Volk*'s own, be assigned the role of Afrikaner interrogator. An ambivalent Afrikaner, Anna is alternately guilt-ridden (she breaks down frequently during the hearings), shocked by the apartheid violence of her people, and the (reluctant but not uncritical) defender of Afrikaners. It is her relationship with the *Washington Times* African American journalist, the too-obviously named Langston Whitfield (so that the name of the black Harlem Renaissance poet stands in juxtaposition, but also in proximity, to that of the Afrikaner poet), which provokes in Anna her sharpest critiques of her people. After a combative beginning, Anna and Langston (Samuel L. Jackson), both of whom are married, engage in an affair that affects both their readings of the TRC and of apartheid South African history.

Through the event of the TRC, the past is made into a place where the nation is reconstituted, democratized, divided from its racist, dictatorial, or genocidal predecessor by bringing those pastoral spaces—the spacious, airy kitchen of the Afrikaner farm, the conviviality of the dimly lit *shebeens* (speakeasies), and the often stuffy, overly affected TRC hearing rooms—to metaphoric and historical life again. These are among those spaces in which, in one way or another, the time of apartheid atrocity has to be articulated, publicly spoken into TRC life. This is the time of the paradoxical confession: enunciating the secret that is not a secret. The power of TRC speech resides not in its articulation but in its power of assignation: naming the event and the perpetrator, making visible the criminality of apartheid, is the (only) power that the TRC, unwittingly, assigns itself. In this way, the apartheid past might no longer be verboten, but articulated through symptomatic fragments.

The political logic of truth commissions is, its founders claim, not to cleanse the nation of its violent, tumultuous past, but to offer the narratological means to come to terms with the past through the force of naming. The act of naming creates the conditions for political accountability—for the perpetrator to accept that name and, then, in the discourse of *ubuntu*, to be historically relieved of that name and absolved into a different political moment: the time of the postapartheid present, the time of a putative *ubuntu*—that African practice of recognizing that all humanity is related, that a (historic) injury done to one is shared by all, that forgiving an apartheid political transgression enables postapartheid reconciliation. For this reason, the TRC can only perform its political function if it suspends the past, if arbitrary temporal barriers, separating the past from the present, are imposed. The TRC freezes the past into its distinct temporality but, as *Country* demonstrates, the past survives as a political, affective, and material remainder in the present. The time of offense, of struggle, and of violence is the past. For this reason the time that was cannot be allowed to stand as the time that was. It must be exculpated, made other to itself, explicated—through narrative—into something other than itself; the time that was must be revealed to itself as a narrative of itself that was insufficient to itself. The time that was must, in effect, betray itself in order to function in the now, to overcome its discontinuity with the present: it cannot be what it was if it is to have any usability in the present.

It is the theme of betrayal—of the individual, familial, communal, and "national" self (if the Afrikaners can be said to constitute a nation)—that provides the narrative thread that runs through *Country*. "Lojale verset" (loyal resistance), Anna proclaims in a contemplative moment, is the only way to be true to the now reconfigured supra-, or nonracial, democratic national self. *Lojale verset* is a term borrowed from the protonationalist early twentieth-century Afrikaner poet, N. P. van Wyk Louw. The act of postapartheid loyalty is imagined as ethically and morally resisting the historic Afrikaner—and, more generally, the white South African—self; *lojale verset* is predicated on the willingness to interrogate the self (or, collective selves) to the point of turning against, "betraying," that Afrikaner self. There can be, then, no act of loyal resistance which does not test the very limits of loyalty, which lays itself open to the charge of its more egregious name, disloyalty, an act Anna's brothers and father routinely accuse her of. The Afrikaner of the time before must confront that (now not-yet anachronistic) Afrikaner self: that Afrikaner self of the time before, once imperiously resident on those Free State farms, must be made knowable in the now. The Afrikaner of the time passed, the passing of which all the Malan men rage against (while Anna and her mother stand by, frustrated in their love for these men, husbands, sons, brothers), must explain why and how it was sustained in the moment of violence—Afrikaner racism that produced the willful, brutal destruction of black life. The event of the TRC is to ensure that the time passed is made unrepeatable.

In order to gain amnesty, the Afrikaner self must announce, in full view of those—or the survivors of those—against whom it committed atrocities, its culpability; its political, not personal, culpability. In the pastoral terms of *Country*, the Afrikaner self can only be absolved, granted amnesty, if it can show itself to have been, in that heinous phrase, "only following orders;" if the Afrikaner self was, as is the case with Anna's younger brother, "Boetie" (Langley Kirkwood), performing a political function. According to Boetie Malan, "I got blood on my hands so we could all sleep safe." Overcome with grief, unable to imagine a life—in a country that is no longer his—where he would have to face his sister after he betrayed her vision of him, Boetie commits suicide in the stable. With his death, one fragment of the time passed is now, literally, passed. However, is not his symbolic death both unnecessary and a political sham? A sham, moreover, that sustains the South African and all other truth commissions?

Betrayal is, for a very good ethical reason, the principle conceit of all truth commissions. These commissions are premised on the faulty, historically unsustainable notion that the time passed was not known. For this reason, it is the political work of the TRC to make it knowable. But how could the time passed not have been known? How could Anna not have known that, if not her brother, then certainly someone in her immediate family, to say nothing of her immediate social circle, was culpable? How can white South Africans ever claim not to have known? How did they imagine their lifestyle, their privileges, their vastly disproportionate wealth, could have been sustained without the structural violence of apartheid? Apartheid's was not a secret violence: the murder of Steve Biko in detention, the murder of the Cradock Four in the Eastern Cape, the assassination of Ruth First, the existence of so-called rogue elements in the police force who took the law into their own hands, the wanton brutality of the police force in their clashes with protestors armed only with bricks and stones. . . .

On the disenfranchised side, who can claim not to have known, or not to have heard the rumors about atrocities committed against dissident African National Congress (ANC) members in the front-line states (Angola, especially)? Who was entirely oblivious about the discipline meted out at those camps? What disenfranchised South African did not believe that Winnie Mandela was involved, to a lesser or greater extent, in the violence carried out in the name of the Mandela United Football Club? Who believes, for an instant, that Winnie Mandela, the symbolic "Mother of the Nation," was not directly implicated in the death of the fourteen-year-old boy Stompie Seipei? Who did not recognize the need for retribution to be exacted from the *impimpis* and the *askaris* (the former were disenfranchised spies for the apartheid regime and the latter captured guerillas who were retrained to kill their own people)?

None of these, or several other such incidents of ANC and apartheid state-sponsored terror, were secrets. The *names* of the security branch officers who killed Biko or who tortured ANC leaders, those may not have been public knowledge. But even if it were difficult, would it have been impossible to obtain those? The rest of the information was the mundane stuff of everyday life in apartheid South Africa. Confrontations between the predominantly white police force and black protesters, Soweto 1976, the insurrection of the mid-1980s, this was shown on state-run TV, reported in the heavily censored newspapers, discussed in workplaces, often between the enfranchised and the disenfranchised, sometimes obliquely, sometimes heatedly. South Africans knew, and they never claimed otherwise. The horror of apartheid was not that it was unknown, but that it refused to make itself private—it had no reason to, such was its repressive force. Very few white South Africans ever believed, even as they feared it (silently and not so silently), that their time (of racist dominance) would pass, so they lived their history in public, never in secret. They did not hide it: Afrikaners and Anglos alike, they trumpeted their control of the black majority; they lived in contempt of international sanction and moral condemnation. There was nothing mea culpa–ish about apartheid governance; that is what made South Africa such a pariah nation. Afrikaners did not live apologetically in a land they considered theirs. They inhabited the apartheid state as a dominant minority. It is this history that compels the recognition in Boetie that, as he so drolly puts it, "this is not our country anymore." This after he, bloodied shirt and all, has just shot a black cattle thief in the leg. Boetie is right, of course, South Africa is not his, certainly not in the unqualified way it used to be. Boetie's is a gnomic sentiment, but a historical pronouncement of Dylanesque proportions nonetheless: the times have gone and changed on the Afrikaner.

The genius of truth commissions is that they allow for the ethical betrayal of the time passed. Because of the TRC, the time known can now be represented as the time unknown, the time unknown until now, until the justice-instituting event of the TRC. The TRC should, because of this cynical historical logic, not be conceived as the revealing of a history so much as the remaking of the apartheid past. The TRC constitutes the act of making the familiar alien: through the submission of amnesty requests, the full disclosure before the commission itself, the admission to the victims, a minority of Afrikaners reveal the atrocities of the past to the nation determined to end the time that was. Now that the past is "fully known," disclosed into public record so that a postapartheid history of the extended apartheid moment can be accurately written, the nation can be pastoralized—prayed, pained, absolved—into postapartheid democracy.

It may, however, be necessary to coin a neologism to more properly describe the process. The TRC allows for the postapartheid nation to be "absoluted" into the nonracial, democratic present. This act enables both the absolution of (mainly) white, but also black, perpetrators and the full absorption of Afrikaner, Anglo-white, and all the disenfranchised into the postapartheid present: now that the past has been made known, now that the victims have publicly named the perpetrators, now that the time that is being made to pass is being narrativized into history, the past can be sutured (in)to the present. The past can be made historically continuous with the present; the past is not denuded of its irruptive capacities, but—through the act of naming, of historic confrontation between victim and perpetrator—articulated into an exceptional relationship with the present. The reconstituted nation makes the past different from, but no longer disruptive of, the present. To be absoluted is to allow for the confession of guilt and the national forgiving of the perpetrators, the erasure of historical erasure, and the coming into absolute oneness of the new nation.

That is the fiction of the TRC, a fiction undone very early by *Country*. During an initial confrontation between Anna and Langston, he challenges the Afrikaner notion of ignorance. Backed into a rhetorical corner, Anna admits: "We all knew things." (This barbed encounter, unfortunately, is one of the few moments in the film in which Langston performs effectively as a historical interlocutor. He moves too quickly from skeptical outsider to *ubuntu* convert, a process that is, of course, coterminous with he and Anna becoming lovers.) *Country* is not a memorable movie, Binoche and Jackson's are forgettable performances, but this is its singular contribution to TRC literature. Even as *Country* tries to validate the TRC as enabling the process of truth revelation, that logic is undone by the ghostly specter of knowledge. The past is not revealed by the TRC; it is betrayed. It is not that the atrocities were not known, but that their occurrence was systemic, vital to the continuation of racist, undemocratic rule. *Country* demonstrates how it is easier for the TRC to pretend (new) knowledge than it is to acknowledge what is already known. It is not truth, but knowledge that the TRC betrays: the past is denied its own epistemological integrity. There are, at most, a few dark secrets, buried in the apartheid past. There is very little of ethical value to be uncovered there that is not already known.

The past is known—"We all knew things"—but despite that, the facticity of knowledge means little in the face of the revelation of state terror. That is why epistemological discovery remains the dominant hermeneutic of the TRC. It authorizes the past as an event that must be interpreted into democratic oneness; the past must be interpreted against itself, the past must be made unrecognizable to itself in order to make it usable to and for the dispensation of the present. The logic of discovery is what governs the work of the TRC. The TRC chair, the Reverend Mzondo (played by Owen Sejake; the character is a poor stand-in for the impishly pious Archbishop Desmond Tutu, the real TRC's head) and his fellow commissioners express, incomprehensibly for any South African who lived the apartheid era, their shock and horror at some new revelation of Afrikaner atrocity.

Read on its own terms, the past is not a secret, but a threat. If no one can claim not to have known—which is what Anna does—then the TRC itself becomes an obsolete and politically inadequate mechanism for political redress. If every member of the previous dominant group knew, if every member of that constituency was complicit, then there is no "truth" to be found: the TRC is superfluous because the truth is already known. The project, then, is a more onerous, unmanageable one: wholesale indictment. How does one grant amnesty to, how does one absolute, an entire political constituency? More to the point: can one undertake such a project? Or is that the unfathomable, unspeakable truth about South Africa's TRC? That it made the fragments, the demonized De Jagers and assorted low- and mid-ranking police and security officials stand in for all of white South Africa? (De Jager was the leader of a notorious security unit that killed activists, a unit composed of both white police officers and black *askaris*.) If everyone did know, then no one can claim not to have known. In order to make the apartheid past palatable, it must be not so much revealed as individualized into a repressive unknown. The postapartheid present is only viable if the apartheid past is betrayed by those not indicted, those who do not, like Anna, ask for amnesty. It is those who claim that they have no truth to reveal who make reconciliation more possible. They stand in contradistinction to the guilty of the *Volk*. If there is no truth to reveal, then there were also, unlike the De Jagers and the Boetie Malans, Afrikaner innocents.

It is the salient feature of this movie that it, unreflexively, brings into political focus the repressed lesson of *Country*: it is Anna and her ilk—as much as the ghostly, ghastly, unrepentant De Jager (Brendon Gleason)—who should be indicted. Anna, her mother, their neighbors—those Afrikaners who knew but did not speak, who knew but did not do, who refused to interrupt the violence of apartheid even though they knew—it is they, too, who are culpable. De Jager is the ghostly figure who haunts the consciousness of the Afrikaner political elite, the man in and with whom the secret that is not a secret of the past resides, the prototypically crude security officer, red-bearded, brandy-drinking, who only talks to Whitfield in his dark, guarded house, away from the public event that is the TRC. De Jager is the metonymic One who has to stand trial while the Many, Anna and her like, are absoluted into the postapartheid present.

These are the questions that truth commissions almost never pose, and it is a line of inquiry that *Country* never makes public: What is the price for knowing? Is there any form of a truth commission that can take on such a project? If "we all knew things," does that make all Afrikaners guilty of transgressing against the disenfranchised? How could it not? If everybody knew, then what is the point of the TRC? What good is knowledge that is already known? If there is a certain truth in the assignation of individual responsibility, what meaning is ascribed to individual responsibility in the light of systemic violence? When the structures of racism make violence against black bodies and psyches mundane, what value does individual responsibility have? What is the political use of indicting the few, the very, palpably guilty few, if the many are—symbolically, materially, and legally—absolved? What good is it to make visible atrocities through TRC testimony if its invisibility was, in any case, minimal? What good is accountability without the possibility of censure? How can there be prosecution of the transgressors when the TRC has no sovereignty, no power over the life and death of the perpetrators?

It may be, finally, that it is in their sovereign political uselessness that the true political value of truth commissions resides. Because it can, politically, do nothing, it must, rhetorically, symbolically, be made to do much. It is, in its epistemological excess—the fact that it reveals "everything," but nothing (or, little) that is unknown—that it can make such moral hay of its supposed findings. It is not in its knowledge, but in the representation of its knowledge that politicians have been able to locate the usefulness of the TRC.

The absence of a cost for Afrikaner knowing, Anna's inner anguish and torment apart, is brought sharply into focus by the bloody and historic street justice meted out at the conclusion of *Country*. Dumi (Menzi "Ngubs" Ngubane), Anna's sound engineer and, we learn as he is about to be killed, an *impimpi*, is executed summarily by one of his former activist colleagues in front of his own home and in front of Langston just hours after the TRC concludes its work. Dumi revealed vital information to the apartheid security forces, thereby ensuring the death of at least two of his fellow activists. For the black South African transgressor, the cost of betrayal is sovereign street justice: the elimination of a life for the other lives it sacrificed because of its complicity with the state. Disbanded black guerillas will have no truck with the TRC because they believe in a more reciprocal, Old Testament modality of public accountability: a life for the lives sundered because of betrayal. Afrikaner betrayal is afforded the privilege of privacy: suicide on the wealthy, if gated, farm; inner trauma and uncontrollable guilt. The costs to the black South African populace for betrayal are, much like under apartheid, immeasurably higher: public death. And yet the space of the black township continues to lie beyond the purview of the state, that space that can make no claims made on the state. Even De Jager, Dumi's onetime associate who is denied amnesty not for his political crimes but for the excessive violence he used in executing his "duties," is afforded the right to trial. Dumi's accusers were also his judges, his jury and, literally, his executioners.

The unexpected brutality of Dumi's death throws into sharp relief not only Anna's uncostly knowing and her betrayal of Afrikaners but also the very notion—that *Country* tries so hard to endorse—of black humanity: *ubuntu*, the term Langston cannot at first pronounce, strange as it is to his American tongue. The shame of Afrikaner violence is public and memorialized in the event of the TRC. The fate of the *impimpi* is rendered as nothing but a tragic afterthought. It is not only that the truth of the TRC is, historically speaking, irrelevant, but that its preferred mode of reconciliation has no purchase on black activist history. In Dumi's case, there is no possibility of amnesty; there is only the most searing critique of *ubuntu*: human lives have political meaning only when they are, structurally, publicly (that is, with the support of the state), guaranteed justice, even if that justice is (politically and physically) postmortem.

Dumi can carouse with the Afrikaner writer and the international journalists covering the TRC, but he cannot run from the time of the black political. The history of black political activism is discontinuous with the *chronos* of the TRC. The remainder of the antiapartheid struggle, so different from the threatened violence of the Afrikaner anti-postapartheid variety, constitutes a time and space of the political where black lives lost demand a reciprocal, not a reconciliatory, justice. In the black townships of the Cape Flats, where Dumi is killed, the One perpetrator cannot metonymize the Many. The black guilty are indicted, one transgressor at a time.

Note

1. Antjie Krog, *Country of My Skull: Guilt, Sorrow, and the Limits of Forgiveness in the New South Africa* (New York: Three Rivers, 2000).

The 9/11 Commission Report

Kim Phillips-Fein

The 9/11 Commission Report: Final Report of the National Commission on Terrorist Attacks upon the United States. New York: Norton, 2004.

Five years after September 11, 2001, it is hard to remember how swiftly guilt was assigned for the hijackings and bombings of the World Trade Center and the Pentagon. At 8:30 that morning, only the most inveterate news junkies in the United States had heard of Osama bin Laden or al-Qaeda. Twelve hours later, everyone knew who they were and what they had done. A moral landscape crystallized almost immediately as Afghani training camps and elusive Saudi billionaires became part of the mental geography of the nation. In the language of President George W. Bush, the conflict was one between good and evil, between love of freedom and contempt for individual liberty.

Not everyone, of course, was satisfied with these abstractions. Some, like Larry Silverstein, the real estate magnate who had leased the twin towers only weeks before they fell, wanted to know the answer to the crucial question: Who can I sue? The disproportion between the small band of attackers and the military might of the United States caused many to wonder why the plot had evaded intelligence agencies and how such an apparently fragile group was able to do such damage. The families of the dead, questioning whether anything could have been done to prevent the attacks or to save their loved ones, pressed for a full investigation. And in the weeks and months following 9/11, conspiracy theories began to circulate on the fringes of

Radical History Review
Issue 97 (Winter 2007) DOI 10.1215/01636545-2006-022

the Left and the Right, whispers that 9/11 was an "inside job," rumors that we were not hearing everything the government knew.

The result was the formation of the National Commission on Terrorist Attacks upon the United States — a bipartisan committee with a large staff and the power to subpoena political leaders, charged with developing the fullest possible explanation of how and why the hijackings happened, and ordered to try, as best it could, to answer the question of what could be done to prevent such violence in the future. With a staff of more than thirty researchers, granted incredible access to all kinds of historical documents and sources, the 9/11 Commission, as it became known, was a historian's dream. In the summer of 2004, the commission's report was published to great fanfare and fulsome praise for its wide-ranging recommendations regarding the reorganization of the intelligence agencies, for its scholarly research, and even for its tersely elegant literary style.

The 9/11 Commission sought to explain why an outside group attacked the United States and to suggest future policies for dealing with such threats — threats defined at the outset as originating well outside of American borders. Nothing in its mandate demanded self-interrogation regarding the reasons for violence or terror, only a debate as to the appropriate response. But despite this, *The 9/11 Report: The Final Report of the National Commission on Terrorist Attacks upon the United States* bears a deep similarity to the underlying logic of the reports of truth commissions in other nations. Even though it presents radical violence as an external threat visited on the United States, the report nonetheless provides an argument for its source: the spread of anomie, social disaffection, and radical ideology through the Middle East and Central and Southern Asia. It then argues that the ultimate answer to this crisis, and the security threats that it poses, is a new international order, one in which the United States (or perhaps a coalition) will protect and promote norms of individual economic opportunity, tolerance, the rule of law, and free markets around the world. The establishment of this new foreign policy, we are told — combined with the reorganization of our national security apparatus to make it more streamlined and efficient — is the only defense against the coming apocalypse. In this way, the report marshals a narrative about past violence in order to project a future social order — one in which the international power of the United States constitutes the final bulwark against fear, against terror.

. . . . .

The first project of the report is simply to tell the story of the bombings. The reviews that greeted its publication made much of its narrative power; it is perhaps the only official document produced by the United States government ever to have been nominated for a National Book Award. And the report is indeed a work of literary force, opening, as it does, with a gripping, minute-by-minute account of how the planes were boarded, captured, and driven headlong toward their targets on a "temperate and nearly cloudless" morning in mid-September 2001 (1). Terrifying descriptions of the attacks themselves take up a full third of the book. The details given in the report are vivid and painful—transcripts of final cell phone calls, descriptions of frightened parents turning on the television only to watch the plane smash into the South Tower, the story of the first New York City fireman to die in the attacks, killed by a body falling from a burning building. Yet while the numb, precise account satisfies one kind of curiosity, it alone cannot grant us insight into how and why the attacks occurred. It is impossible to read the report without feeling afraid—one of its major arguments, after all, is that "in the new age of terror . . . we [civilians] are the primary targets" (323). In its visceral description of the destruction of 9/11, the report operates, on some level, as a call to action. The narrative of the horrors of 9/11 steps in for an argument about our foreign policy—it is all the argument that is needed. The frightening story of the violence of that day transcends any political or historical analysis; complete unto itself, it seems to demand the strongest imaginable response.

What kind of people could cause such destruction and pain? The report states that the "new terrorism" against which we must be on guard is not simply terrorism in general—it is explicitly *Islamic* terrorism. This new terrorism differs from the old political terrorism of the Irish Republican Army and the Palestinian Liberation Organization. While these older movements deployed terrorism to achieve specific political gains, the report suggests that Islamic terrorism is more deeply ideological and hence more dangerous. The new terrorism is at once messianic and nihilistic, its violence that of pure sadism, seeking only to destroy. Its religiosity gives it the intense quality of an all-consuming, rapturous passion, albeit one that thrives on suicide and murder. It has no political goals or ambitions. We cannot "bargain or negotiate" with it; as the report puts it, "it can only be destroyed or utterly isolated" (362).

But not so long ago, Islamic fundamentalism was viewed by the West as far preferable to the old "political" opposition to colonial rule: the secular, Marxist-inspired radicalism with its fraught ties to the Soviet Union. To historicize the so-called new terrorism, the report might have placed al-Qaeda in the context of the well-known role the United States played in Afghanistan following the Soviet invasion. The United States, still reeling from Vietnam, no longer wanted to use the conventional methods of state warfare in the struggle against the Soviets. Instead, the country began to covertly fund nonstate armies in the region. The doctrine intensified in the Reagan years. As in El Salvador and Nicaragua, the United States poured vast sums of money into funding the bloody war in Afghanistan. This was the context in which Osama bin Laden began to build al-Qaeda, gathering tens of thousands of Arab supporters of the Afghanis to wage jihad against the Soviet Union. Mahmood Mamdani has argued that if today al-Qaeda poses special dangers to people around the world as a transnational organization, one with no loyalties to a particular state, and hence with no restraint on its actions, it owes its structure largely to American foreign policy in the late years of the Cold War, when the United States was specifically attempting to privatize its wars and avoid taking action through the nation-state.[1]

The sinews that bound the anticommunist warriors of the Reagan administration to those who fought the Soviet army in Afghanistan were ideological as well as financial. The religious militancy of the Islamic warriors who fought "godless communism" greatly appealed to the faithful of the Reagan administration. As Steve Coll has reported in *Ghost Wars*, his epic depiction of the Afghan wars, William Casey, the director of the CIA under Reagan, admired the noble ferocity of the Afghan fighters in the fight against communism. After all, Casey's own anticommunism was the product in large part of his ardent Catholicism, and he recognized in the language of jihad his own crusade against Soviet communism. A scant two decades ago, the Reagan administration encouraged and sympathized with the quality that now seems to render the new terrorists beyond negotiation, almost beyond reason itself. As scholars of political violence have observed, during the late years of the Cold War, religion was thought to render people immune to the real ideological virus of the day—that of communism.[2]

The report ignores these kinds of complexities, devoting a mere four pages to history and political context. We are given to understand that the poor economic prospects of Middle Eastern nations (the product, in large part, of "unprofitable heavy industry, state monopolies and opaque bureaucracies") in the larger context of modernization and the decline of older mores and traditions leave young men vulnerable to the allure of terrorism (53). "Eccentric and violent ideas [sprout] in the fertile ground of political and social turmoil," according to the report (48). A couple of paragraphs mention the role of the United States in Afghanistan, mostly to tell us that Osama bin Laden never took any money directly from the CIA—a denial that omits so much that it is meaningless.

. . . . .

In place of historical analysis, we learn a great deal about the day-to-day life of the members of the cell groups of hijackers: their difficulty securing apartments within the United States; the perpetual visits that Ziad Jarrah, one of the pilots on 9/11, kept making to his Turkish girlfriend back in Germany, even after he was supposed to cut her off; the warnings Mohammed Atta gave not to call family members (which he violated himself, telephoning his father a final time on September 9). Most of this information is drawn from the testimony of detainees, many of whom the commission was not permitted to question directly, forced instead to rely on investigators' reports. Still, the report manages to give a peculiar humanity to the nineteen hijackers through its careful reporting of their lives in the United States. At one point, the reader turns the page to find photographs of the young hijackers staring out, the only portraits of people who died on 9/11 in the book.

But we are given only the barest interpretation of their motives, which the commission deems inexplicable. The entire analysis of the appeal of jihad for these rootless young men is reminiscent of Hannah Arendt's description of the lure of totalitarianism: modern humanity, cast adrift in an impersonal and rapidly changing world, desperately seeks comfort within the rigid strictures of ideology.[3] As the report puts it: "When people lose hope, when societies break down, when countries fragment, the breeding grounds for terrorism are created" (378). The report cites political criticisms raised by the jihadists, such as their objections to the sanctions against Iraq after the first Gulf War and U.S. policy toward Israel. But they are quickly submerged in the broader account of malaise. The report instead tells us that there is no purpose to the violence of al-Qaeda; the only motive of the radically meaningless new terrorism is to destroy American life on as spectacular a scale as possible. At the end of the book, the reader is left with the understanding that one day, nineteen men decided to commit suicide and mass murder by flying planes into American landmarks—an unfathomable act of evil. The report, in other words, leaves us exactly where we began.

Yet one does not have to discount religion entirely to see that people are likely drawn to al-Qaeda at least in part because of the specifically political ideology of the organization, and especially its criticism of the foreign policy choices of the United States, not simply out of general resentment or a vague quest for meaning in life. Unless these political objectives are at least acknowledged, it will be immensely hard to respond to the threat of violence.

. . . . .

What, then, of the final strand of the report—the evolution of U.S. policy toward terrorism? Could the United States have somehow prevented the attacks through more careful detective work or by trying to catch Bin Laden? Or by mandating locks on cockpit doors and installing air marshals on planes? According to the report, throughout the 1990s and before September 2001, political leaders were increasingly aware and anxious about the possibility of an impending attack. Yet they were reluctant to take sustained military action (although as the report points out, the Clinton administration did bomb Afghanistan, while also continuing the decade's low-level air war against Iraq). No matter the enthusiasm for pursuing Bin Laden, the country always drew back from a sustained military assault. The camps in Afghanistan, after all, were viewed as primitive "jungle gym" camps, in the words of one general. They were not seen, the report says, as "worthwhile targets for very expensive missiles" (120). The deputy national security advisor recommended after the 1998 bombing of Afghanistan that such a strategy offered "little benefit, lots of blowback against [a] bomb-happy U.S." (120).

The report adopts an understated attitude toward this position. But implicitly, it seems to suggest that taking military action sooner would have been preferable and efficacious. We knew what horrors were coming—we just could not take the action needed to protect ourselves. It is the old timidity of the liberals that always brings a sneer to Dirty Harry's lip. In this sense, the report seems likely to be used to justify future military adventures. Newspaper editorials in publications like the *Investors' Business Daily* interpreted the report in precisely this way: "The 9/11 Report bolsters President Bush's war on terror and his efforts to spread democracy in the Middle East . . . . We must know our enemy, and confront it. If we fail to do so, we'll have no one but ourselves to blame for the damage done."[4] Or, as an Arkansas paper put it, our attitude toward potential terrorists should be: "We find them. Then WE strike first—using all elements of national power."[5]

The report proposes a highly idealistic foreign policy to counter the spread of Islamic terrorism. The United States must "define what the message is, what it stands for" (376). The nightmare of terrorism should be met with economic and political liberalization. To hasten economic growth in the Middle East, the report recommends a Middle East free trade area. Echoing Friedrich Hayek, it argues that "vibrant private sectors" have "an interest in curbing indiscriminate government power" (378). The historic mission of the United States, after all, is to embody and vigorously broadcast a vision of "individual educational and economic opportunity" (376), of political participation and the rule of law and the toleration of different faiths. In a way, the report comes across as mildly critical of the Bush regime: it calls for "more than a war on terrorism," suggests that the United States should agree that detainees be treated in accordance with international law, and demands a "preventive strategy that is as much, or more, political as it is military" (363, 364).

Yet the report remains strangely quiet about the most dramatic new foreign policy effort of the post-9/11 international order—the war in Iraq. Although the report makes it clear that the Bush administration was obsessed with fighting Iraq in the absence of any clear information linking Saddam Hussein to al-Qaeda, it says little about the ensuing war, except to note that a "failed state" in Iraq will create a haven for future terrorists. This suggestion implies the impossibility of American withdrawal from Iraq. In addition, the report strongly endorses and celebrates the successes of the Afghanistan operation, and argues that the United States and NATO must remain in the region to oversee reconstruction (367). Aside from the obvious political difficulties an open discussion of the Iraq war might have caused for the commission, there may be deeper intellectual reasons for this silence. In telling the story of the events that led up to 9/11, the report chose to paint the threat of Islamic terrorism in stark and existential terms—the rootless anxiety, envy, and dislocation of the Middle East facing the modernism of the United States. This emphasis allowed its authors to avoid discussing the history and politics of U.S. ambitions during the Cold War, and their connections to the current terrorist threat. In the same way, in its description of the ideals the United States is supposed to uphold in the world, the report evades the hard reality of U.S. military force, saying nothing about the role that military occupations could play in spawning new waves of violence. The explanation of 9/11 given by the report seems to justify the rise of a new kind of international power for the United States—one in which the country uses its military to defend a world order of freedom and peace against dark forces that threaten death and violence. But one need look no further than Baghdad or Guantánamo Bay to see the dangers of this kind of Manichaean utopianism in which the United States has all the light—and the other side, all the dark.

Notes

1. Mahmood Mamdani, *Good Muslim, Bad Muslim: America, the Cold War, and the Roots of Terror* (New York: Three Leaves, 2005).
2. Steve Coll, *Ghost Wars: The Secret History of the CIA, Afghanistan, and bin Laden, from the Soviet Invasion to September 10, 2001* (New York: Penguin, 2004). See also Robert Dreyfuss, *Devil's Game: How the United States Helped Unleash Fundamentalist Islam* (New York: Metropolitan Books, 2005).
3. Hannah Arendt, *The Origins of Totalitarianism* (New York: Harcourt Brace, 1951).
4. "Winning the War on Terror," *Investors' Business Daily*, July 26, 2006.
5. "The 9/11 Report: On First Reading—Well, Skimming," *Arkansas Democrat-Gazette*, August 14, 2004.

The Abusable Past

R. J. Lambrose

Folding Chairs?

Endowed chairs are perfect examples of cultural materialism: although they rarely take physical form — with appropriate legs, backs, stretchers, and so on — their presence in the university is unequivocally material, not to say materialist. And like an ordinary chair, an endowed chair can on occasion begin to look, well, tarnished. So it was with the Kenneth L. Lay Chair in Economics, endowed in 1999 by a $1.1 million gift to the University of Missouri–Columbia from the former chairman and chief executive of Enron. Given to the university at the height of the Enron "miracle," the chair became something of an embarrassment when the company tanked and its chiefs were hauled into court.

Lay's gift was in legal terms irrevocable, yet in September 2005, as the former CEO was desperately trying to buff up his public image in advance of his trial, he wrote a letter to the chancellor of UM-C, urging him to distribute the monies to fourteen different charities then assisting the relief efforts for victims of Hurricane Katrina. When the university conferred with the Texas-based trustee in charge of Lay's remaining legal assets, it learned that Lay had earmarked none of them for Katrina victims. So much for his moral epiphany. No deal, the university replied.

In February, 2006, Lay again asked that his gift be returned, this time to pay his legal expenses. Again no deal. The Lay chair remained in place — and empty. The university has made at least three offers, all of them declined. Lay's guilty verdict appears to have frozen this particular asset. After all, what respectable economist would want to occupy the contemporary equivalent of the Ponzi chair?

Radical History Review
Issue 97 (Winter 2007) DOI 10.1215/01636545-2006-023

So why not change the name of the Lay Chair of Economics, just as the University of Missouri changed its own brand name to "Mizzou?" Call it the Chewco Chair or the Jedi Chair as homage to the off-the-books partnerships for which Enron became infamous. Or simply leave the name as it is so that Kenny-Boy may contemplate its permanently (and appropriately) virtual status from his grave. Who could object to that? Certainly not Lay's former employees, every one of whom would have loved to see him get the chair.

Misery Loves Company

Here's a scenario: It is dark and you are running through the forest. Suddenly you break out of the woods into a moonlit clearing, where you see (good God!) Donald Rumsfeld and Dick Cheney, each with a shotgun. They look at each other and then begin to raise their guns. . . .

Nightmare vision? Maybe, but not totally implausible. If you were to find yourself some weekend in the woods near Saint Michaels, Maryland, on the Chesapeake Bay, you could in theory run into the Bush Buddies, each of whom has purchased a large waterfront estate in the so-called Church Neck area of the Bay. Three years ago, Rumsfeld laid out $1.5 million for Mount Misery, a former red-brick bed-and-breakfast built in the early nineteenth century and situated on four and a half acres of prime riverbank. A year later Cheney moved in next door, paying a cool $2.6 million for a thirties-era Cape Cod on nine waterfront acres, complete with formal gardens and a 145–foot dock in San Domingo Creek.

What do the pals do at what *New York Times* columnist Elizabeth Bumiller calls the Hawks' Nest? A little water-skiing? Maybe. Some discreet water boarding? Perhaps. Hunting seems more likely, though. Cheney has been known to visit the local gun shop in Easton to pick up some ammo, and Antonin Scalia, his old hunting companion, has come down from time to time. Of course an FAA-imposed no-fly zone of a nautical mile protects the duck buddies—and whatever innocent plane may come in range.

Cheney does have another vacation home in Wyoming, while Rumsfeld has two other houses of his own, one in Washington and one in Taos. Rumsfeld, it appears, was encouraged by his wife to buy Mount Misery as a weekend getaway. And it was she who supervised the renovations that led to the discovery of two War of 1812 vintage cannonballs. Rummy proudly displayed these by his fireplace—until warned that they might still be live.

That an Improvised Fireside Device (IFD) briefly threatened Rumsfeld is the least of Mount Misery's historical ironies, however. There is also the fact that the place was built by Edward Covey, the notorious slave-breaker whose tortures Frederick Douglass describes at some length in his *Narrative*. Forget the cannonballs. Place a pair of shackles by the fireside and a German Shepard curled up on the hearth, and you'll have a perfect photo-op.

Smallville

"There he goes again." That was what historians and documentarians across the country were saying last March after Larry "The Franchiser" Small, secretary of the Smithsonian Institution, announced a new, thirty-year deal with the CBS-owned Showtime Division to provide it virtually exclusive access to its vast library and archives to service a new joint Smithsonian Networks venture in documentary programming. The first initiative is to be the Smithsonian on Demand channel, scheduled to launch in December 2006. Of course "on demand" means for a price; admission to the Smithsonian itself is still, for the moment, free.

Showtime agreed to pay the Smithsonian some $500,000 a year over the life of the contract, in return for which the division received the right of first refusal over commercial documentaries that draw substantially on Smithsonian holdings and staff. The Smithsonian retained the right to exempt six documentaries a year from these strictures, but this exception only brought home to filmmakers and scholars the grim fact that no film that made more than incidental use of the Smithsonian archives and expertise could promise it to, say, PBS.

Many of these details did not become known until April, after an open letter of protest to Larry Small, signed by more than two hundred filmmakers, historians, and media scholars, was published and a House Subcommittee on Appropriations demanded that Small make the secret contract public. The American Historical Association president Linda Kerber, in a letter endorsed by the AHA's governing council, reproached Small for the "obfuscation" surrounding the Showtime deal, as well as for the equally "confidential publishing contracts" that the Smithsonian Press had earlier signed with HarperCollins. "Both arrangements," Kerber concluded, "raise compelling concerns about how the management at Smithsonian is exercising its responsibilities over the public trust it holds." The secrecy itself seemed an augury of what public history would look like under a proprietary regime.

The Showtime press release was hardly more comforting. "It's hard to find a great brand that has not been exploited on TV," said Matthew Blank, chairman and CEO of Showtime Networks Incorporated. "We feel that Showtime Networks has the resources and market knowledge to bring the Smithsonian brand to television audiences." "This isn't 'Museum TV,'" Blank assured journalists, "it will blend Showtime's gift for story telling with the Smithsonian's integrity and treasure trove of fascinating resources."

Readers were left to wonder what the shelf life of integrity would be in the face of Showtime's gift for storytelling—and secrecy. The network's general manager, Tom Hayden (!), promised that on-demand programming would likely highlight "Indy and NASCAR racing," as well as something on George Bush's favorite space theme: Mars exploration. Perhaps Karl Rove could do the voice-overs.

Critics were also left to muse about the alternatives that Small's deal forecloses. At the very moment that the BBC is planning to make its public archives freely available for downloads, here is the Smithsonian locking up its holdings for thirty years, and for a mere $500,000 a year! The national patrimony sold for a mess of pottage and a pot of message. As of this writing, Debra S. Ritt, the inspector general of the Smithsonian, has just resigned. To reporters she noted of Smithsonian Business Ventures (where the Showtime deal was fashioned): "There isn't a lot of transparency over what it does, how the revenues are spent that they generate."

Back in June, Ritt was reported to have resigned her inspector generalship in order to take a senior executive position in the audit office of the Small Business Administration. To some observers, though, it appeared that she had just *left* the Small Business Administration.

The Family Romance

Spam scams are a literary genre of their own, and as with any genre, slight changes in any of its features—theme, mode of address, and so on—can be made to speak to larger changes in the culture. Some appeals may have the feel of permanence—the marrow of tradition, so to speak; promises of organ and asset enlargement, for example, not to mention that elusive low-interest mortgage. On the other hand, we thought the Nigerian Gambit (a scam promising access to millions of stolen government deposits) had legs too, but it appears to be giving way to a new, nearly self-parodic appeal a lot closer to home: South Carolina, to be specific.

The e-mail announces itself as coming from the principal attorney for the estate of the "late Senator Strom Thurman" and seems to have specifically targeted labor and radical historians. "We write to notify you," the message begins,

> that my late client made you a beneficiary to the bequest sum of Nine Hundred and Fifty Thousand Dollars in the codicil to his will and last testament. He died at the age of one hundred years. This bequest is to support your activities, humanitarian services, help to the less-privileged and research work. In accordance with our inheritance laws you are required to apply for claims through this law firm to NatWest Bank United Kingdom, where this fund was deposited. We are perfecting arrangements to complete the transfer of this inheritance to you.

The kicker: "You are required to forward the following details of yours; full names, address, occupation, age and phone numbers for verification and re-confirmation."

The message concludes with a potted biography of Thurmond that lists his four children by Nancy Moore Thurmond but, interestingly, makes no mention of Essie Mae Washington-Williams, the daughter that the twenty-two-year-old Thurmond had by Carrie Butler, a sixteen-year-old black maid in the family household. A 1998 biography of "Ol' Strom" had identified Washington-Williams, but the facts of the case were not confirmed until 2004—a year after the segregationist's death — when she (and the Thurmond family) stepped forward to acknowledge Strom's paternity. On this point, the scam is discreetly silent.

Such calculated tact amounts to a broad wink directed toward the spam scam's addressee: if he or she has no memory of Strom's dalliances, no harm done; there's always the "humanitarian services" and "research work" to be subsidized by a Thurmond legacy. On the other hand, if the recipient (hereafter known as "the Mark") does remember Essie Mae Washington-Williams, then, hey, maybe the connection goes deeper. Ol' Strom lived for a century, after all, far longer than Ol' Tom Jefferson. Black or white, we may all be Strom's children.

The Correct Award

The presidential presentation of the annual National Humanities Medals is always a challenge in a conservative Republican administration. One imagines that that the National Endowment for the Humanities staff is sent scrambling to find public figures (e.g., Midge Dechter or Lew Lehrman) or academics (e.g., Gertrude Himmelfarb or John Lewis Gaddis) who can meet the Bush administration's political smell test, as well as the award's criteria of providing a body of "work [that] had deepened the nation's understanding of the humanities, broadened citizens' engagement with the humanities, or helped preserve and expand American's access to important resources in the humanities." In the process, the staff inevitably begins to the stretch bounds of the meaning of "the humanities" — or perhaps pull the legs of their political bosses in the White House. Three years ago, for example, we puzzled over the selection of Art "Kids Say the Darndest Things" Linkletter (see *Radical History Review*, no. 88).

This year, the choice that left us scratching our heads was Judith Martin, better known as "Miss Manners" and described in the award citation as "the pioneer mother of today's civility movement." A worthy achievement, to be sure, but not a staple of the humanities curriculum at most universities. But then we noticed that another winner this year was Alan Charles Kors, the University of Pennsylvania intellectual historian known for doggedly fighting any restrictions on free speech on campus. The symmetry was beautiful: Bush was handing out one medal to someone who opposes political correctness and another to someone who's made correctness her life.

Felipe Agüero is an associate professor in the Department of International Studies at the University of Miami and was a 2005–6 fellow at the Woodrow Wilson International Center for Scholars working on a project on business and the politics of corporate social responsibility in Latin America. He is the author of *Soldiers, Civilians, and Democracy: Post-Franco Spain in Comparative Perspective* (1995), and the coeditor of *Faultlines of Democracy in Post-transition Latin America* (1998), and, most recently, of *Memorias militares sobre la represion en el Cono Sur: Visiones en disputa en dictadura y democracia (Military Memories of Southern Cone Repression: Contested visions in Dictatorship and Democracy*) (2005). He has been a fellow at the Kellogg Institute at the University of Notre Dame and at the Institute for Advanced Study in Princeton, NJ.

Sally Avery Bermanzohn was a labor organizer in Durham, North Carolina, when her husband Paul was critically wounded in the Greensboro Massacre. Pregnant at the time with their second child, she fought poverty and physical danger to raise her family. She is now a professor and the chair of the political science department at Brooklyn College, City University of New York, where she teaches courses on the politics of violence, race, class, and gender. She authored *Through Survivors' Eyes: From the Sixties to the Greensboro Massacre* (2003), an oral history of six survivors of the Ku Klux Klan murders. The book was honored by the American Librarian Association and granted the Creative Achievement Award by Brooklyn College. She coedited *Violence and Politics: Globalization's Paradox* (2002), which includes her chapter on violence and the U.S. civil rights movement. She is currently writing a book about terrorism and the Ku Klux Klan.

Alejandro Castillejo-Cuéllar is a professor of anthropology at the Universidad de los Andes, Colombia, and a research associate at the Direct Action Center for Peace and Memory, South Africa. He holds a PhD in cultural anthropology and an MA in peace and conflict studies. His doctoral dissertation was awarded the prestigious Stanley Diamond Award in the Social Sciences, the highest honor the New School for Social Research bestows a PhD graduate. He was a research fellow at Columbia University, New York, and at the Solomon Asch Center for the Study of Ethnopolitical Conflict at the University of Pennsylvania. Between 2001 and 2004, he was a visiting research fellow at the Institute for Justice and Reconciliation, in South Africa. He is author of a number of articles and books, among them, *Anthropology, Postmodernity, and Difference: A Latin American Debate* (1997) and *Poetics of Otherness: Towards an Anthropology of Violence, Solitude, and Internal Displacement in Colombia* (2000). His book, "The Archives of Pain: Violence, Terror, and Memory in Contemporary South Africa," is currently in preparation.

Grant Farred is an associate professor in the Program in Literature at Duke University. He is author of *Phantom Calls: Race and the Globalization of the NBA* (2006), *What's My Name? Black Vernacular Intellectuals* (2003), *Midfielder's Moment: Coloured Literature and Culture in Contemporary South Africa* (1999). His forthcoming books include *Long Distance Love: A Passion for Football* and *Bodies in Motion, Bodies at Rest.*

John J. Fitzgerald is a retired teacher from Longmeadow High School in Massachusetts, where he taught social studies and served as the department chair. During the Vietnam War, he served in the U.S. Army as a combat infantry platoon leader, where he was wounded in action and awarded the Bronze Star for Valor and the Purple Heart. An early member of Vietnam Veterans Against the War, he joined the antiwar movement in 1967 and supported Eugene J. McCarthy for president in 1968. He is the coeditor of *The Vietnam War: A History in Documents* (2002).

Greg Grandin is a professor of history at New York University and is the author of *The Blood of Guatemala* (2000), which won the Latin American Studies Association Bryce Wood Award, *The Last Colonial Massacre: Latin America in the Cold War* (2004), and, most recently, *Empire's Workshop: Latin America, the United States, and the Rise of the New Imperialism* (2006). He worked with the Comisión para el Esclarecimiento Histórico, the Guatemalan truth commission, and has recently been awarded a John Simon Guggenheim Fellowship. He has written for *Harper's*, the *New York Times*, the *Boston Review*, and the *Nation*.

Thomas Miller Klubock is a member of the *Radical History Review* editorial collective and is an associate professor of history at the State University of New York, Stony Brook. He is the author of *Contested Communities: Class, Gender, and Politics in Chile's El Teniente Copper Mine, 1904–1951* (1998), as well as of a number of articles on labor and gender in Chile. He is currently writing a social and environmental history of Chile's temperate rain forests.

R. J. Lambrose, having just learned from his new department chair that he has been entitled to a sabbatical since 1987, will be taking leave from the "Abusable Past" to pursue research into his family legacy on a Strom Thurmond Fellowship.

Elizabeth Lira is a Chilean clinical psychologist, researcher, and professor at the Center for Ethics, Jesuit University Alberto Hurtado in Santiago, Chile. She has been honored with several prizes internationally for her work with victims of human rights violations and has published widely on the impact of political violence. She was a member of the National Commission on Political Imprisonment and Torture in Chile (2003–5). Since 1996 she has collaborated with Brian Loveman on a research project investigating patterns of political reconciliation and resistances of memory, especially in Chile. She is currently the president of the Consejo Superior de Ciencia de Fondecyt.

Brian Loveman is a professor of political science at San Diego State University. He received an MA and a PhD from Indiana University, and a BA in history and political science from the University of California, Berkeley. His major fields of interest are Latin American politics, inter-American politics, international relations, and human rights. He has written a history of Chile widely read in English: *Chile: The Legacy of Hispanic Capitalism* (3rd. ed., revised and updated, 2001). Among his recent publications are two edited volumes: *Addicted to Failure: U.S. Security Policy in Latin America and the Andean Region* (2006) and *Strategy for Empire: U.S. Regional Security Policy in the Post–Cold War Era* (2004). With Elizabeth Lira he has authored and edited ten books and various articles in Spanish related to the themes treated in the article published in this issue of *Radical History Review*.

Mary Nolan is a professor of history at New York University. She is the author of *Visions of Modernity: American Business and the Modernization of Germany* (1994), and coauthor, with Omer Bartov and Atina Grossmann, of *Crimes of War: Guilt and Denial in the Twentieth Century* (2003). Her articles on German memories of Nazism and the Holocaust include "The Politics of Memory in the Berlin Republic" (2001) and "Air Wars, Memory Wars" (2005).

Elizabeth Oglesby is an assistant professor of Latin American studies at the University of Arizona, Tucson. She has conducted research in Guatemala since 1986, and in the late 1980s she was a researcher at the Association for the Advancement of Social Sciences in Guatemala (AVANCSO). She has written on rural counterinsurgency, refugee resettlement, postwar elite politics and corporate social responsibility, and labor restructuring. She is coauthor of *¿Dónde está el futuro? Procesos de reintegración en comunidades de retornados (Where is the Future? Processes of Reintegration in Returning Displaced Communities)* (1992). Her recent articles include "Corporate Citizenship? Elites, Labor, and the Geographies of Work in Guatemala," *Environment and Planning D: Society and Space* (2004); and "Machos, machetes y migrantes: Masculinidades y dialécticas del control laboral en Guatemala (Machos, Machetes, and Migrants: Masculinities and the Dialectics of Labor Control in Guatemala)," *Estudios Migratorios Latinoamericanos* (2003). She is former editor of *Central America Report* in Guatemala City, and a former associate editor of *NACLA: Report on the Americas*. She was on the staff of the Guatemalan Commission for Historical Clarification in 1997 and 1998. The essay presented here is based on research supported by a fellowship from the Carnegie Council on Ethics and International Affairs.

Paul Ortiz is an associate professor in the Department of Community Studies at the University of California, Santa Cruz. He is the coeditor of *Remembering Jim Crow: African Americans Tell about Life in the Jim Crow South* (2001) and *Emancipation Betrayed: The Hidden History of Black Organizing and White Violence in Florida from Reconstruction to the Bloody Election of 1920* (2005). He has published articles on farmworker movements, slavery reparations, and an essay on Hurricane Katrina that appears in *Hurricane Katrina, Un-natural Disaster: Reflections and Prospects* (2006), edited by John Brown Childs. He was an advisory committee member for the First Annual César Chávez Celebration in Watsonville, California.

Kim Phillips-Fein is an assistant professor at New York University's Gallatin School, where she teaches twentieth-century American political and economic history. Her first book, on the role of business in the rise of the conservative movement in the postwar United States, is forthcoming.

Charles F. Walker teaches Latin American history at the University of California, Davis. He is the author of *Smoldering Ashes: Cuzco and the Creation of Republican Peru, 1780–1840* (1999) and three edited volumes in Spanish. He has just completed a book on a massive earthquake and tsunami that devastated Lima in 1746.

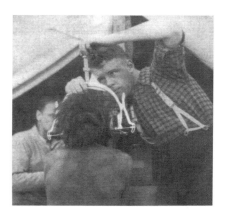

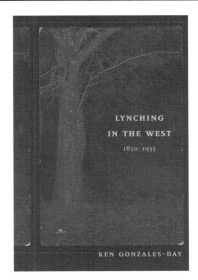